Screening Gender on Children's Television

Screening Gender on Children's Television offers readers insights into the transformations taking place in the presentation of gender portrayals in television productions aimed at younger audiences. It goes far beyond a critical analysis of the existing portrayals of gender and culture by sharing media professionals' action-oriented recommendations for change that would promote gender equity, social diversity and the wellbeing of children.

Incorporating the author's interviews with 135 producers of children's television from 65 countries, this book discusses the role television plays in the lives of young people and, more specifically, in developing gender identity. It examines how gender images presented to children on television are intertwined with important existential and cultural concerns that occupy the social agenda worldwide, including the promotion of education for girls, prevention of HIV/AIDS and domestic violence, and caring for "neglected" boys who lack healthy masculine role models, as well as confronting the pressures of the beauty myth.

Screening Gender on Children's Television also explores how children's television producers struggle to portray issues such as sex/sexuality and the preservation of local cultures in a profit-driven market which continually strives to reinforce gender segregation. The author documents proactive attempts by producers to advance social change, illustrating how television can serve to provide positive, empowering images for children around the world.

Screening Gender on Children's Television is an accessible text which will appeal to a wide audience of media practitioners as well as students and scholars. It will be useful on a range of courses, including popular culture, gender, television and media studies. Researchers will also be interested in the breadth of this cross-cultural study and its interviewing methodology.

Dafna Lemish is Professor of Communication at Tel Aviv University and editor of the *Journal of Children and Media*. Her books include *Children and Television: A Global Perspective* (2007); *Children and Media at times of Conflict and War* (co-edited with Maya Götz, 2007) and *Media and the Make-Believe Worlds of Children: When Harry Potter Meets Pokémon in Disneyland* (with Maya Götz, Amy Aidman, and Hyesung Moon, 2005).

Screening Gender on Children's Television

The Views of Producers around the World

Dafna Lemish

Routledge
Taylor & Francis Group

LONDON AND NEW YORK

First edition published 2010
by Routledge
2 Park Square, Milton Park, Abingdon, OX14 4RN

Simultaneously published in the USA and Canada
by Routledge
270 Madison Ave, New York, NY 10016

Routledge is an imprint of the Taylor & Francis Group, an informa business

Typeset in Sabon by Taylor & Francis Books
Printed and bound in Great Britain by
CPI Antony Rowe, Chippenham, Wiltshire

British Library Cataloguing in Publication Data
A catalogue record for this book is available from the British Library

Library of Congress Cataloging in Publication Data
Lemish, Dafna, 1951-
Screening gender on children's television : the views of producers around the
world / Dafna Lemish. – 1st ed.
    p. cm.
Includes bibliographical references and index.
1. Television and children. 2. Children's television programs – Social aspects. 3.
Gender identity on television. 4. Sex role on television. I. Title.
    HQ784.T4L357 2010
    302.23'45083 – dc22
              2009037887

ISBN 10: 0-415-48205-4 (hbk)
ISBN 10: 0-415-48206-2 (pbk)
ISBN 10: 0-203-85540-X (ebk)

ISBN 13: 978-0-415-48205-9 (hbk)
ISBN 13: 978-0-415-48206-6 (pbk)
ISBN 13: 978-0-203-85540-9 (ebk)

To Peter S. Lemish
for "sharing, caring, daring."

(Pete Seeger, *Wonderful Friends,* from *Pete Seeger at 89,* 2008)

Contents

Figures

Acknowledgements

I owe a great deal to many people who helped me envision and materialize this project. It was spawned in the inspiring, fertile ground of years of friendship and collegiality of my fellow scholars in the Feminist Scholarly Division of the International Communication Association (ICA) who were there to teach, stimulate, nurture, support, and inspire. Here, I would like to cite and to thank, in particular, Carolyn Byerly, Cindy Carter, Vicki Mayer, Sharon Mazzarella, Marian Meyers, Norma Pecora, Lana Rakow, Karen Ross, Linda Steiner, and Angharad Valdivia.

I am grateful to cohorts of students who challenged my thinking and kept me on the tips of my toes, and in particular to my former Ph.D. students who widened my intellectual horizons and are now feminist scholars in their own right, starting chronologically with Amit Kama, Einat Lachover, Hagar Lahav, Shilrey Shalev, Sigal Barak-Brandeis, Diane Levin-Zamir, and Arielle Friedman; and continuing with Ornat Turin, Shiri Reznik, Michal Tirosh, and Shelly Geffen, who are currently completing their graduate studies.

Several of my Israeli colleagues have unknowingly contributed to this project in various insightful ways: Linda-Renee Bloch, Jerome Bourdon, Akiba Cohen, Nelly Elias, Anat First, Nurit Guttman, Rivka Ribak, Chava Tidhar, and Limor Shifman. I am indebted to them for their support, wisdom, and patience with me.

Special thanks to the following people, who facilitated my participation in the events where much of this research was conducted, for their solidarity, advice, and encouragement: Firdoze Bulbia (Chairperson of the fifth World Summit, Johannesburg, South Africa); Robert Ruoff (General Manger of the Basel-Karlsruhe Forum, Switzerland-Germany) and Markus Nikel (Program Manager of the Forum); Shigeru Aoki (Secretary General of the Japan Prize, NHK, Tokyo, Japan); Geena Davis (Founder of the Geena Davis Institute on Gender in Media, US); Lic. Juan María Naveja de Anda (Director General of Educational Television, Mexico City, Mexico); Sylvie Lamy (Events & projects coordinator, The Alliance for Children and Television, Montréal, Canada).

Michael Rich (Head), and the entire team of CMCH (Boston, US) – David Bickham, Amy Branner, Ariel Chernin, Karen Fisher, Brandy King, Isabel Lopes, Sally Persing, Julie Polvinen, Lauren Rubenzahl, and Laura Sherman, deserve special thanks for providing a stimulating and friendly environment as well as logistical assistance while I was writing this book during my sabbatical with them.

I thank the three anonymous reviewers of the book proposal for their valuable comments and enthusiasm for this project and Sharon Mazzarella who reviewed the full draft of the book for her encouraging and insightful suggestions. Special thanks go to Annegret Lassner at Prix Jeunesse for helping secure copyright permissions for the photos presented in this book. At the Routledge team I am most grateful to Senior Editor Natalie Foster for having the foresight to approve this project as well as for her encouragement and advice along the way; to Emily Laughton, Editorial Assistant, for her patience, good humor, and efficiency in working through the logistics of bringing the book to print; and to Andrew Watts, Production Manager, for a smooth, friendly, and professional production process.

Most of all, I am deeply indebted to Maya Götz (Head of Prix Jeunesse and of the International Central Institute for Youth and Educational Television IZI, Munich, Germany), a colleague and friend, for providing both intellectual and partial financial support for this project, but most of all, for her commitment, creativity, originality, and enthusiasm for it. Our collaboration started in 1995 when I was in transit at the Frankfurt airport and has continued since – across years, continents, and projects. Traces of our many hours of exchanges on gender in children's television can be found throughout this book.

Finally, I am forever grateful to my life partner, closest friend and colleague, Peter S. Lemish, for sharing the process, experiences, and ideas at the heart of this project; for his constant support and intellectual stimulation, and for professionally editing the entire manuscript for academic rigor and quality. But more than anything else, I am deeply indebted to him for being an inspiring, live role model for "gender-bending," and for his uncompromising belief in the possibility of deep social change.

This project could not have come to life without the generosity and deep care of the hundreds of television professionals who agreed to share their professional and personal lives with me and to join forces in exploring the role television can serve in promoting gender equality around the world. I am indebted to them not only for making this book possible, but for significantly enriching my own life. This book is dedicated to them with affection and gratitude.

Preface
The Journey

As I write this preface in my sabbatical office at the Center for Media and Child Health (CMCH; Children's Hospital Boston, Harvard School of Public Health, and Harvard Medical School), I find myself staring nostalgically at a poster for *Gone with the Wind*, one of the most formative movies of my childhood. I have criticized this film for its warm and romantic portrayal of the US South during the time of slavery, its emotionally exploitive constructions of the Civil War, and its stereotypical depictions of men and women. But at this moment I reflect on the poster's reproduction of the famous romantic scene in which the handsome Rhett Butler (Clark Gable) assertively carries the submissive Scarlett O'Hara (Vivien Leigh) in his arms, and recall that soon after this famous scene Rhett forces himself on Scarlett in an act that will result in her impregnation. And then I realize with shock that my cherished childhood cinematic memory is actually of a rape scene!

Each one of us carries powerful visual images from our childhoods of film and television characters that made lasting impressions on us, for whatever reasons, in different circumstances. We may envy them, aspire to be like them, identify with them, or wish to have them as friends. For over two decades now I have been researching these images and their gender stereotyping in media texts, teaching critical analysis skills, and working to raise critical consciousness about the power of visual images among students, media producers, teachers, parents, and my own relatives, friends, and colleagues. I have learned that many studies of portrayals of women and men on television point to a social world that differentiates between the two quite systematically, as well as providing children with restricted images of what it means to be a boy or a girl and limited visions of the kinds of men and women they can grow up to be.

As I reflect on images I have analyzed, many anecdotal episodes come to my mind from the period when I was gathering the data presented in this book. For example, jet lagged in my hotel room in Tokyo during the Japan Prize event of October 2006, I was zapping mindlessly among the available channels when I came across an interview on CNN's *Larry King Live* with Zhang Ziyi, the Chinese actress of Ang Lee's hit film *Crouching Tiger, Hidden Dragon* (2000). Ziyi (who was twenty-seven years old at the time of the interview) has become extremely famous, rich, and influential. Indeed, she stands out as a film role model, presenting a strong young woman with unique martial-arts competences who fights successfully for the values and people in which she believes. Yet, in contradiction to her film image, the interview constructed her as delicate, lacking ambition, and shy. She recalled never having dreamt about becoming an actress, but rather she had envisioned herself as a kindergarten teacher like her mother (because she loves to sing and play with children, and tell them stories) or as a flight attendant (because they always seemed to her as a child to be so gorgeous looking). Larry King reminded her – and the audience – that she is one of the most influential women in culture globally – and concluded with a question about her dreams for the future. Ziyi answered very gently and shyly that she is hoping to find a man, settle down, have children, and go back to her dream of becoming a kindergarten teacher. What does it mean when a cultural icon rehearses the most traditional dream of all for women? And even if her text was clearly scripted in order to produce a particular image for publicity purposes (as suggested by several media-savvy colleagues with whom I discussed this interview), what is the impact of a representation of a "desired" vision held by an extremely successful, well-known young woman on young people around the world?

A year and half later, I participated in a conference organized by the Geena Davis Institute for Gender in Media in Los Angeles (January 2008). Davis, a famous Academy-award-winning actress and the founder of the institute – known for her many roles of empowered women in films such as *Thelma & Louise* (1991), an American road movie that features two lead females breaking away from male oppression; and more recently as the President of the US in the TV drama series *Commander in Chief* (2006) – opened her lecture by relating a personal story about watching TV with her daughter: ... *and I immediately noticed that there seems to be a really substantial gender gap, not much better than what it was when I was a kid. I was pretty stunned by that.* She went on to describe how she realized while watching with her daughter the animated Disney film *Finding Nemo* (2003) that all the fish in the sea were male ...

Linda Seminsky, Director of Children's Programming at the US Public Broadcasting Service (PBS) and a well-respected authority in the community of children's television professionals, shared the following observation in her keynote address at the closing of the event: *I was watching television with my son one day, and at the end of it I said, "You know, there was not a single good, strong female character in any of those shows." All the female characters were secondary characters, or they were mean girls, or they were unlikeable for some reason. So, I first became interested in how few girl characters there were, and then, how awful they were.*

Examples abide. We all probably have a story to share about our viewing of, and critical reflections about, traditional portrayals of girls and boys, women and men, on television. What indeed could be alternative portrayals of male and female role models for children, models that would offer them, as well as us, the adults in their lives, a vision of a possible more gender-equal world, a vision ripe with possibilities for themselves? And how can these images be changed?

Over the years, critiques and calls for more equal and humane gender portrayals offered in the academic and intellectual literatures have left me unsatisfied and frustrated. Indeed, bookshelves are laden with critical analyses of gender portrayals in popular media, the arts, and literature. The Internet offers many conscious-raising sites. But I could hardly find an answer to the "what next" question; that is, we know what we do NOT want to see, but DO we know what we WANT to see? Does it have to be the case that academics are much better at critiquing existing images than we are at making practical recommendations for how to do things better? Indeed, in many of my interactions with well-intended producers and students of media, I found myself challenged by such familiar statements, as: *OK, I get you. I accept your criticisms of existing images. You've convinced me. I want to do things differently. So what do you suggest?*

In reflecting on such challenges, I realized that while I am very passionate and clear about what is wrong with gender images for children, I had not developed a compelling, positive, concrete vision of what I wish to see on the screen. Would it be the all-too-familiar role reversal of "crying boys who share their feelings and assertive girls who fight back?" Would we be content with just showing boys washing dishes and girls studying math? Such proposals, while certainly well intended, are not sufficient to advance significant change, socially and among the community of media professionals, as they are too limited and limiting, too binary, and unreflective of the nature of identity development in boys and girls. What I was searching for is a more authentic, complex, and creative vision. Perhaps, I speculated, insights into these issues could be obtained by speaking with those directly involved in producing images – the media professionals involved in producing quality television for children.

Critical studies of the production domains of television for children are few and far between. For example, we know very little about what media professionals assume and expect of their child audiences, and what roles they assign themselves.[1] What we do know for certain is that these are the professionals whose thinking and actions lead to the creation, and in many cases perpetuation, of these images. Therefore, I decided to investigate what media professionals think about issues related to the presentation of gender in children's television. This book is the result of such an effort – to discuss and to learn from the experience of media production professionals.

Once launched, this project became more ambitious and demanding than originally envisioned, but also much more exciting and inspiring. Over the course of five years, as I spoke with media professionals throughout the world, I took their observations, claims, advice, frustrations, dreams, and questions with me to the libraries in an attempt to integrate grounded professional knowledge with academic analytical and theoretical frames. Thus, the book that evolved shares their views and also seeks to demonstrate the potential benefits of integrating professional and academic ways of knowing about the media and social world. In doing so, it extends and adapts the feminist adage "the personal is political" into academic life, as proposed by Angharad Valdivia: "The intellectual is the personal is the political."[2]

Overall, then, this book is about processes of change – those that are taking place and those that need to occur – in the global television industry's presentation of gender in productions oriented to young audiences. In doing so, it also makes a bold attempt at reconciling cultural studies with political-economy analyses through a feminist lens. Through citations from the interviews I conducted, we come to learn about transformations in producers' gender ideology and its extension into production practices, their experimentations with more equal gender models, as well as the interviewees' alignment with the discourse of social responsibilities and how they advance visions for social change. As a presentation of this action research project, the book mobilizes the expertise of professional producers of quality television, allows their voices to be heard, and in doing so enables them to contribute to debates within the community of critical approaches to media studies.

In this spirit, I draw upon my Jewish heritage and the principle of "Tikkun Olam" (translated from Hebrew as "repairing the world" or "perfecting the world"). According to the rich Jewish history and traditions associated with this principle, humans are responsible for repairing a world made unjust by them and in doing so collectively increase the chances for the longevity of their transformations. Combined with my deep commitment to a feminist perspective on life, I embrace the concept of critical consciousness[3] as a prerequisite for resistance and for the possibility of change through a rejection of the naturalization of systems of social repression. I attempt to contribute to social change via introducing change in the social structures producing gender inequality in the area of my own work – children and media. One of the salient characteristics of feminist theory is its commitment not only to contribute to research and social theory, but also to be a catalyst for a deep social change, thus emphasizing the emancipating potential of combining knowledge and action. It recognizes that all knowledge is partial and socially situated, and all forms of scholarship are ideological by nature and political by implication. It values the researcher's own subjectivity and reflexive abilities and is ethically committed to promoting the wellbeing of those studied. Most of all, it is committed to obtaining, disseminating, and integrating knowledge in regard to specific change recommendations, thus assisting in liberating and empowering underprivileged segments of society.[4]

As a consequence, I have intentionally adopted an accessible writing style, free as much as possible from academic jargon. My goal in doing so is to make the text as friendly as possible to professionals, educators, and students of media, as well as to the scholarly community. It is not my intention to write a theoretical, Cultural Studies type of book. Rather, one through which the reader will see how theory can be applied in action in order to enhance our understanding and meaning-making in the empirical world. The breadth of the investigation required is so wide that it could include almost everything that has to do with gender and culture. Clearly, this is beyond the scope of any book, but I hope I have not neglected the most significant and central theoretical issues and that the references and suggestions for further readings will be helpful to those who wish to explore in greater depth the many issues raised in this book.

Chapter One begins with an integrative review of the main issues addressed, summarizing what we already know about portrayals of gender in children's television and the impact these images might be having on children's developing identities. This chapter forms the theoretical background and rationale for the study and leads to stating the main research questions. Chapter Two follows with a detailed presentation of how I went about exploring these issues and the methodological complexities of generating knowledge from interviews conducted with persons from around the world. Chapter Three engages the intersection of gender and culture in television for children to reveal the many concerns being bred by representations, locally and globally, and the main social-change challenges producers are addressing – or would like to address – in their work. This cultural-comparative discussion leads us to addressing, in Chapter Four, the thorny topic of sex and sexuality in television for children, perhaps one of the most contested issues among the professionals interviewed. Chapter Five grounds this study in political-economy debates: that is, the gendered nature of employment in the field, on one hand; and the professionals' envisioning of their audiences, on the other, as both impact the process of production of television for children. Chapter Six seeks to integrate all of the previous discussions by articulating eight working principles for changing gender presentation on children's screens. Finally, Chapter Seven presents a strong and I hope persuasive argument for pursuing the social change called for in this book.

The five years I have spent on this project were years of professional as well as personal growth, as traveling the world and meeting so many dedicated professionals has widened my own cultural experience and thought me lessons about tolerance, respect, compassion, understanding, and most of all academic and personal humility. In a continuous effort to develop a more sensitive cultural consciousness, I had to work hard to process through my own prejudices, misinformation, and stereotypes, to reflect and even to "unlearn" about race and ethnicities while acquiring the cultural knowledge and sensitivities necessary to interpret – I hope in authentic ways – and to make sense of the grounded knowledge made available to me. I was constantly challenged in this process by the need for introspection and self-reflexivity about my own cultural positioning and the power relationships between myself and those I was interviewing, and a desire to search for more egalitarian participatory styles of interviewing. In particular, I had many enlightened exchanges with colleagues from "enemy" countries, from the perspective of my own deeply conflicted Israeli home, colleagues I would have never had the opportunity to meet, let alone truly listen to, under different circumstances. These experiences gave me hope for a possibility of a better future for our children around the globe.

Chapter 1

Gender Representations and Their Socializing Role

What Do We Already Know?[1]

What do media representations of gender, those images that *re-present* females and males to us, contribute to children's understandings about themselves and who they should strive to be? How do the media construct what is portrayed as normative femininity and normative masculinity in our societies? We begin to address these key, general questions by reacquainting ourselves with what exists in practice. This will be followed by presenting a broad conceptualization of these issues, grounded in scholarly thinking and research, that serves as the rich resource for interpretations presented throughout this book. The chapter concludes with a discussion of the implications of gender representations for children's socialization and then, given all of the above, a brief presentation of the project's research agenda.

Features of Gender Representations in Children's Visual Media

Most visual media present characters that can be assigned to one of the two gender categories – be they humans, cartoon figures, animals, or science fiction characters. Collectively, such characters constitute a pool of models with whom children can negotiate, use to make meaning, identify with, and imitate – should they chose to do so. They define for them what is "normal" and accepted in their society. Consequently, adopting such models earns positive reinforcement, while those deemed exceptional, even deviant, are negatively sanctioned.

Findings from studies that have examined the portrayals of females and males on television, in movies, computer and video games, and advertisements point to a social world available to children that differentiates between the two genders quite systematically, in a manner much in line with representations in adult programming.[2] On the whole, like adult males, boys are identified with "doing" in the public sphere that is associated with characteristics such as action, rationality, forcefulness, aggressiveness, independence, ambitiousness, competitiveness, achievement, higher social status, and humor.

Girls, like adult women, are associated with "being" in the private sphere and are characterized, generally, as passive, emotional, caregiving, childish, sexy, subordinate to males, and of lower social status. Their "girly" personality traits are depicted as being fundamentally different in nature from those of boys. Girls, by contrast, are portrayed as being more romantic, sensitive, dependent, vulnerable, and continue to be defined more by their appearance than by their actions. Such dominant media messages in texts designed for children continue to promote the same restrictive ideologies of femininity and masculinity that characterize media in general, and say little about the multifaceted aspects of girls' and boys' lives, capabilities, and potential contributions to society.

Males – both younger and older – are the main heroes of most children's programs. They succeed in overcoming everyday problems, deal successfully with all sorts of dangers, and have many adventures. Even non-gendered imaginary characters – such as creatures and animals – are considered "naturally" to be male, unless they are specifically marked as female through processes of sexualizing their appearance (e.g. hair ribbons, long eyelashes, colored lips, waspwastes, long legs, short skirts, high heels). Female characters in most media texts for children are there to be saved and protected by the males and provide the background for the adventure. Above all, their position is defined by their meaning for the male heroes. Certain symbols, such as horses, dolphins jumping in front of a sunset, bunnies, and flowers are gendered in our societies and reinforced by market forces as "girlish." Other areas, such as technology, action, or fighting are almost always framed as male, hence reinforcing viewer expectations of masculine dominance in these domains. Marketing, and more specifically, television advertising and merchandise packaging for children, applies gendered clichés excessively in presenting goods for consumption by signaling gender intention via means such as glittery or pastel colors for girls and action-packed dark hues for boys.[3]

Thus, contemporary children's visual media continue to offer a significant underdevelopment of female characters. But what is even more striking, is the fact that the bulk of content presented to children continues to systematically promote quantified underrepresentation of females as well. For example, a study of gender prevalence and portrayal of G-rated (general viewing) films in the US (those deemed appropriate for children) found that only 28 percent of the speaking characters (both real and animated) were female; and only 17 percent of the films' narrators were female. Similarly, male characters constituted twice the number of female characters in television created for children in the US.[4] These findings are hardly unique for the US. A cross-cultural comparison involving 24 countries that analyzed over 26,000 characters in over 6,000 children's fictional programs broadcast for children 12 years old and under during 2007[5] reinforced these conclusions. First, and most striking, is the fact that the sample included twice as many males as females (68 percent and 32 percent respectively), reiterating the marginality of girls in all realms of life. This gender imbalance was evident all over the world, in public and private television, in international and domestic programming, in animated and real-life formats. Female characters were even more noticeably under-represented as non-human characters (animals, monsters, and robots), where the biological sex of a character is clearly an arbitrary choice: whether an animal, monster, or robot is a boy or a girl is a choice producers make. It seems that the greater the degree of creative freedom, the more the gender ration is biased towards male characters. The study also documented the fact that girls appear much more often in groups while males are independent loners and antagonists.

Furthermore, the study clearly suggested that Caucasian characters dominate children's TV screen around the world (72 percent), with the reality of ethnic diversity being repressed in most of the participating countries. That race and gender are heavily conflated in these images is strongly evident in the dominance of exaggerated Western body-types presented on children's television. Major gender differences related to body size were also found: Girls tended to be very thin, twice as thin as boys, who were twice as frequently overweight. This is particularly the case in animated programs marketed on a global scale. Analysis of 102 animated girls and young women in such programs points to alarming findings:[6] Globally, close to two in three young female characters have extremely unrealistic figures, with entirely unnatural small, wasp-like waists and long legs. What is more striking in these fabricated, unattainable figures is that they are so much alike, creating a unified model that puts even the heavily criticized Barbie figure behind as too curvy and full.[7]

These bodily characteristics are strongly related to an additional central feature of visual images of characters, which is the tendency to hypersexualize the appearance of young females. Females 11 years and under on TV for children were found to be almost four times as likely as males to be shown in sexy attire. Here, too, animated stories tended to exaggerate even more the unrealistic small waist and sexy appearance of girls, while at the same time animated action males were more likely to have a large chest and unrealistically masculinized physique than their live-action counterparts.[8] And, once again, we see how the restrictive "truism" of "girls appear" and "boys do" take up form and shape in presenting oversexualized girls and overactive boys in animated content consumed by children around the world.

Over-sexualized portrayals of girls in popular culture have continued to attract public and scholarly attention, including recent studies.[9] This phenomenon has been designated the "Lolita Effect,"[10] after the famous novel by Nabokov, which describes a complicated relationship between a mature man and a seductive teenage girl. The frequent presentation of sexy little girls or fun-fearless-sexual teenagers is entangled with myths of sexuality that link these portrayals to particular ideal body types and youth (i.e., only girls who look a particular way are "cool" and "sexy"), as well as to beliefs about girls' exhibitionism and manipulation that attract the male gaze and potential sexual violence toward them.[11] Scholars argue that the "Lolita Effect" suggests that the media circulate and contribute to the cultivation of distorted sets of myths about girls' sexuality that work to both undermine girls' healthy sexual development and at the same time to keep girls in their subordinated place in society.

Of course, we find changes over time[12] as well as exceptions in the domain of children's programming, as in adult media. The exceptions include some features (but not all, as their body images remain unchallenged) of Disney's female lead characters in more recent films such as *Pocahontas* and *Mulan* (and others discussed in the following chapters) as well as the global success of *Dora the Explorer*,[13] the Latina girl in the hit Nickelodeon pre-school program. Indeed, Nickelodeon, the commercial cable network for children, has been cited for the creation and inclusion of many new, multidimensional girl characters (e.g., *Clarissa, As Told By Ginger*).[14] While these exceptions, too, have been the subject of criticism (e.g. Disney's Pocahontas, for example, has been criticized for the continued romanticization of Native American women, particularly in relation to her love for a white man[15]), they serve to highlight, by way of contrast, the routine gender bias of everyday commercial popular media around the world.

One trend of new images noted is the shift of perspective from girls as victims to girls as active subjects and creative media producers themselves (e.g. of blogs, digital images, etc).[16] Of particular interest are depictions of strong but feminine girl heroes in children's television and video games, such as the animated series *The Powerpuff Girls, Kim Possible, Atomic Betty*, and others that have been inspired by the emergence of the concept of "Girl Power." While supergirls may be brave, smart, and independent, most of them also embrace the centrality of physical attractiveness (supposedly for their own pleasure) as liberated and empowered strong characters, and not as passive objects that are posing in order to please a male gaze.[17] The highly successful *Powerpuff Girls* animation series is exemplary of this evolving strategy, as it contains many contradictory messages about the coexistence of strength ("power") and femininity ("puff")[18] while nourishing itself on the themes of "girl power" and power feminism associated with third-wave feminism. Accordingly, being strong, brave, successful, and independent while fighting evil forces does not necessarily negate the pleasure of embracing "girlishness."

While the Powerpuff Girls are only five years old, analyses of other programs featuring "tough girls" – as warriors and superheroines – suggest that the range of socially accepted physical appearances offered by supergirls is restricted, hypersexualized, and Westernized. Girls who do not conform to these expectations are often socially sanctioned, even ostracized as outcasts. Thus, popular culture seems to be involved in an ambivalent process, wanting to depict strong girls in a manner such that they do not pose too dramatic a challenge to the traditional association between men and toughness. As a result, female toughness, while growing in scope and widening in character, is still greatly restricted and regulated in a variety of ways, including the over-emphasis on sexy appearance, never being tougher than the male partners, and the inclusion of overtones rendering a potential lesbian reading.[19] Female friendships among strong characters are rare and those that exist are over-shadowed by female rivalry. The exceptions – such as *Xena: Warrior Princess* and *Buffy the Vampire Slayer* – exemplify the possibility of toughness and female friendship and solidarity as feeding each other.[20] However, while successful young women characters like Buffy have attracted extensive scholarly and public attention,[21] the textual narrative and other visual markers relate the message that even strong empowered young females continue to offer girls lessons about normative feminine beauty as a key to success, popularity, and an exciting life.

Another emerging issue in images of girls and women discussed in the recent literature cites the presentation of more "brainy" characters who break away from the negative depiction of clever girls as unattractive and unpopular. Scholarly critique of this move argues that these portrayals maintain clever women in a subordinate position to men, as women whose cleverness and intelligence is a sexy asset and not an obstacle. Recent characters in children's cartoons (e.g. the PowerPuff Girls, Lisa in *The Simpsons*, Daria, Dora) as well as in family drama heavily consumed by children (e.g. *Gilmore Girls, Buffy the Vampire Slayer*) challenge this notion, suggesting that being smart and "cool" are not mutually exclusive nor do they cancel out one another.[22] This argument is aligned with a third-wave feminism notion that the feminist and the feminine are not necessarily binary positions, and that one can be an independent and smart girl and still enjoy displaying girlish sensibilities and feminine performances.

Irrespective of these changes, in most of the television fare viewed by children around the world we find ambivalence about girls' intelligence and the threat it might pose to the normalized gender order, as expressed among others by the resilience of the "dumb (or bitchy) blonde" stereotype and the presentation of girls who are not as clever as their male friends. Being clever is often signified by unfashionable clothing, wearing glasses, a lack of self confidence, and the like, and is juxtaposed to romance and female nurturance. Alternatively, smart girls often use "subversive niceness" to make their intelligence less noticeable and more palatable.[23] The problem with such strategies is that they match the preconceived notions that women are "manipulative" and "conniving," using their feminine traits to get what they want.

Race has also been an area of exploration and change in children's TV, with a growing blurring of racial differences. Here, rather than presenting a binary categorization of black/white, there is a tendency for hybridity and ambiguity that allows for open interpretation as to the racial identities of characters.[24] The hugely successful *Bratz* characters and dolls exemplify this phenomenon, as do the *Cheetah Girls, Dora,* and Gabriella from *High School Musical* and various other "brown" characters that speak to many races and "travel" success-fully internationally. What seems like a fluidity of the category of "Whiteness" and the "browning" of characters is perceived, apparently, by producers and audiences alike, as more inclusive and universal. This strategy may seem to be less threatening than clear racial distinctions, and thus it serves marketing purposes quite well.

Male images in children's television have been showing some signs of change as well. One trend is the growing numbers of buffoons and not particularly handsome "geeks" portrayed as techno-oriented wizards who are going to rule the world through their brains and mastery of technology (modeled, for example, after Bill Gates, Chairman of Microsoft and one of the world's wealthiest people). Yet, scholars have noted a stronger trend towards the hypermasculinity of animated male characters, portrayed through the growing size of their bodies, for example by huge biceps and shoulders. One consequence is that such "beefy men" assume more space (both physically and symbolically) on the screen. Some researchers argue, as well, that these characterizations are a form of backlash to the perceived threats to traditional masculinity posed by the feminist and gay movements as well as a reaction to the Vietnam War and the perception of "weak Americans"[25] reinforced since with the events of 9/11 and recent military actions.

In conclusion, while we find a decrease in some types of traditional gender stereotypes on television for children, other stereotypes are emerging and becoming more prominent. Clearly, one major limitation of this review is that it is based entirely on scholars studying programs that are produced in the US media and are circulated around the world. All too often, we know very little about the representations of gender in locally produced programs, to which much discussion will be devoted in the following chapters. Overall, American television continues to offer restrictive images of young people, female and male. This is particularly surprising given the fact that professionals involved in the production of children's television in leading organizations report increasing awareness and concern for the social world they are portraying. For example, one such senior professional wrote in 2007: "The reality is that children's programs are – and always have been – very strongly self-policed by broadcasters and by producers themselves;" adding that they regularly employ consultants with backgrounds in developmental psychology and education.[26] Similarly, another senior professional reported the details of collaborative efforts between academic advisors and producers of television programs for children at NBC, one of the major US networks. Although violence was the predominant issue of concern at the time, gender stereotyping was addressed as well.[27] Such testimonies intensify the complexity involved in understanding the continued prevalence of gender stereotypes in children's television at the beginning of the twenty-first century.

Furthermore, this situation emphasizes the important roles of the visual media, and particularly television, as social-change mechanisms. On the one hand, many would argue that the media can be employed to advance actions oriented to achieving greater gender equality, while conversely, others seek – consciously or unconsciously – to preserve the existing social order, and hence the media become a mechanism of social control.

Theoretical Conceptualization and Framing

Given the development and present status of gender representations in children's media, our next order of business is to define the theoretical issues underlying them, the mechanisms driving the construction and distribution of these representations, and the dynamics involved in their possible change. The conceptualizing of these phenomena will also provide us with concepts and principles to be drawn upon in interpreting the study's findings.

The study of representations assumes that gender is socially constructed, involving an ongoing process in which learned sets of behaviors, expectations, perceptions, and subjectivities are applied by individuals, social institutions, and societies in defining what it means to be a woman and what it means to be a man. The main critiques of this Cultural Studies school of thought are that, first, a hegemonic cultural ordering presents gender differences as biologically determined and "natural," and therefore immutable. Second, the concealed patriarchal ideology driving this process seeks to naturalize beliefs and practices that advance the supremacy of men over women. The French philosopher Simone de Beauvoir's[28] formative statement – "One is not born a woman, but becomes one" – captures the essence of this process. Accordingly, gender is not viewed as something originally existent in human beings, but rather it is a set of understandings that organize how we relate to our bodies that is produced through behaviors and social relations in the practices of daily life. As such, gender is distinct from the biological, sexual differences that characterize humans from birth.

Accordingly, gender is considered to be a product of "social technologies"[29] that include, among others, media texts, the arts, and institutionalized discourses about appropriate behaviors, appearances, belief systems, personality characteristics, and every other aspect of our lives. Accordingly, while it is a biological fact that women can give birth, it is a social construction that women in most societies are expected to be "natural mothers" and are the gender better suited to be children's dominant caregivers.[30] Some feminist and queer scholars problematize these issues even more when they suggest that the body, too, is not a natural, biological constant but something that is interpreted culturally, and thus the distinction between sex and gender is once again blurred, with sex being perceived as a social construction as well.

In many ways, such theorizing undermines what most people take for granted as natural: a relationship between our sex, our gender, and our sexuality (e.g., that having female sexual organs, also means that we behave in a way that is construed as "feminine" in our society, and that we are also sexually attracted to men and engage in heterosexual relationships). It also opens the human experience to all possible intersections of the three (e.g., that there is no necessary relationship between our organs, our appearance, who we perceive ourselves to be, who we are attracted to sexually, etc.).[31] The taken-for-granted nature of this understanding is a marker of the success of the patriarchal ideology.

Working on the basis of these fundamental assumptions, the media have been criticized for their role in legitimizing and reinforcing gender-related stereotypes, and in doing so, for their contribution to the continuation of gender inequality and discrimination. At the core of this critique is the claim that media portrayals of social life continue to function as a primary mechanism in retention of the binary view of gender, according to which there is a "forced" separation between the public sphere of the open, rational, political world of men and the private sphere of the closed, emotional, caregiving world of women. The media continue to produce such portrayals in spite of the general advancing state of social change challenging gender inequalities around the world and specific attempts to change media representations.

In order to explain and expand on this critical interpretation, the following sections present an integrative overview of research and the theories that have evolved from it about the ways the mass media portray gender and the potential for change.

Media and Gender

Researchers are in general agreement that the media are a socializing force that have significant influence on how we learn to define ourselves and others by our gender and so develop our subjectivities about our own and others' gender. As a result, feminist scholars have focused their research, analyses, and critiques on the roles of the mass media. The premise driving these studies is that media representations are contemporary expressions of deeper ideological assumptions and discourses, rooted in worldviews and belief systems that produce a particular view of gender. Such representations have been blamed for reaffirming and supporting gender hierarchies existing worldwide, as well as for maintaining the social *status quo* and the general subordination of women by reproducing social perceptions that legitimize dominant ideologies, such as patriarchy (based on gender differences), capitalism (based on economic-class differences), and colonialism (based on ethnic differences).

However, given that representations are discursive constructions (i.e. they are realities constructed through discourse), they are not perceived to be enduring practices. Rather, they assume different forms and meanings in different places and times under varied political, cultural, social, and economic contexts, and within diverse ideologies. As a result, gender representations are understood to be dynamic, fluid, changeable, and contested sets of social practices and perceptions. Accordingly, the investigation and analysis of representations serves as a central way to understand gender. And, as advanced by feminist media researchers, such investigations are an important part of the feminist project of problematizing and critiquing ways of knowing, as well as taken-for-granted assumptions about our lives.

Representations and Reality

The complex relationships between gender representations and reality have been the focus of much academic debate, particularly in the Cultural Studies tradition, in general, and more specifically the branch that developed in England since the 1950s. The latter tradition, and specifically the Birmingham School, was important in the formation of second wave social and cultural feminist thought, particularly in drawing insights from structuralism and post-structuralism. These approaches take the view that representations do not have an original, authentic "reality" that can be represented or misrepresented accurately (i.e. a concrete reality of being a woman and a concrete reality of being a man), but rather see gender as a form of "performance" involving the acting out of expected social scripts.[32]

Since gender itself is understood to be a construction, rather than material reality, gender representations in the media are understood to be *representations of representations*, standing for the *meaning* of the original subject, rather than the material subject itself.[33] In contrast to studies of sex-role stereotyping and images of women, this approach does not assume that there are right or wrong, good or bad ways of representing a woman or a man. Rather, this perspective moves the emphasis from concerns for individuals to the larger categories of femininity and masculinity and shifts the burden of responsibility from critique of the "accuracy" of representations to challenging the systems that construct and create them – their political economy, power hierarchies, ideological infrastructures, and goals. Accordingly, the question asked is not whether particular images of men and women (e.g. in advertising, news, or drama) are "accurate" portrayals of the way men and women "really" are in the concrete world, but rather – how are specific images constructed and what are the mechanisms driving them? As we proceed in this book, we will see that this is exactly the question we are attempting to answer here: That is, not whether a particular image of a girl or a boy in China, Bolivia, Sweden, or South Africa is "accurate" and "true to life" in these countries, but rather are the gender representations constructed by producers an ideological mechanism transmitting image-messages about social life via television, and if so, how can they be changed?

Building upon the work of Indian literary critic and theorist Gayatri Chakravorty Spivak, who extended Karl Marx's nineteenth-century socialist arguments, feminist media scholars claim that media gender representations have two complementary meanings:[34] According to one meaning, media representations are "portraits" or the "making present" of women and men and their gendered realities. An investigation of such a meaning illuminates the ideologies, interests, life circumstances, and privileges (be they class, race, sexuality, and others) that influence the way gender is constructed. The second meaning relates to "proxy" or "speaking out for" women and men. In this regard there is a need to ask: Whose voice is allowed in the media? Who speaks on behalf of whom? And, who gets to represent themselves?

The case of women and the news illustrates the difference between these two meanings and their interdependency. The first meaning refers to women as news subjects; that is, the ways in which they are portrayed (e.g. as victims, trophy wives, celebrities, politicians). The second refers to women as producers of news (e.g., reporters, editors, spokespersons for organizations). These two meanings are also interrelated, involving issues of culture and politics, and combined to challenge dominant power systems that influence both who and how gender is "made present" as well as how and who is "speaking for" oneself and others. Following the French philosopher Michel Foucault, the study of representations recognizes that power operates in cultures through its various discourses and is located in the analysis of the symbolic systems through which people communicate and organize their lives.

The underlying premise driving many of these intellectual readings is that representations are related to subordination and oppression in the material world. More specifically, in regard to certain media genres of representations, such as pornography for example, there is a compound set of inter-relationships between reality and representations. This is due to the fact that in pornography, women are abused, humiliated, harassed, and raped not only in the symbolic but also in the material world in the process of its production.[35]

Femininity versus Masculinity

One of the primary critiques of popular media's gender representations argues that the historical construction of femininity and masculinity has been conducted through binary as well as hierarchical oppositions.[36] While generally men have been presented as "normal," representing the majority of society, women have been presented as the minority "other," the "second sex" – the exception, the incomplete, the damaged, the marginal, and sometimes even the bizarre. Such dichotomization is a form of dualistic thought rooted in the Enlightenment worldview that includes such binary divisions as those constructed between rational/emotional, spirit/body, culture/nature, public/private, subject/object, West/East, modern/traditional. In accordance with this perspective, men and women have been constructed, systematically, as inhabiting opposing sides of these dualities, with the masculine associated with the highly valued rational-spirit-culture-public-subject-West-modern and the feminine with the devalued emotional-body-nature-private-object-East-traditional.

Examinations of media representations conducted throughout the second part of the twentieth century revealed the existence of the same fundamental principles of patriarchal thinking across cultures around the world, including relegation of the feminine to the private sphere, restriction of the presentation of women to the bodily functions of sex and reproduction, and the location of women within the world of emotions – where rational thought is lacking and behavior uncultivated. Furthermore, personality traits of women are depicted as being fundamentally different in nature from those of men: On the whole, women have been represented as subservient as well as less logical, ambitious, active, independent, and heroic. In contrast, they have been represented as more romantic, sensitive, dependent, emotional, and vulnerable. Critics have argued that such representations perpetuate another dichotomy – one reserved in patriarchal culture for women: The "Madonna," on one hand, and the "whore," on the other. As "Madonna," women are cast in the role of mother – the one who gives birth, nurtures, raises, sacrifices herself, and finally the one who mourns her loved ones. As "whore," they are pressed into the mold of a sexual object, the essence of whose existence is tantalizing and threatening to the male, and whose ultimate fate is to be punished as a victim of violence and exploitation. Such media representations, claim critics, legitimize the dehumanization of women, and relate to them as objects lacking consciousness and individuality.

Masculinity, too, as the hegemonic cultural form, has been constructed as a "natural" state of being that is commonly conceived and framed within several normative expectations: Physical domination and subordination of others (humans and nature alike); occupational achievements and purposeful and rational attitudes; familial patriarchy in which the male is protector and provider; daring and staying outside the domestic sphere; sexual lust with heterosexuality as the dominant model.[37] Deviation from these norms is prohibited, socially as well as psychologically, as any departure is seen to threaten hegemonic masculine identity. As a result, media representations emphasize a masculinity associated with the public sphere and the world of occupation, competition, achievements, and social status. In comparison with women, men have been largely portrayed as more rational, individual, independent, as well as those who have difficulty in the expression of emotions and in displaying weakness. They are represented as more culturally and technologically oriented than are women, demonstrate self-restraint and tend to dominate both women and nature. Male expressions of the emotive are cast through forms of bonding, with "men in arms" as expressions of solidarity, loyalty, determination, and sense of purpose. They are constructed in association with action, adventure, aggression, competition, and preoccupation with vehicles, technology, and weapons. The male subordination of women is presented as related to their sexual drive. In contrast to the emphasis on women's appearance, men are defined by their action: women "appear" and men "do."

Social "myths" are one of the primary mechanisms through which these constructions of femininity and masculinity are maintained and perpetuated. As explained by the French literary critic and semiotician Roland Barthes,[38] myths are ways of conceptualizing gender within particular historical and cultural contexts in ways that make it seem natural; that is, as a taken-for-granted, common-sense lived understanding of what it means to be a man or a woman. In this way, myths perform as mechanisms that disguise the ideologies and the power systems driving them. In terms of media research, the argument offered is that the media produce and reproduce these myths through the gender representations they offer to their audiences.

One such prevalent myth is the ever popular "beauty myth," discussed by the American writer Naomi Wolf.[39] This myth constructs a certain kind of femininity, masculinity, and the relationship between them, according to which women are defined and assessed by the beauty of their appearance and men by their desire to conquer such women. This emphasis on a particular form of beauty (largely rooted in White feminine forms characterized by a limited range of external, physical attributes, such as big breasts, slim wastes, long legs, flawless skin, blonde hair, and blue eyes) has been accused of sending women on an endless quest for a "look" that is unattainable and guarantees a life of frustration, feelings of inadequacy, and a wasteful exploitation of emotional, intellectual, and material resources, as a woman's happiness and self fulfillment become dependent on her appearance.

The glorification of external appearance as the most central characteristic of a woman's essence is related directly to the media's overemphasis on the portrayal of women as sexual beings whose central function is relegated to being objects of male sexual desire and pursuit. Accordingly, such dominant media messages continue to promote restrictive ideologies of femininity, glorify heterosexual romance as a central goal for women, encourage male domination in relationships, and stress the importance of beautification through consumption, while dismissing the validity of women's own sexual feelings and desires apart from masculine desire.

Difference and Diversity

Through the evolution of feminist theorizing, we recognize now that gender can be an unstable and highly contested social category, and that gender experiences and identities are heterogeneous, fluid, ambiguous, incoherent, and ever-changing. This is because gender is always situated in a particular cultural context and historicity, and conflated with other social categories such as race, class, ethnicity, religion, and sexuality. As a result, the process of gender representation is strongly linked to other socially constructed systems of difference and exclusion.

The problematization and rejection of binary concepts, especially the critique of the East–West binary by the Palestinian-American theorist and activist Edward Said,[40] brought to the forefront an interest in multiculturalism and diversity. This critique challenged social systems that privilege men's representations of women and their speaking on behalf of women, and led to the reconceptualization of other forms of subordination. For example, texts in which the colonizer represents and speaks for the colonized, and the resulting process of "internalized colonialism" through which the subordinates incorporate such constructions into their self-imagined subjectivity. As the UK cultural theorist Stuart Hall argues,[41] use of dominant representations has the power to impose on audiences a perspective on themselves as "other," much in the same way that women are taught to view themselves as "other" in comparison with men.[42]

The contributions of post-colonial and postmodern theorizing to feminist studies of representation led to the recognition that there is a need to confront the challenge of representing marginalized others, to unravel the relationship between diversity and inequalities, as well as between representations and the power systems driving them. The discussion of the need to "decolonize" representations and to develop a transnational perspective[43] is also related to the question of representational "silences:" what and who is not represented, what and who is missing? Critical analyses of "White femininity," as reproduction of the supremacy of White culture, for example, evident in a variety of cultural icons (e.g., the original Barbie dolls; portrayals of the late Princess Diana; the news coverage of the American soldier Jessica Lynch's captivity and rescue in Iraq; or the many prime-time American serials, and commercial heroines, traveling globally) highlight the conflation of gender and race and the complexities of the power systems involved. This has reinforced the well-established claim that while women around the world suffer from varying degrees of subordination, they do not have the same options and choices, due to variance in their location in the power structures. As a result, the gaps between popular representations and the life of the majority of women around the world are often inconsolable.

Changing Trends

More recent studies have found evidence of gradual change seeping into gender representations used in the media. For example, women have been appearing more frequently in media texts in professional roles, in addition to being maintained in their roles as keepers of the private sphere. Men, too, have appeared as partners and caregivers in the realm of the family, along with being maintained in their other, dominant male roles. This gradual transition within representations of Western, middle-class society can be attributed to cultural changes in the real world and to cumulative influence of the feminist revolution. Thus, there is evidence that contemporary struggles faced by women are raised and examined by the media, including explorations in issues of gender politics and feminism and its goals

The growing diversity of gender representations and the constructions of multiple variations for what it means to be a woman and a man in popular culture have resulted in offering an array of gender options, some contradictory.[44] Often referred to as "post-feminist," proactive media representations offer portrayals of females who are complex and distinct from one another on a variety of variables, including those mentioned above – such as race, ethnicity, sexuality, class, and religion, but also education, age, marital status, motherhood, personal abilities and disabilities, and the like. The rupturing of dualities can include, for example, female characters who "want it all" rather than making a choice between family and career; who refuse to choose between feminism and femininity, such as leading an active, independent life but choosing to cater to traditional requirements of appearance and norms of conduct. Furthermore, representations of "power feminism," which move from women's oppression to celebration of women's abilities and achievements, are becoming more commonplace in popular media. Deconstructing binary categories of gender and sexuality, in particular, and perceiving them to be flexible and indistinct, allows for growing experimentation, as well, with representations of gay, transgender, transsexual, and bisexual lives.[45]

Two complementary interpretations have been offered regarding these developments. First, it has been noted that there is a strong tendency for "categorical exchange:" women are shifted into categories of masculine representation, as independent and powerful, for example, as typified by a number of women politicians and female journalists holding senior positions; as tough action-adventure heroines in computer games; or as preoccupied with lust and sex. Similarly, men are presented in ways usually perceived as feminine: as sexual objects in advertisements; or as tearful, broken-hearted, repulsed lovers in dramas. However, the use of categorical exchange, while interesting to analyze in its own right, does not necessarily allow for the identification or expression of unique female and male experiences, worldviews, and values.

Second, the influence of commercial forces has been offered as an explanation for the emergence of innovative representations of women as well as men. According to this view, the growing emphasis on "career women" or "sensitive men," as well as the presentation of sexually active women and men as objects of desire, may be more a reflection of consumer culture pressure than of deep structural changes in ideological underpinnings. As a result, the "new" woman is acceptable as long as she is not only strong, but also sexy; and the new type of sensitive man is becoming more acceptable as long as it is clear that he is not only sensitive but also successful.

Despite such developments, there are few signs of a deeper structural change. Many scholars of gender representations argue that these changes are not more than added nuances that leave the patriarchal ideology intact, as they continue to "naturalize" as well as justify male domination while contributing to the internalization of this ideology. As a result, differences between men and women continue to be accepted as real, essentialist, and natural. On the whole, such a representational system is detrimental to both women and men, albeit in varying degrees, since it teaches both to adopt particular perceptions, roles, and practices that reinforce their differential placements in the social hierarchies as they continue to perpetuate the supremacy of the White male. Accordingly, feminist analysis of gender representations points out the need to continue to engage in reflexive critique and deconstruction of representations as well as of the institutions that produce them.

Construction of Gendered Identities and Roles

Accumulatively, one of the most pervasive conclusions from research and theorizing on representations is the implications they have as dominant agents of socialization in children's lives today.[46] Studies of the influence of such gender images as described above on children's developing identities found evidence that they play a significant role in children coming to adopt traditional perceptions of gender roles. Overall, the research on television's role in developing gender stereotypes among children is not unequivocal. This is due, among other reasons, to the difficulty in identifying the specific contributions television makes to developing gender stereotypes from those of other socializing agents such as parents, educators, or religious institutions. Cultural perceptions of gender are so deeply embedded in all human societies that children have ample, daily, first-hand experiences and opportunities to internalize them. However, when restrictive perceptions of gender are advanced on a massive scale and on a daily basis, as is the case with the distribution of many American-based media products for children, the constant presentation of values and role models may serve as a significant contribution to reinforcement and internalization as well as normalization and legitimization of the current social structure and its underlying patriarchal ideology. This may explain how the media contribute to children learning what are considered to be appropriate gendered norms of behavior and expectations regarding gender roles, such as: the range of professions available to them, specific expectations regarding romance, how to manage sexual relationships, marriage and family life, and so forth.

For example, young girls, in particular, may be learning self-effacement through these texts and so be encouraged to direct their emotional and physical resources to the attainment of unrealistic expectations in order to gain peer acceptance (such as the constant disciplining of the body in order to ensure physical perfection associated, among other things, with eating disorders and other forms of self-mutilation).[47] Indeed, young girls continue to be a primary target audience for the Western type of advertising that instills the "beauty myth" from an early age. Through continued exposure to such messages in popular texts, young girls learn to seek an "improved" self through a continuous cycle of regulatory practices (e.g. dieting, exercising, grooming, removing hair, etc.) and product consumption. The research evidence related to the predominant theme of sexualization of girls suggests that they internalize self-objectification, develop lower self-esteem, and assume the belief that their body is the key site of their femininity and that attractiveness rather than personality and achievements is the best path to social acceptance, romance, and status. These beliefs are carried out in their social relationships that include, among other roles, policing other girls' conformity to the specific constraints of the beauty myth, competing for boys' attention through self-sexualization, and legitimizing patriarchal "blame the victim" attitudes regarding sexual harassment and abuse.[48]

In a similar manner, the research evidence suggests that the target audience of young boys learn to associate masculinity with physical domination and subordination of others, humans and nature alike, with occupational achievement, a purposeful and rational attitude, as well as with sexual lust. For example, media superheroes popular throughout the world – such as characters in the animated as well as live-action *Superman*, *Batman*, and *Spiderman* series – play a primary role in many boys' development of male identity. They are the embodiment of the "perfect" traditional man: most heroes are strong, brave, muscular, always on the lookout to defend the weak, undefeatable, active in the outdoors, full of adventure, and are adored by females. Viewing and internalizing these superheroes enables boys to evolve their own desires, and so establish relevancy to their own lives. At the same time, storylines involving dominance and aggression situated in the context of conflict and threats restrict young males' identity development and limit their ability to experiment with emotions and experience other possible social scripts.[49] For example, many of the action-adventure animations, dramatic series, and video and computer games directed at young male audiences equate masculinity with physical strength, aggression, and weaponry. Collectively, the overwhelming message they convey is that "toughness" is the most valued masculine quality in need of cultivation. This "tough guise"[50] can be viewed as the male equivalent to the female "beauty myth" – as both offer very restrictive social scripts and visions for what it means to be a woman and a man in our times.

At the same time, the current literature emerging out of the Cultural Studies tradition suggests that children are active meaning-makers and have the potential to be self-conscious and reflexive in their approach to popular media texts. However, it also recognizes that children are constrained by their cultural milieu and so oriented to the ideological workings of the patriarchal, capitalist, and colonialist hegemonies driving these media texts. Scholars surmise that most stereotypical popular media fare may constrain the inner worlds of both girls and boys and contribute to the reproduction, via children's responses, of a limited range of cultural expectations.[51]

Consequentially, the approach adopted in this book does not embrace the "strong effects" tradition in media research (i.e., one that assumes casual effects of these gender images on their audiences) in an uncritical manner, but rather the "construction of meaning" tradition of Cultural Studies.[52] The arguments presented take their point of departure from the claims that, first, the meanings of gender images are not self-evident or immanent in the texts; and, second, they are not simply transmitted from text to child, but are established and negotiated actively by individual children who are socially and culturally situated. Evidence of such processes is often found through reception studies that inquire into the ways audiences – in this case children – make meaning, interpret, and relate media contents to their own lives.

Much Cultural Studies research has centered on women and girls in the context of media content traditionally associated with them (e.g. soap operas, teens' and women's magazines, romance novels, pop music, and advertising). These studies have revealed the dynamics of how female viewers gain pleasure, sometimes even a sense of empowerment and control, from content that is seemingly oppressive to them. Research of pre-adolescents and adolescents focused on the role of the media in central developmental tasks in this period. In particular, identity development and learning to deal with social pressures, both of which are important in evolving perceptions of femininity and masculinity. One approach advanced argues for a view of media texts as "sites of struggle" between conflicting social forces including traditional patriarchal forces versus female resistance; capitalist value systems versus alternatives such as socialism, Marxism, or religious moralities; uncritical acceptance of the adults' way of life and worldviews versus the cynical, critical visions of the younger generation.[53]

These conclusions are instructive, too, for those interested in exploring the potential of popular texts for children in order to advance feminist-oriented structural change regarding identity, in general, and gender, in particular. Television (in all its forms – including video, DVDs, cable and satellite reception, computer downloads, etc.) is, as noted, still the most dominant medium in children's lives and is highly accessible around the world, including in developing societies. Viewing television is perceived as a voluntarily leisure activity associated with pleasure and stimulation of emotional involvement. Actors and actresses provide meaningful and adored role models for identification, wishful thinking, and imitation. The accumulated body of knowledge has established that incidental non-intended learning from television is highly significant. No other socializing agent – be it the family, formal and informal educational systems, or religious institutions – has such appeal. In addition, the trend for media convergence suggests that television images are commonly found in other media, including Internet images, computer, video, and mobile-phone games.

Thus, focusing on visual media is an advisable strategy for advancing deep social change in the perception of gender among the greatest number of children from many diverse backgrounds and life circumstances. "Edutainment" genres (i.e. those which integrate education with entertainment)[54] that address a variety of issues – such as health, literacy, and peace building – have been constructed and employed around the world to advance such change. One such approach recruits popular television texts to advance awareness of social issues, with the ultimate goal of contributing to the empowerment of young viewers by providing them not only with information and knowledge, but also with role models, reasons, values, and the motivation to be involved in shaping attitudes and actions that can be incorporated in their own everyday lives The effectiveness of most such efforts has yet to be studied in a systematic, comprehensive manner, although from what we already know about the relationship between children and media, there is reason to believe that such an approach does have great potential to contribute to the wellbeing of children viewers.[55]

Asking New Questions

Given what we know about dominant gender representations, as summarized throughout this chapter, including the roles of the media as socializing agents, the study reported in this monograph set out to explore the following questions:

- What alternative portrayals of male and female role models for children can be offered, models that will offer children as well as the adults in their lives a vision of a possible more gender-equal world?
- How can these gender images be changed?

Media studies have traditionally explored the three complementary realms of inquiry: the content of media texts, the audiences that receive them, and the producers that produce them. The aim of this project was to focus on the latter component of this chain: The producers and their reflexive thoughts about their everyday practices of producing gendered texts. Put in a different way, this book investigates the less studied side in Hall's famous encoding/decoding model of communication – the process of encoding meanings about gender into messages in children's quality programming.[56] Restated in the language of the research literature, we ask: Is it possible that producers of television for children can resist use of conventional gender representations? Can – and should – television stimulate significant change in our perceptions of what it means to be a girl and what it means to be a boy? Can – and should – it attempt to cause "gender trouble," to use Judith Butler's provocative book title, by exposing the problematics of gender as a category defining human beings and de-naturalizing it (denying its "natural" qualities), as well as locating different possibilities of resistance to normative definitions of gender?[57]

   As we embark on a journey in the following pages to find and to assess satisfactory answers to these questions, you will read about the experiences and opinions of producers of quality television programs for children from around the world. In all honesty, this is all too rare an opportunity – at least in academic circles. Indeed, in spite of their shared interest in television for children, it has been my experience through many years of work in this field that academics and producers hardly speak to each other, and commonly treat one another with suspicion, even disrespect. Producers often believe that academics are trapped in ivory towers and are ignorant of how the television world really operates; for example, the kinds of organizational constraints that tie their hands and limit their creative freedom. Academics, for their part, often believe that producers are not interested in what research has to say, are mostly motivated by the pursuit of profit and personal fame, and are too vain to seek relevant knowledge that could inform their work. When members of these two communities meet in professional gatherings, their stigmatization and mutual distrust often collide or create tense interchanges. In this book I hope to initiate a different type of meeting – dialogical in nature, in the spirit of Martin Buber's "I – Thou" conception, hence involving open and empathetic listening ground in mutual respect, building upon shared interest in and devotion to the wellbeing of girls and boys around the world.

Chapter 2

Studying Producers of Quality Television Around The Globe

Methodological Issues

Between June 2004 and June 2008, I sought out and interviewed media professionals involved in producing quality television for children in the following six international gatherings of professionals:

- Prix-Jeunesse International Competition (Munich, Germany), June 2004; June 2006; June 2008;
- The Japan Prize (Tokyo, Japan), October 2006;
- The Basel-Karlsruhe Forum (Basel, Switzerland), January 2007;
- Fifth World Summit on Media for Children (Johannesburg, South Africa), March 2007.

Altogether 135 interviews were conducted with professionals from 65 countries involved in producing media for children. A detailed account of this process and the major issues it entailed is provided in this chapter, as I believe this background will assist the reader to contextualize the themes and interviews as well as assess the value of the findings.

Quality Television for Children

We begin with discussing the nature of one of the primary characteristics employed in defining all of these conferences: All of these events claim to be involved in advancing quality television for children.

The meaning of quality television is a much debated issue in both the professional and the scholarly worlds. It is entangled with issues of power hierarchies: who defines what quality is and on whose behalf? How is quality judged differently for different audiences? Furthermore, the criteria for judgment of quality may shift across cultures as well as through time. For example, new television genres and aesthetics as well as innovations in television production techniques may have created a need to adjust definitions of what quality might mean. Furthermore, all discussion of quality recognizes that the criteria employed are colored by value judgments, personal taste, and emotional responses to television content.[1] To complicate things even further, several scholars have argued that "quality" television can be distinguished from "good" television: While the former is based on quality criteria related to genre, the latter is based on critical judgment regarding what is actually good or bad.[2] Others have added that quality also depends on the usefulness to the consumers of the program and whether it fulfills its viewers' expectations.[3]

For the purposes of this study, "quality television for children" was defined operationally as any television program accepted for presentation in one of the events specified above as well as those produced by educational and public broadcasters around the world. In addition, a few commercial programs were discussed, when interviewees chose to define them as "quality television for children." One might say, then, that I adopted a professional "self-definition" approach to quality television. Clearly, this is a very restricted, yet grounded definition, one that relieved me of the responsibility of attempting to make impossible decisions about "quality" in relation to hundreds of television programs produced in dozens of languages around the world.

At the same time, the description of the events that follows builds upon what I have found to be commonly accepted, self-adopted guiding principles for developing quality children's television:[4]

- Provide children with programs prepared especially for them without taking advantage of them; programs that entertain, but at the same time try to advance child viewers – physically, mentally, and socially.
- Develop programs that allow children to hear, see, and express themselves, as well as their culture, language, and life experiences in ways that affirm their personal identity, community, and place. This is promoted by taking steps to protect and encourage programs that reflect local cultures and those with minority languages.
- Recognize differences between children that are a result of their cognitive and emotional development, their talents, interests, personality characteristics, interpersonal relationships, and their social environment.
- Avoid unnecessary presentation of violence and sex in programs.
- Offer children a variety of genres and content, and do not reproduce programs according to a successful formula.

In addition, more specific criteria are used in the literature to evaluate quality television programs for children from a production-values point of view:

- Does the program invite children to see things they have not seen in the past; to hear things they have not heard before; and most importantly – to think or imagine things that they would otherwise not have thought about or imagined?
- Does the program tell a good story? Does it rely on the familiar to bridge to the new and unfamiliar ? Are verbal and visual components compatible?
- Does the program offer characters that children really care about? Is there a struggle between good and bad that is not too extreme? Are the children in

the program capable of overcoming difficulties in a reasonable manner? Is the end of the story dependent on the generosity, fairness, honesty, caring, and responsibility of the main characters?

- Does the program avoid preaching to children or talking down to them in a condescending manner? Does it avoid presenting adults as behaving in an unfair, irrational, or foolish manner? Does it undermine children's trust in the adult world?
- Does the program expand the children's world of experiences in an aesthetically appealing manner?
- Does the program include a degree of wittiness and humor that does not exploit others?

The Events

Familiarity with the unique nature of the events during which data was collected via interviews and the kind of people they attract is crucial to understanding the professional, social, and cultural context in which these interviews took place, and thus we devote attention to describing them in detail. I have purposefully maintained the idealistic discourse and celebratory tone associated with these events in order to reflect the kind of atmosphere and self-image they project/carry, as I believe such a narrative may help readers to appreciate the discourse elicited and situate the knowledge gained.

The Prix Jeunesse International Festival[5] takes place in Munich biannually and brings together more than 350 children's television producers from over 60 countries. With entries from telecasters around the world, the festival is a showcase and competition to honor the world's best television programs for children aged 2–15, paying tribute to programs that, within their cultural context, help young people to develop physically, mentally, and socially to their fullest potential. Prix Jeunesse, a foundation at the Bavarian Broadcasting Corporation supported by the Society for the Promotion of International Youth and Educational Television, led by an International Advisory Board,[6] endorses the idea that television should be attractive to the target audience, should enable children to see, hear, and express themselves and their cultures, and should promote an awareness and appreciation of other cultures. Prix Jeunesse has enhanced its initial role as an international festival and competition since its inception in 1964 by becoming a global organization actively involved in lobbying for quality in children's television and media worldwide. The Prix Jeunesse has also extended its role in international children's television by sharing winning festival programs and professional content with producers all over the world through the Prix Jeunesse Suitcase, a series of workshops for media professionals, and the Item Exchange (in collaboration with the European Broadcasting Union) that facilitates the exchange of low-budget, quality programs across national borders in several regions of the world.

The Prix Jeunesse is a festival with a workshop character. All the participants view and evaluate the 90 films selected for the competition, submitted from all over the world. Participants watch the program screenings in small groups followed by an exchange of views in twice-a-day discussion groups about the quality of the seven to ten programs viewed during the last session. All producers may participate in the program competition voting process by submitting their ranking of the program according to criteria that address production values as well as substance concerns such as whether the program respects children and empowers them. The top entries selected by the participants in the different age and genre categories are awarded a Prix Jeunesse International Prize at the end of the six-day event. Other awards include a Prix Jeunesse Children's Jury Prize (awarded by the children's jury of over 600 kids) and special prizes sponsored by UNICEF, UNESCO and BMW. The festival has also added a Web Prize for websites that accompany television programs.

Each festival has a specific theme that is also part of in-depth discussions held in the diverse festival events. For example, the 2004 festival focused on "Children Watching War," in 2006 the theme was defined as "An International Comparison of Children's Humor," in 2008 "Girls and Boys and Television," and the theme in 2010 is "Different and the Same: Celebrating Diversity." The workshop approach creates an open atmosphere for the exchange of ideas and discussion of projects, all of which aided me in gaining cooperation and agreement to be interviewed for this project.

The Japan Prize International Educational Program Contest[7] was established in 1965 by NHK – Japan Broadcasting Corporation, Japan's nationwide public broadcasting organization. With its primary focus on educational programming, entries for the Japan Prize contest include educational fare developed for a range of target audiences (from pre-school children to adult viewers), and cover multiple distribution outlets (content developed for use in schools or at home). Over the years, the Japan Prize has expanded to include new interactive media platforms and has launched an award for excellent educational television program proposals. The contest has become a global competition for educational programs that seek to contribute to advancement of educational programs around the world, and the promotion of international understanding and cooperation. Contest entries provide a clear reflection of contemporary issues, addressing such topics as the environment, poverty, war and peace, understanding cultures, bullying, drugs and alcohol, and delinquency, or highlighting distinct educational issues within a country. Starting in 2002, the Japan Prize contest began to include a Web Division to acknowledge leaders in the field and to evaluate the overall educational effects of combining television programs with web content. To commemorate the thirtieth anniversary of the Japan Prize, the organization established the Program Proposal Division in 2003 to help support excellent proposals by highly motivated producers whose ability to produce programs is limited by a lack of financial resources and technical facilities.

Recognizing the importance of international interaction and the exchange of ideas among people involved in education and media, the Japan Prize Contest schedules screening and discussion sessions for contest entries so that delegates from around the world can exchange opinions and ideas directly with producers of the programs screened and also with other participants coming from different backgrounds. However, the actual rating of programs and web sites, as well as the selection of winners, is undertaken by international juries of professional and academic experts selected annually by the organization.[8]

The Basel-Karlsruhe Forum[9] was established 45 years ago as the Basler Seminar, sponsored by the Swiss Broadcasting Corporation, with the goal of bringing together teachers and professionals in education who wanted to work as television producers and directors. Since 2003, when it was joined by Südwestrundfunk SWR and the city of Karlsruhe in Germany, the Basel-Karlsruhe Forum (BaKa) is hosted alternately in the two cities every other year. Today the BaKa Forum is a meeting point of global reach for professionals in educational, science, and societal television and other media committed to global education through media, with a stated vision of conviction that sharing knowledge and new technologies, discussing and developing common values and working on common formats, co-producing, and producing for exchange are in the common interests of all cultures around the globe.

The BaKa Forum offers screenings of outstanding new productions from around the world followed by discussion by international delegates. In addition, it consists of a contest in which an international jury selects excellent television programs and multimedia productions of high educational value as winners of special awards. The meetings also offer seminars to the participants on global issues, such as the theme of the 2007 seminar – "Producing Peace," which included discussion of issues such as the media's coverage of war and peace, and its role and responsibility in promoting peace.

The World Summit on Media for Children[10] was initiated by Patricia Edgar in May 1993 when she presented the idea to a Round Table meeting hosted by Prix Jeunesse. It was clear at that time that children's programming was rapidly changing and that the increasingly globalized nature of broadcasting meant that children's programming considerations could not remain a purely domestic issue. With support from various donor organizations, governments, and broadcasters in the respective hosting countries, World Summits have been held every three years and bring together producers, broadcasters, researchers, children's media regulators, and other professionals and community leaders committed to the improvement of quality media for children. Unlike the Prix Jeunesse Festival and Japan Prize, each Summit is hosted by a different country, with interested organizations bidding to have upcoming Summits within their country. Regional and World Summits have continued since the First World Summit in Australia (1995), including World Summits in England (1998), Greece (2001), Brazil (2004), South Africa (2007) and the Sixth World Summit in Sweden (2010). In addition, regional Summits in Asia (1996) and

Africa (1996, 1997, 2000) have provided an ongoing exchange of ideas and collaborations.

The Summits' goals are: to raise the status of children's programming; to emphasize to key players in broadcasting the importance of issues relating to children; to achieve a greater understanding of developments in children's television around the world; to promote a charter of guiding principles in children's television; to ensure that the provision of programs for children will be guaranteed as the communications revolution proceeds; and to assist the developing world by providing opportunities for quality children's programming in the future.

South Africa hosted the Fifth World Summit on Media for Children, based on the theme "Media as a Tool for Global Peace and Democracy," in March 2007. To honor the Summit's debut in Africa, it showcased the diversity of Africa's media environment, but also featured global needs and collectively explored possibilities. The agenda for the 2007 World Summit in South Africa included Round Tables, workshops, panels, masterclasses, plenary sessions, exhibitions, and an international children's summit and film festival with the theme "Peace and Democracy." Key themes and concepts concerned issues such as the globalization of children's media, children's access in the information society, children's media rights, investing in children's media, comparative regulatory approaches, the role of content providers, children and media at times of war and conflict, health, HIV/AIDS and its impact on children's media, South-South partnerships, training for adult and youth producers of children's media, and how children participate meaningfully in the creation of their own media. The manifold issues discussed called for a varied and professional attendance including policymakers, regulators, children's rights organizations, producers, filmmakers, radio specialists, researchers, academics, Internet service providers, web designers, new-technology specialists, content developers of traditional and new media platforms, Cultural Studies specialists, commercial as well as public broadcasters, and children from around the world.

Additionally, several interviews took place outside of these events, taking advantage of my own additional professional trips. These included planned encounters with US producers who, while being a dominant presence and maintaining their status as members of the world's largest children's television industry, have a relatively low level of attendance at these global events (a fact that in of itself deserves attention). Additional interviews were integrated into other professional trips in Germany, India, Israel, and Taiwan. A few interviews also took place during the European Broadcasting Union (EBU) news exchange meeting in Jerusalem (Israel) in April 2008.

Finally, as is customary with ethnographic research, I was fortunate to have an opportunity to share the initial findings as well as evolving interpretations with professionals at later stages of the work, while participating in three additional international events: The Geena Davis Institute on Gender in Media conference in collaboration with the Annenberg School for Communication at the University of Southern California, as well as a closed-door workshop of top children's television industry experts in January 2007 in Los Angeles, US; the annual meeting of The Alliance of Children and Television in Canada, in Montreal, Canada in November 2008; and The Muestra Iberoamericana de Television in Mexico City, Mexico in November 2008. Undoubtedly, preparations for these presentations as well as the feedback and input from participants assisted me to coalesce and crystallize my understandings and interpretations of the emergent findings.

The Interviewees

The 135 formal interviews were conducted with professionals from 65 countries, 90 females and 45 males. A detailed breakdown of the interviewees' backgrounds is presented in Tables 2.1 and 2.2.

As is evident from these tables, a conscious effort was made to interview professionals from as many countries around the world as possible. Collectively, interviewees represent a diversity of cultures, religions, races, historical backgrounds, political régimes, technological advancement, media systems, and a host of other variables that may affect the realities of life for women and men as well as their representations. This having been noted, no claim is made that this is a representative sample of either the composition of human societies around the globe or of the interviewees' societies. Clearly, not one nor even ten professionals from any one country represent thinking about and assessments of the entire offering of images on quality television for children in a particular society in a remotely satisfactory manner. Nonetheless, the argument put forward here is that analysis of the collective interviews from this diverse population has produced insights into a rich collage of issues involved in existing general trends and directions of development of gender portrayals around the world.

A special small subgroup of seven "migrant" interviewees shared the fact that they were born, educated, and advanced professionally in a particular culture, but were working at the time of the interview in a different region in the world. For example, a Canadian man working in South Africa; a Korean woman working in Malaysia; a Lebanese woman working in Qatar; a North-American man working in Ethiopia; among others. This sub-group represents a form of "work-migration" in the field of media production. In summarizing the demographic information on the interviewees, I coded them in relation to the country in which they were working, as they were discussing their current experiences there. However, admittedly, this is somewhat biased, as their perspective integrated their familiarity with their native cultural background and was often comparative in nature.

Despite painstaking efforts to provide a balanced mosaic of voices from around the world, it is clear that the US voice is most frequent in the quotes selected in the following chapters. There are at least five reasons that explain

Table 2.1 Interviewees by country

Country	Number of interviewees	Gender	Reported Name
Argentina	2	M	Roberto
		F	Elenora
Austria	1	F	Sarah
Australia	1	F	Hildegard
Bangladesh	1	F	Sumita
Bhutan	1	M	Jigme
Bolivia	1	F	Emma
Botswana	1	F	Mpule
Brazil	4	F	Elaine
		F	Grasielle
		F	Christiane
		F	Larissa
Canada	4	M	Eric
		F	Vicky
		F	Meghan
		F	Carla
Chile	1	F	Valentina
China	6	F	Mei
		M	Yu
		F	LiYang
		F	Jing
		F	Ningfang
		F	Xiya
Colombia	1	F	Adriana
Croatia	1	F	Maja
Cuba	1	M	José
Denmark	1	M	Casper
Ecuador	1	F	Beatriz
Egypt	1	F	Nabila
Ethiopia	1	F	Senait
France	2	F	Nathalie
		M	Nicolas
Germany	4	F	Brigit
		F	Renate
		F	Silvia
		M	Uwe
Ghana	1	F	Suzzy
Hong Kong	1	F	Nicole
India	4	F	Amita
		M	Gautam
		F	Rumeli
		F	Devika
Iran	1	F	Zahra
Ireland	1	F	Meggie
Israel	4	M	Benny
		F	Dikla
		F	Noga
		F	Dana

Table 2.1 (continued)

Country	Number of interviewees	Gender	Reported Name
Italy	3	F	Paola
		F	Leticia
		M	Antonio
Japan	4	M	Yamagishi
		F	Miyama
		F	Yuko
		F	Akiko
Jordan	1	M	Amer
Kazakhstan	1	M	Yegor
Kenya	3	F	Suzana
		F	Margaret
		M	Fundi
Korea	4	F	Ki-Hyun
		M	Chan-ho
		F	Si-yeon
		F	Mi-jung
Kyrgyzstan	2	M	Boris
		F	Irina
Malaysia	1	F	Nasing
Mexico	2	F	Leonora
		F	Erika
Mongolia	1	F	Dorjsuren
Nepal	1	F	Manisha
The Netherlands	2	F	Kim
		F	Famke
Nigeria	2	M	Obinna
		F	Dominique
Norway	2	M	Svein
		F	Hanne
Pakistan	2	F	Salma
		F	Alizeh
Palestine	1	M	Jamal
Papua New Guinea	1	F	Josephine
The Philippines	1	F	Leona
Poland	2	M	Radoslaw
		M	Jakub
Portugal	1	F	Augustina
Qatar	1	F	Maria
Serbia & Montenegro	1	M	Milan
Slovenia	2	M	Mitja
		F	Alanka
South Africa	3	F	Paradise
		F	Samora
		M	Virender

Table 2.1 (continued)

Country	Number of interviewees	Gender	Reported Name
Spain	2	M	Carlos
		F	Isabel
Sri Lanka	1	M	Edmund
Sweden	2	F	Karolina
		F	Anneli
Switzerland	1	M	Hermann
Syria	2	M	Omar
		M	Halil
Taiwan	3	F	Chia-che
		F	Ying
		M	Yuan
Tanzania	1	M	Taylor
Thailand	1	F	Kornvika
Tunisia	1	F	Amina
Turkey	3	M	Ibrhaim
		F	Esmeral
		F	Yaesmin
UK	3	M	Greg
		F	Julie
		M	Tony
Ukraine	2	F	Katherina
		F	Nelly
Uruguay	1	M	Carlos
USA	19	F	Caroline
		F	Lindsey
		F	Tina
		F	Kristine
		M	Brad
		F	Kate
		F	Lori
		F	Hope
		F	Abby
		F	Cindy
		M	Matt
		M	Dan
		M	Todd
		M	Chris
		M	Steven
		F	Laura
		M	Jerome
		F	Sally
		M	Mike
Yemen	1	M	Mohammed
Total: 65	**Total: 135**	**Total: 90 F 45 M**	

Table 2.2 Interviewees by continent

Continent	Number of countries	Number of interviewees
Africa	9	14
Americas	11	37
Asia	25	49
Australia (+ Islands)	2	2
Europe	18	33
Total	65	135

this: First, the US television industry is the most dominant producer and dis-seminator of television for children in the world, with the richest accumulated professional experience in the area. Second, of all countries included in the study, the US comprises the largest group of interviewees. Third, given the use of English as the interview language, this group of interviewees was privileged to be able to communicate without any language barriers. In addition, they also have access to particular modes of analytical discourse directly related to this study, including familiarity with Western debates about globalization, children, and media. Undoubtedly, this assisted them in formulating their responses in the context of an academic research interview with a fellow Western interviewer. Finally, the Anglo-Saxon and European communities in which these profes-sionals work have a rich social–cultural heritage of change in regard to gender that has been experienced at first hand by many of the interviewees from these regions. The reader is cautioned not to interpret this quantitative presence and ease of discourse as a stance by the author, recalling use of the justifiably cri-tiqued lens of a cultural deficit model of the "developing" or "third" world, but as a consequence of a privileged form of Western intellectual discourse.

The predominance of female interviewees (two thirds) is, however, reflective of the professional make up of the field of media production for children. Indeed, many interviewees commented that female professionals dominate the specialty of children and youth as well as educational television within the world of television production. This observation is consistent with and reflects traditional occupational segregation, which perceives such professional invol-vement as an extension of traditional private-sphere female specializations. While aspects of the gendered occupational world of quality television for children are not the focus of this study, they do have implications for the issue at hand and were raised in numerous interviews, as will be discussed in Chapter Five. Collectively, such segregation is associated with lower status and financial rewards as well as limited professional resources, as in other media occupations.

The age of the interviewees ranged from early twenties to mid-sixties, with the majority from mid-thirties to mid-fifties, reflecting, probably, an estab-lished professional status that allows for travel and international networking.

The official language of all of the major events was English and so, too, was the language of interview. However, the linguistic skills of the interviewees ranged from that of native speakers of English (interviewees from Australia, Canada, India, Ireland, South Africa, UK, US) to a lack of any English knowledge whatsoever, which required the use of an interpreter (some of the Chinese, Japanese, and South Korean interviewees). Most interviewees from The Netherlands and Scandinavian countries spoke fluent English, as did several of the interviewees from African and Latin American countries. As a general rule, more language difficulties where encountered with Southern Europe, Middle Eastern, and Asian producers; yet it was the case on many occasions that interviewees from these countries surprised me with an excellent command of English. Generally speaking, then, English proved to be a workable language for most interviewees, despite the fact that it is not their native language, nor is it my own. Undoubtedly, this fact resulted in a less accurate or precise expression of ideas. However, the dominance of the English language at these events is itself indicative of the nature of the interviewee population, as many had either been educated in English-speaking cultures, networked with other professionals in international settings, and/or traveled enough to have attained a fairly high capability in the use of English.[11]

Indeed, interviewees' linguistic capabilities in English are related to the broader matter of their educational background. The vast majority of the interviewees had earned a BA degree, in a wide range of fields; most in the arts, humanities, education, and social sciences. Thus, their professional background and experience was quite varied as were the personal circumstances that brought them to the media industry world: Those who studied television and film moved naturally into the industry. Others came from the field of education or academic teaching from such diverse backgrounds as archeology, advertising, computer science, engineering, journalism, management, marketing, the performing arts, psychology, and public relations. Interviewees held a variety of professional positions in the television world at the time of the study. They were producers, directors, animators, scriptwriters, editors, head of divisions, and executives. Seeking a generic term of reference, I refer to them in this study loosely as "producers" or "professionals."

Finally, many of the interviewees had children of their own and referred to them in the interview when discussing various aspects of the programs available on television, in relation to their exposure to gender portrayals, and in expressing wishes for better gender images for the sake of their own children. Often, familial references occurred as a means of illustrating a more general point: "For example, when I think of someone like my own daughter … " Interviewees often framed responses as being enriched by personal experience as parents in addition to their professional experience in the media industry.

The collaboration of the interviewees in agreeing to being interviewed as well as in producing the interview spanned from outright enthusiasm and a desire to converse, as well as willingness to share ideas and dilemmas, through to rare occasions of outright antagonism (although these few incidents do not seem to have anything in common). I was happy to find many willing interviewees from around the world who wanted to cooperate, including interview candidates from countries officially at war with my own country, Israel. Most expressions of reluctance to be interviewed were related to concern about inadequate linguistic skills and an overburdened schedule during the events. What was clearly helpful for my project was the atmosphere and expectations of conduct in these international events: Professionals who attend these events come with a predisposition to interact, network, meet new people, talk about their work, and demonstrate tolerance for, and interest in, the work of others. These events are characterized by a friendly, outgoing atmosphere among strangers who work intensively in small groups, eat meals together, and even perform in karaoke parties late at night with newly acquired acquaintances. So, being approached by a total stranger who presented them with a request to meet was a completely normative and accepted situation. Therefore, on the whole, interviewees were agreeable and in the majority of the cases seemed delighted to have an opportunity to talk about themselves and their own work, as well as to express their views on the work of others to which they had been exposed during the event or outside it. Thus, the nature of the social context facilitated the interviews even when the specific logistical circumstances where obtrusive (e.g. high-level background noise, lack of comfortable seating arrangements, limited free time).

Each of the 135 interviews was unique, creating, collectively, a wide range and diversity of responses. Interviewees employed various types of response techniques that included the use of diversion, confrontation, and avoidance strategies as well as advancing personal agendas. Overall, it is impossible to summarize their nature in a unified manner, except to say that they required a great deal of flexibility on my part.

I use pseudonyms when quoting or referring to interviewees. These fictional names reflect the specific gender and culture as well as their other individual characteristics. For example, the use of a Christian name (such as "Christine") for an interviewee from a mostly Muslim country means that the original interviewee had a Christian name; and an English name assigned to an African interviewee means that their original name was indeed an English one. In order to protect the anonymity of all of the interviewees, particularly those who took personal risks in critiquing their cultures in general and the institutions that employed them more specifically, I choose to disguise also the names of those who might have wished for me to give them open credit for their contribution to this book. Yet I do hope that all interviewees will recognize themselves in the following pages and feel that I have done them justice in representing their ideas.

In addition to referencing and quoting many of the 135 interviewees, I have integrated in the following chapters many of the voices and insights shared in discussion groups and interpersonal exchanges that took place during these events, along with many of my own participant observations. While the former were not counted as interviews, they nevertheless lend an additional depth to the study.

The Interview

The Interview Guide

The interview guide included several groups of questions that centered on the following areas, usually addressed in the following order:

1. My aim in introducing the study and in the initial warm-up questions was to establish rapport and mutual acquaintance. The general purpose of the study was presented directly: How boys and girls are presented in quality television for children (at this point no specific references to terms such as "gender" or "feminism" were mentioned, in order to limit the entry of bias into the interview). Entry questions were directed to the interviewee's own perspective, experience, and opinions on the topic. I explained that this would be an open-ended interview and that I did not believe there were "correct" answers. Interviewee anonymity was guaranteed. Interviewees were asked about their background, work experiences, specialty areas, roles at the event where the interview was taking place, their experiences at the event so far, and the like.

2. Next, interviewees were asked to discuss a specific program that they had submitted to the event or a program submitted by colleagues from their home country, a submission to a previous international event, or one they hoped to submit in the future. My aim in moving from the familiar to the abstract was to gather concrete images while enabling the interviewee to feel secure in his/her expertise and to talk about his/her own (or his/her station's) productions. Initially, interviewees were asked for details about the program (e.g. genre, topic, narrative, goals, age group) and then to describe the main characters (gender, ethnicity, age, appearance, behavior, personality, relationships with other characters, something unique about them). From here we proceeded to discuss if the main characters were typical or untypical of how boys and girls were presented on the interviewee's national television for children of that particular age group; considerations in designing these characters; any particular concerns in relation to the characters' genders. This concrete anchoring of the conversation usually led to divergence to additional topics of discussion in any of the directions sketched below, as well as in other unique ways.

3. Next, we engaged in a general discussion of gender images of locally produced programs for children in comparison to both local prime-time television as well as commercial and imported programs for children in the

interviewee's country. Interviewees discussed gender stereotypes that were produced frequently in their country along with similarities/differences to other regions of the world in both quality and commercial television. This led to an attempt to unveil the underlying explanations for such stereotypes: Unique cultural characteristics, structures, belief systems, history and the like that the interviewees believed explained prevailing images in their culture. If not raised spontaneously by the interviewee, questions were asked about whether gender issues were related to other diversity issues such as ethnicity, disability, class, and if so, various ways in which this was the case.

4. The discussion of changes in gender images was based on the interviewee's personal views, motivations, involvement, and ideas shared. Interviewees were asked about their own attitudes and feelings about existing gender stereotypes; if they viewed it to be the responsibility of television to serve as a change agent; and if change was indeed possible. Obstacles for change were discussed and ideas for different images were introduced. Specific examples of different gender portrayals in the interviewee's own or in a colleague's work were discussed, as was the notion of "ideal" images of girls and boys.

The Interview Format

The interviews varied from brief twenty-minute exchanges in smoky corridors or at a bar to leisurely two-hour discussions followed up later with additional conversations and email exchanges. I met several of the interviewees at more than one event and was able to follow up on conversations held a year or more earlier. All but four interviews were audio-recorded, with the permission of the interviewee, and transcribed verbatim.[12] Summaries of group discussions and observations were recorded, live, by taking notes on a laptop.

As is usually the case, each interview developed in a different manner. This was a function of the professional and personal characteristics of the interviewees, the flow of the discussion and examples provided by the interviewees, their command of the English language, logistical circumstances (described below), the personal rapport that emerged, and many of the other intervening variables that form and shape interpersonal interactions. The interviews were also deeply colored by the interviewees' own personal biography and life history. Many interviewees interspersed stories about their own children, episodes from their personal experiences, viewing habits, spousal disagreements, and the like.

Over the years, my concerns about the nature of the power relations that can exist between myself as a researcher and those being researched, as well as my commitment to promoting the wellbeing of those I approach as sources, has led me to try to frame such interviews as conversational exchanges between professionals dedicated to the wellbeing of children around the globe, in which each of us contributes different expertise and knowledge. In doing so, I have sought, to the best of my abilities, to create a friendly, open, relaxed, informal, and respectful atmosphere. I listened attentively and sought to be, and felt that I was, genuinely engaged and interested in the interview. The conversational as well as interviewing techniques used in this process included: prompts ("this is very interesting;" "can you tell me more about this?" "can you give me an example?" "I would like to understand more about what you just said;" "can you elaborate?" "this is very helpful;" etc) and mirroring back to the interviewee his/her own ideas by using his/her own words in the next question. I avoided the use of judgmental comments until late into the interview, when I quoted other interviewees (anonymously) who had suggested competing or critical ideas, allowing time for the interviewee to respond to such challenges or issues. For the most part, I maintained a flexible interview schedule, following the interviewee's stream of thought until the last part of the interview when I attempted to cover those central topics that did not surface spontaneously.[13]

In order to explain the privileged position I had at these events, one that granted me free entry and access to all participants, I need to share the fact that I held professional academic roles at all of these events (as an advisor, lecturer, program judge, and academic journal editor) and thus I was not an anonymous participant. While this status greatly facilitated the recruitment of interviewees, it may also have influenced them; for example, producers might have hoped that my position would somehow advance their own professional interests and ambitions. While I made clear that my research was totally independent of the organization of the event itself, I was clearly an "outsider" of sorts, being among the few academics at each of these events and not part of the international professional community of television for children. At the same time, this position granted me the possibility of assuming the participant–observer role as a "detached–concerned" interviewer, a role that balances intimacy and rapport with a certain degree of detachment and personal disinterest.

About my general participation in these events I should also acknowledge the fact that my privileged position as a middle-class, educated, White researcher is often a matter of contention in international settings that celebrate diversity. Furthermore, being an Israeli academic can lead to my being ostracized or relegated to the margins in the eyes of some participants. Yet, in many ways and for many others, I was like any other participant at the events – a person whose multiple identities were involved in multiple ways during different interviews; for example: A Latin-American Jewish female producer felt an immediate bonding with me; a male producer from an Arab country insisted on diverting our interview to political issues connected to the Arab–Israeli conflict; an interview with a female producer from China required an interpreter and both were clearly operating through a "diplomatic face" – making special efforts to convince me that there was no gender inequality in their country and being unwilling to engage in any personal exchange that might hint at any kind of difficulties; an interview with a female North American executive turned into comparing notes about our daughters' media consumption; and an African producer seemed to have an ulterior motive as she kept directing the conversation to asking for assistance in helping raise funds for her new project. Thus, I was never "just" an interviewer, but my many roles – academic, Israeli, Jewish, mother, woman, Westerner – were all brought to bear on the process.

The four-year interviewing period was characterized, throughout, by involvement in a continuous process of developing my own cultural consciousness through self-reflection on my positionality as a privileged educated White woman in the status of researcher. I constantly challenged myself by asking questions and reflecting on my own stereotypes, biases, misinformation, and misunderstandings; as well as questions about my relationships with my interviewees and the need to unpack the hierarchies[14] (both in places where I was clearly perceived by my interviewees as being in a superior position of "the expert" and those where I perceived myself to be in an inferior one to high-power industry executives).

The Setting

Interview settings were quite diverse and presented many social and technical challenges. When interviews were scheduled weeks in advance, we could arrange for a quiet meeting place and free up time in our schedules so that a lengthy interview could unfold under optimal circumstances. However, many interviewees were recruited at short notice and the interviews conducted in a quiet corner alongside the hustle-bustle of event activities. Other interviews developed spontaneously, on the spot, when unexpected opportunities rose, and presented a "now or never" situation requiring great flexibility and the overcoming of logistic difficulties like noise, interferences, competing attractions (for example, an interview on the bus in an outing; an interview during a social dinner; an interview while waiting in line).

All of these factors contributed to a dynamic and unpredictable research process in which no interview resembled another. Clearly then, the length and depth of the interviews, the quality of the responses, the degree of confidentiality, and personal rapport were significantly affected by the circumstances of the interview. However, I believe that it would be a mistake to assume that short, spontaneous interviews were by definition less productive than lengthy ones. Often insights were provided in a rather brief and focused exchange, while lengthy and relaxed interviews ended up being a personal celebration of the interviewee's professional achievements that produced limited input into the topic of study.

The Interview Analysis

All interview transcripts were read and reread in an emergent process that led to the crystallizing of the central themes of the study. While clearly the interview guide dictated in advance the major topics of inquiry, the thematic organization of the discussion presented in the following pages was grounded in the interviewees' collective responses. The themes that emerged through my repeated reading of the transcripts evolved as more empirical evidence became evident and accumulated with each reading. As is common in such an analytical process, thematic categories were shaped and reshaped, interrelationships between them clarified, and meaningful exemplars selected to allow for representation of the authentic voices of the interviewees.[15]

A complementary empirical base for this study is a general thematic analysis of many of the media texts referred to by the interviewees, including some of the children's programs screened at the six events, the interviewees' own programs, and other programs mentioned by interviewees to illustrate central points in the interviews. Since no systematic analysis of these media texts was conducted, the accumulated knowledge on gender portrayals presented in Chapter One, as well as interviewee interpretations, served as the lens through which the presentation of gender and gendered issues in these texts are seen.

The collective interpretations, critiques, and creative ideas shared by interviewees that evolved in the thematic analysis were then linked to and interpreted through the theoretical body of knowledge presented in the previous chapter.

Presentation of Results

Empirical studies of this nature produce vast quantities of verbal output that is interesting, sometimes repetitive, and all too often overwhelming in its complexity. This is particularly true in a project that involves interviewing 135 individuals from 65 different cultures around the world! I have attempted in the chapters that follow to illuminate the questions at the core of this project from different perspectives. Thus, each chapter could be likened to a light shown on a different cut of the prism-like research corpus. The "generative themes" created through this problem-posing process[16] enable us to gain a deeper understanding as well as a more comprehensive mapping of the complex relations between gender, media, and culture.

Also important in this presentation is the inclusion of extensive quotations from the interview transcripts. These quotations illustrate the findings as well as serve as a partial remedy for the political issue discussed in the first chapter – "who speaks for whom?" This use of selected, often extensive, quotations enables the producers to speak for themselves rather than me, the privileged researcher, attempting to represent their views in my own voice. I am well aware that some would argue that it is impossible for the Anglo-American academy, of which I am part, to speak for the "third world." As Gayatri Spivak (a leading postcolonial feminist, discussed in Chapter One) argued, for example, the voice of non-Western subjects is muted through the multiple filters of theory and discourse used in the academy.[17] I have made painstaking efforts, therefore, to retain the interviewees' strands of thought, ideas, and personal style, correcting only gross English mistakes to make the text accessible. Additionally, the extensive presentation of selections from the interviews also enables the reader to join in the process of problem-posing, interpretation, and conjoining additional layers of meaning and understanding.

Yet, selecting specific parts of an ongoing conversation to illustrate a finding or interpretation is bound to eviscerate various strings of contextual meanings. In addition, it involves choice and interpretations that already reflect broader theoretical assumptions and expectations. Finding the appropriate balance between "raw" quotation and theoretical interpretation is always a challenge. I hope that the balance I have arrived at here is insightful as well as respectful of the interviewees.

Chapter 3

What Does Gender Mean?

Understanding Gender in Cultural Context

Introduction

What does gender mean for producers who construct the programs that appear on the flickering screens enjoyed by children, and from which they learn? Early in the interview process it became clear that producers of quality television for children from around the world view gender issues in quite different ways, as revealed in the wide range of topics and concerns raised in response to interview questions: What does gender mean to you? What are the most burning gender issues in your society? And what gender issues should quality television for children make an effort to address? The diversity of views is not surprising given what we learned in Chapter Two about the different societies and individual characteristics of the producers interviewed in this study. Discussion of gender, as we have learned from feminist and queer theories, always intersects with other discourses of identity – be they racial, ethnic, class, sexual, or geographical. And indeed, as the process of analysis and reflection continued, it gradually became clear that the specific issues interviewees raised were far from being eclectic or coincidental. Patterns gradually crystallized containing similarities that seem to be culturally and regionally grounded.

Indeed, theorists of critical schools of thought argue, first, that gender and multiculturalism share the same intertwined social sources[1] and that, second, they breed binary oppositions, such as male/female, Black/White cultures, Western/Eastern worlds, high/low cultures, public/private spheres. Since gender is constantly constructed through cultural contexts and processes, it is not surprising that producers' views differed greatly in gender assumptions, perceptions, the status ascribed to gender equality, and the diverse issues they associated with gender in their various societies. While prevailing media stereotypes and inequalities are shared in most of the cultures represented by the interviewees (as presented in Chapter One and discussed in later chapters), most of their interpretations were imbedded in specific cultural differences. Indeed, in many ways, it is impossible to understand the meaning and implications of the concepts of gender in one society without comparing it with other societies, as the richness and diversity of the following interview selections make clear.

The analysis of these varied culturally grounded perspectives on gender illuminates recent critical approaches to media globalization by examining local responses to transnational cultural flows that are often ground in local cultures as well as in indigenous traditions, heritages, and values. For example, we gain insight into how advancing innovative images of gender perceived to be appropriate in one part of the world can be irrelevant, or even damaging, to girls and boys in other parts of the world.

More specifically, I noted that producers were cognizant of the unique gendered "feel" of their local productions, as they were constantly comparing their work to that of others in their profession, particularly, those in the "imagined production center" of what they referred to as the Westernized television screen. This social practice of "imagination," to apply Appadurai's conceptualization, refers to the construction of collective aspirations for some global sense of place.[2] Thus, the much debated tension between "local" and "global" and the perceived consequences of cultural globalization, as well as differing conceptual varieties of Americanization and Westernization,[3] were salient in reflections on their own work. Global, as used by the interviewees, rarely meant universal. Indeed, globalization seemed to refer to the spread of Western mediated products and images from which none of the countries involved in this study was immune.[4] Thus, the notion of "The West and the Rest" came out very clearly in their discourse, together with a form of cultural particularism through which producers attempted to assert their own unique identities.

The claim that we live in a world increasingly characterized by Americanization has been put forth repeatedly in intellectual and political thought.[5] Indeed, objections to the erosive power of globalization on local cultures have been frequently referred to among the fears of Americanization: The influence of the US, and more specifically, of its values, ideology, economics, political interests, and culture. As in other realms of discussion, the critique put forth by the producers here is strongly entangled with admiration of things American as well as a desire to perform at a similar professional level.

We start, then, with producers' general reflections on these cultural differences, as they pertain to their specific concerns for the meanings and consequences of gender. Following this discussion of the "local/global" tension, the second part of the chapter delineates specific locally grounded themes related to children in producers' discussions of the meaning of gender as elicited in the interviews.

Gender Between a Rock and a Hard Place: The Local and the Global

Many interviewees were aware of their conclusion that gender assumes a different "look" and its portrayals on screens have a different cultural "feel" in different countries. As Kasper (Denmark) explained: *There is a difference, a cultural difference. If you look at television programs from Sweden or Holland it is more or less the same. If you look at Mongolia or Asia or China it is a different way of portraying ... the difference [is] in the culture ... I don't know if it is good or bad ... but they portray their children differently.*

Nathalie (France) shared a similar sense in her attempt to explain cultural differences: *Programs have a cultural feel to them ... when you see, for example, programs of the northern European countries or the German programs, there is a deep cultural difference. They are not the same feeling, they are darker ... the Latin countries have nearly the same feeling ... and there is the same cultural approach between Spain, Italy, and France. England's got more humor but harder than we are. And northern countries are very pessimistic and darker in seeing the world. But I think in our TV making we are mainly inspired by Anglo Saxon pictures ... can't really explain it ... but we never found a Danish or Swedish program portraying boys and girls that fit our audience ... and I presume that a French program for American people, for example, may look very exotic.*

Dominique (Nigeria) was even more specific in identifying the unique features of African productions: *We do a lot of traditional storytelling, animal stories, where the animals are archetypes.* Employing traditional narratives evolving around animals was a feature identified by other African producers as their own voice coloring the screens of children's television.

Whether, indeed, the Nordic look is "darker," the French more "exotic," or the African more "mythical" is of course beside the point, as the overall impression is that producers were quite confident in their ability to "tell" where a given program came from, in general terms, by its cultural "look." Some producers were also quite self-reflective regarding their own cultural look on the screen and did not hesitate to expose, openly, their own cultural biases. Nasing (Malaysia), for example, was very straight forward about local cultural constraints on gender portrayals in her country: *To be honest, there is no discussion of boys and girls and their roles on TV ... it all depends on the culture and society and also on how they handle and manage these issues. Because women's issues or children's issues or gender issues – no matter how modern we think we are – they are still very culturally based and it is very difficult to break a culture that has been there for thousands of years, and I don't want to use the word oppression, but ... you wouldn't see an Asian program where the man is in the kitchen helping the wife with the dishes, but in the Western programs you would see that ...*

While some producers had a tone of self-critique in their voice, for others it was a sense of acceptance accompanied often by an undertone celebrating their uniqueness. The suggestion by Chan-ho (Korea) is an example of such thinking: *We have expectations that girls would be polite, nice, sweet ... As a producer for small children, I think we need to keep to our own culture. We need to filter that kind of foreign influence in a way, but not all of it [...].*

Maria (Qatar), a representative of Al Jazeera's Arab satellite programming for children, illustrated the channel's desire to advance local values: *We cannot ... you will not see on our channel a kid insulting his father or mother or mistreating them ... so it's all about values that we respect and we want to convey to our kids, you know. So as I told you, we have a huge editorial policy.* Even when it is not explicit, the undertone in such quotations suggested strong criticism of other television programs that are not attuned to these local values – such as girls' "sweetness" in Korea or children's respect of the elderly in the Arab world.

"We" Versus "Them" (American) Binary

This cultural "feel" was framed, frequently, within the local/global tension, highlighting a clear "we" versus "them" binary, as the above quotations demonstrate. Mapule (Botswana) expressed it quite bluntly when she said: *We, as a developing country, we train in the West ... we do what the West is doing. They're sort of being the leader, and we are being the followers. It is only now that we are trying to find out our own voices within the global village. To say what is really our need as a country, as Botswana; what are our cultural values and then are they having any negative or positive influence on how women, girl child, boy child, and men are portrayed in media.* Mapule recognizes the dependency of her society on the resources and training offered by the developed West, but she suggested that this comes with a price to the cultural authenticity of the images on the screen.

Manisha (Nepal) brought up quite concrete examples when she talked about an Asian flavor: *Like, suppose, I have seen in one program a girl wants to put on lipstick and see what it is about, at the age of seven or eight or nine. But, in my country, they don't put on makeup when they are kids. Also the Chinese don't do that kind of stuff, that is for adult people. So there are some similarities in Asia that are quiet different than other parts of the world.*

Interestingly, the "we" versus "they" was not unique to non-Western societies, as many of the interviewees from European countries, as well as Australia and Canada, too, defined themselves as "we" in contrast with a specific American "they." For them, globalization trends are clearly synonymous with American imperialism, as they do not perceive themselves to be part of the Westernization cultural trend. While it is impossible to measure the intensity of the responses in this type of study, my reading of the interviews suggests that the interviewees from non-American Western countries were as concerned and critical of American television as were the non-Western producers. Sarah's (Australia) argument is paradigmatic of such views: *We get so much American TV ... I don't think we get a balance, our kids are watching mostly American shows and a lot less Australian ones ... like the whole American high school scene is so completely different in America ... I think the peer thing is different, the whole structure of high school, you know, junior high etc., we don't have it ... the lifestyle is similar but different, the accent ... Slang ... and you know, they are wearing baseball caps, and they are wearing them backwards, and they are wearing baggy American trousers ... There are programs with the Black American family that have no relevance to Australia at all ... it doesn't mean our kids don't enjoy them, the comedy or whatever, but it certainly does not look like their own homes or their families, the way they speak, there is a difference ... they are not reflecting our culture but somebody else's. And, since most of adult television is American, they [children] will get that soon enough – so we [producers of television for children] try to keep a bit of Australian culture.*

Comparing one's television programs to the American ones was a common discursive strategy adopted spontaneously by many of the interviewees, regardless of the topic of discussion. Kasper (Denmark), for example, compared his culture to the American screen: *Yes, definitely American programs look differently. I don't think the American ones are bad. I used to have this feeling that this is not real, that no Danish school kids have a convertible car to drive to school in, and none of the school kids live in a house together with other school kids. So, I was thinking what was this doing to our kids, and how could they identify, and I realized that the Danish children look at it, they liked it, but they knew that this is not their world and they held it at a distance, but they identified with the different characters and their problems ... They just saw through that, but it helped give the program the glamour that made it nice to watch. And Friends, which is a very big serial, has a lot of morals in it, and a lot of issues that the children learn. But, I can never do one like that, first, because I don't have the budget, and second, because it doesn't really look the same when it is not in America. So whenever we do something we will go the other way, we step back and make real drama or real series about our own life, true identity.*

Similarly, Hanne (Norway) talked about the problems encountered in *trying to offer something that is different from the look of the American high-school scene and American programming that is highly rated like* Friends *or the Olsen twins* [6] *or MTV ... that's why it is really important to spend money on producing things ourselves instead of just buying the American shows and putting the rating through the roof.*

The longing for more visibility of their own culture, as expressed above, was shared by many of the producers and was interwoven with a deep concern for issues related to the political economy of local production, as Leona (Philippines) explained: *In the context of media landscape, where you have dominantly imported programs seventy to thirty percent, it becomes imperative to develop something that is indigenous, that is theirs* [our children's]; *that speaks in their language and deals with topics that are about their lives, not only as young children growing up in a particular stage in their lives, but as Filipino children.*

Valentina (Chile) recounted in her own voice what she understood children to be saying, based upon their participation in a workshop conducted by her station: *Children said, "I want to see me there! I want to see a Chilean boy there. I want to see my culture there. I don't want to look like a boy in Manhattan, because this is not my life, this is not my style of living, I don't feel me if I watch a guy on a motorcycle. That's not my reality."*

Some producers took this desire for cultural visibility a step further and translated it into their actual work. Suzanna (Kenya), for example, was more proactive about the ways in which they attempted to highlight cultural uniqueness: *The whole thing about this animation project is that we are not drawing from an obscure content base. We are going for African stories, myths, heroes. We are not necessarily just picking issues from the air, so that's the one thing, creating a cultural grounding in the first place. We need to pay attention to our culture, our language, our needs ... we have, for example, a big problem with female mutilation. Some issues are not necessarily addressed by the programs that are imported ... We have issues that are very particular for Kenya and we would like to have programs that address them. We think our children will relate more to the stuff that they see everyday rather than things like Powerpuff Girls. They are good because they say that girls are heroes but at the end of the day you want to bring up a citizenry that knows their country, these are our leaders of tomorrow.*

Interestingly, Suzanna, like many of her colleagues who I interviewed, is not blind to the potential valuable contributions that some American television for children is providing, as her example of *The Powerpuff Girls* implies. Again, like most other participants in this study, she is also quite familiar with the "big hits" traveling around the world and attracting children all over. Yet, she nevertheless positions the specific needs of raising the "leaders of tomorrow" in her Kenyan culture in clear opposition to what American productions can offer them. And, in exemplifying her claim, Suzanna raised a major concern mentioned by several producers from African societies – female genital mutilation and cutting, which according to UN estimates is a widely practiced tradition: Around 70 million girls and women aged 15–49 in 27 countries of Africa and the Middle East are estimated to have undergone this painful and debilitating practice.[7]

Indeed, on occasion, discussion of discrepancies between the local and the American were perceived as cultural clashes and took a clear form of critique. Direct blame was directed at American television and its role in perpetuating inappropriate values. Some interviewees even critiqued approaches employed by American producers to change gender inequality, claiming that it flooded the children's television market with stereotypical representations of the supposed American way of life and associated gender roles. While producers representing countries throughout the world voiced these concerns, the most succinct critique was offered by producers from traditional societies, those most likely to be ranked low in gender equity on many socio-demographic criteria. The critique they directed at these US efforts claims that they do not provide positive role models and, furthermore, they even undermine local efforts to advance social change. For example, Samora (South Africa) said: *The problem if you talk about values and morals is in the language used. We fail to see how much culture is embedded in language. Like, in one of the American programs, a girl smoking a cigarette asked her mother for more allowance and the mother says to her cynically: "You can go to work on one of the sex lines to make more money." You don't talk like that in our country. And if you purchase those kinds of programs, you … normalize an abnormal situation … the problem about buying programs in this American type of language and American culture [is that] we are subconsciously colonizing ourselves culturally. Children learn from other countries' programs … how a woman dresses, how nice macho men behave. The way gender is represented is being modeled here …*

As the conversation unfolded, Samora raised a second, more culturally specific issue pertaining to racial differences in gender portrayals: *On American TV you would see a White woman heading a company, have relationships and enjoy her life, and that's fine. And the Black woman is home or she is a secretary, and she has to go home and cook for her husband. In the series we have the White woman – she is rich, her husband died. But on the other side of town there is this Black woman, from the rural area, that joins her husband in their little business … but at home she is still the submissive wife that her husband decides things. So what does this tell a Black girl-child about her future?* Samora's bitter tone alludes to a well-investigated phenomenon that many scholars interpret as being at the intersection of gender and race: the quite restricted repertoire of women's roles on Western television traveling around the world. For example, African-American women are often relegated to stereotypes such as "mammies," "matriarchs," "welfare mothers," or "hyper-sexed," and Far Eastern and Latina women as exotic and sexual.[8]

Quotations such as Samora's above, too, can be interpreted through the "cultivation hypothesis" that suggests that viewing particular images on a regular basis is likely to contribute to the cultivation of a worldview similar to the one reflected in them.[9] In this particular case, the dual inscription of gender and race reinforces inequalities, presented routinely as "the way things are." And, it continues to perpetuate these images as legitimate, normalized, and "natural." In this sense, the critique of the power of the affluent White American to represent and to speak for the minority Black woman echoes Edward Said's theory of Orientalism[10] (mentioned in Chapter One). According to Said, Westerners articulate perceptions and assumptions about the Orient, and in this case about the African Black race. As Samora argued, the presentation of Black women in American programs broadcast in South Africa brings a White perspective to the screen that speaks to Black girls from a colonizing point of view.

A different twist on the entanglement of race, culture, and gender was expressed by Emma (Bolivia) in her discussion of the dominance of the White female role model: *And, of course, when all the North American programs show blonde women with very blue eyes, and you see, we are not, and of course in rural areas, and in the cities, the girls are very anxious, they are very frustrated because they are not.*

The discussion on what constitutes a beauty model for girls will be addressed shortly, as it emerged as a central theme in the interviews. Yet this is a good point in the discussion to note that the truth value of this claim (that blonde women on television make Bolivian girls anxious), like many other similar claims made by producers presented here, was not investigated empirically in this study and therefore cannot be confirmed. However, the point of this "witnessing" is not to verify and to confirm producers' arguments, but rather to give voice – to share – their thoughts, concerns, and insights. Furthermore, we should recall that what counts here as evidence is not necessarily what actually happens in the real world; but, rather, these are statements and findings about what producers believe to be happening, and as such what may be driving their work and fueling their creative energies.

A very different critique was expressed by Nasing (Malaysia): *Some of the programs we have seen are very cookie-cut formula, like American TV. They all have the same formula of high-school setting, boy–girl relationship. And, a few of us are quite upset by this. It is the same thing repackaged in a different way from different organizations. I think teens, adolescent children, they have other things besides the relationship aspect. They have rivalries, problems with authorities like parents, or how to deal with schoolteachers and how teachers deal with them. There are so many other perspectives that could have been addressed, and some of the programs do, but some remain conventional, run-of-the-mill kind of programs ...*

Sarah (Australia) complained about the age appropriateness of American programs for children: *I think they do a lot of stuff that is for an older age. I think they are bringing issues at a much younger age than we would have chosen to ... a lot of what we do is fun, comedy, adventure, fantasy. We want them to be teens at that age. They can deal with reality later. Let's keep their imagination going. Let's feed their imagination, rather than what they can see outside their door ...*

Thus, American programming was criticized on many levels: For being stereotypical of gender and race; for perpetuating a particular, unattainable beauty model for girls; for being irrelevant to indigenous cultures; for being too limited in scope of content and issues for children as they mature; for unnecessarily accelerating adulthood. True, these critiques echo many of the themes that dominate the discourse in the literature about cultural imperialism. Yet, these are not the views of academics but rather statements by practitioners, people who populate the production professions in the television industry around the world, most of whom are far removed from the heated intellectual debate flowing through academic journals and argued over in conference halls. That is, these are the views of hands-on television producers who watch a lot of television for children from around the world and who struggle to create their own.

"We" (Americans) Versus "Them"

The 19 US producers interviewed for this study (all of whom define themselves as professionals working outside the realm of mainstream American commercial television, excluding three from Nickelodeon) are far from oblivious to critiques of cultural imperialism. Hope (US) who works for a large educational production company said: *The interesting thing about seeing TV from around the world is trying to understand the cultural subtext that is in the shows, because I think many times the politics and the social behavior of the country are embedded in the picture ... because that's one of the things that people are proud of and want to express ... so I think that one of my criticisms of American TV is that mostly everyone seems to live these perfect lives. Their problems are about boys and girls, not necessarily about the more difficult things that children are facing around the world ...*

Also from the US, Matt reflected on the production policy in his own company, one whose aim is to distribute their programs globally. He provided the following ideological rationale for their marketing goals: *You need to make as much an effort as possible to embrace all kinds of local signs of culture ... to be as neutral as possible and digestible as possible for as many cultures ... look, there are two ways to approach this. One is that, do you make it, you know, homogenous? That's one way to look at it. The other way to look at it is that you try to find that emotional connection that's in all of us around the world and appeal to it. Both are saying the same thing, but one sounds like a devastatingly negative thing, and the other sounds more like a positive thing, an inspirational thing to try and do. I do think today, on the anniversary of John Lennon's death, we are one world and at the end of the day, yes there may be local cultural institutions but television in and of itself is a mass medium, it's a global medium just like the Internet is potentially a global medium. And so, as for television, yes, we need to think about the content as a global content, and therefore it has to be neutralized, if you will, as opposed to localized, in order to succeed on a global basis.*

As this particular conversation unfolded, I shared a number of quotations and the arguments employed by producers around the world in their critiques of US television. Matt picked up the challenge, with the following response quoted at length: *You know, what is the Americanization of the world? Is it our values? What are American values? Okay, that's an interesting question. So ... there are parts of this culture in America that are trying to find that place where we can all share and we can all assimilate. There are other factions in American culture that are right, or left, or sideways, or ups, or downs or whatever, but those, those content creators are not in the mainstream, they can't be. So, you know, again, that's why, you know, it's exciting to see a kids program like* Caillou *created by a child developmental psychologist center in Montreal, Canada, a book that was turned into a television show, that airs in, I don't know, 90 countries around the world right now and that is a success globally. It's exciting to see a program like* Teletubbies *that emerged from the UK and finds its way to the US or* Totally Spies, *that starts in France and finds its way to broadcasters around the world or* Pokémon. *You know, Japan was the largest producer of animation next to the United States for 25 years and no one maybe outside Italy saw those programs until* Pokémon *happened and then all of a sudden there's a demand for Japanese Anima around the world, which, when you look at it, is very identifiably Japanese. So, does that mean they're trying to permeate the world with Japanese culture?*

Matt's defensive tone can be interpreted as a form of self-rationalization and a dismissal of the critiques posed to US producers in encounters with non-US colleagues, audiences, and intellectuals. He dismissed the notion of "American values," claiming that the US culture itself is heterogeneous, and disregarded the conflation of economical interests with cultural influence, claiming that it is all in the eyes of the beholder (as he said, above: "*there are two ways to look at it* ... "). His explanation also relates strongly to what a colleague and I termed "The Megaphone Effect:" "true acceptance of a cultural product seems to come from crossing the Atlantic and becoming a success in the United States [following which] items seem to acquire an ever-expanding sphere of appeal extending across the globe."[11] The *Pokémon* example cited by Matt is a case in point. It began as a video game for Nintendo's Gameboy, became a popular TV series, a card game, a movie, and then the subject of massive merchandizing. From Japan it traveled to the US and from there to the rest of the world, becoming an instant hit, dubbed Pokémania. The international commercial success of *Pokémon* was based on the effective use of localizing (this included the omission of five episodes deemed unacceptable to American child audiences due to the overt sexual objectification of a female character; changing the names of characters so that they would have a more appealing sound to the American ear; and changing color schemes).[12]

Direct reference to localizing was provided, for example, by Dana (Israel) who explained in her discussion of purchasing Japanese animation that *all of these series go through American adaptation, as there is a need to censor them here and there ... it is a completely different world of concepts and values ... different taboos ... for example, they had secondary narratives relating to homo/lesbian themes, or open sexual themes. There was once a scene with a grandfather type who pinched a young woman's ass, which I thought was very serious, more so than a battle scene. So we buy them from the Americans and not directly from Japan, because we are closer in culture to the American culture.*

Dana's explanation illustrates how the US serves as a cultural megaphone for products whose origins lie elsewhere. However, it also became clear as the interview process unfolded that many localized products offer very diverse interpretations of gender on children's television that are locally unique and require a lot more than a "megaphone" and localization to adapt them in terms of relevancy to other audiences. We turn now to the discussion of such themes.

Local Cultural Perspectives of Gender

Attempts to mobilize children's television as a tool for social change by means of constructing an alternative social reality on the screen have been practiced all over the world. The trend to deliberately incorporate social issues (health, literacy, risk behavior, conflict resolution, racial tolerance, etc.) in entertainment programming of all genres (including soap operas and telenovelas, cartoons, drama, talk shows, quiz shows, and reality-TV genres) viewed regularly by children and youth is particularly evident in the non-Westernized world, and is referred to in the literature as Edutainment (see Chapter One).[13] Many creative, well-intended quality edutainment programs for children are being developed worldwide. What is unique about the discussion that follows is that it focuses on social change related to what is perceived as the most important perspective on gender in interviewees' respective societies.

The five themes discussed below emerged in the analysis of interviewees' responses to the question: "What are the most important issues related to gender in your society that television for children has attempted to (or should) deal with?" Most producers' initial responses to this question differentiated between themselves and others, mainly Americans. Having made this point, they proceeded to discuss cultural particularities; that is, aspects of the "us" unique to one's own society. As presented here, in wide brushstrokes, the following are the five most prevalent themes that emerged from analysis of the transcripts.

Two notes of caution: First, while the following discussion highlights issues prominent in regions of the world that share similar social-cultural characteristics, these themes were not entirely exclusive to these regions, as echoes were identifiable in reflections of producers working in entirely different societies and against entirely different backgrounds. Second, regional-focused discussion is bound to be generalized and risks glossing the uniqueness of each of the cultures; and, hence, missing a comparative analysis of the many nuanced differences between these cultures. Thus, I re-emphasize that the purpose of this discussion is to highlight general themes that surfaced in the interviews that seem to be the central concerns shared by producers, regardless of their diverse and particular backgrounds. Needless to say, the following should be understood as the dominant themes perceived by this group of professionals, rather than restrictive generalizations about these cultures and their perceptions of gender.

Schooling and Early Marriage

Perhaps the most traditional, clear-cut, and primary ambition and aspiration that producers claimed to advance was to find ways through which television could be used to encourage schooling for girls. They did so by offering role models of both girls and parents who value education and believe in the rights of girls for equal opportunities.

Recalling the revolutionary work of pioneer feminists at the end of the eighteenth and throughout the nineteenth century in Europe and the US,[14] and a right realized in many societies around the world, advancing schooling for all children, and in particular girls, was a major issue for many of my interviewees, particularly those from societies with extensive rural areas. Their concerns were validated by data provided by the United Nations: Young women represent 59 percent of the world's more than 130 million illiterate youth. Worldwide, more than 60 million women aged 20–24 were married before they turned 18, and if the present trends continue more than 100 million girls will probably be married as children in the next decade. In addition, 15 million adolescent girls become mothers each year.[15]

The basic premise characterizing early feminist thought was that a lack of education and the acquisition of literacy skills is responsible to a large degree for women's lower status in all societies. Thus, providing equal education for girls is key to confronting their inequality and oppression, but also educating women contributes to development of their future families and society at large. As Jordan's Queen Rania said in her special message in a video distributed through YouTube on International Women's Day, March 7, 2009:

> [...] This is what happens when you educate girls: They are less likely to be victims of violence and exploitation and more likely to be empowered; less likely to marry early, more likely to pursue higher education and productive work; less likely to have children who die prematurely; more likely to raise healthy, educated, sons and daughters. But right now, 41 million girls are shut outside of school gates because of poverty and prejudice; because there is no sanitation in schools; water wells are not built close to their village; classrooms are at dangerous distances from home. If we don't help them soon, they will join the half a billion women who are illiterate.

The priority of the struggle to advance girls' rights for schooling as the most important gender issue was most evident in interviews with producers from Muslim countries (such as Egypt, Syria, Turkey, Yemen), but also in countries where there are extensive rural areas (such as Ethiopia, Ghana, India, Kenya, Kyrgyzstan, Nepal, Nigeria). Producers from these societies were concerned about girls dropping out of school and entering traditional early marriage arrangements. For example, Manisha's description of the situation in Nepal represents many of the stories interviewees shared with me: *In some families, in the villages where there is a lower level of literacy, if they have to chose between a boy and a girl, they will chose the son to go to school. Girls who don't go to school help their parents, help in the farm, get married at a younger age ... even though it is changing slowly.* Similar prioritizing of sons was related by Senait (Ethopia): *Girls are underprivileged, you see. With the large number of kids in the family – girls are usually the ones left behind to take care of their siblings.*

Interviewees made a point of emphasizing that the problem is not just enforcing mandatory schooling, since, as was pointed out by Omar (Syria), girls often drop out of school after six years to become domestic helpers or to enter into early marriages. In order to confront the dilemma between ensuring schooling for girls and meeting the economic needs of the family (for extra hands at home or early marriages as a way to lessen the economic burden of feeding another mouth), Esmeral (Turkey), as well as Taylor (Tanzania), explained that television campaigns about schooling for girls did not dwell on the issue of human rights and social justice, but instead emphasized pragmatic concerns: Schooling guarantees better job opportunities and is thus a fine economic investment for the family. As Senait (Ethiopia) put it: *if you educate one girl, it's like educating the whole family, because she is the first educator of her children ... she is like the pillar of the family ... that's the reason we chose a girl as our main character, and we called her* Tsehai [see Figure 3.1] *which means sunshine in Amharic, because she is very inquisitive, and we portray her as a bright and intelligent character.*

Caroline (US), a researcher and policymaker working with coproduction teams for *Sesame Street* in many developing countries, described the situation as follows: *In those cultures there are real practical issues that come into play in terms of girls' education. If you just look at the basic statistics, the number of illiterate women versus illiterate men, the disproportion there is huge, it's striking. So, on those TV programs, there's an active voice trying to move the needle in terms of girls' opportunities. So they've developed very strong female characters that are role models for kids. In Egypt, for example, we have Khokha*[16] *who is this vibrant little girl who loves learning and who loves to read, and she actually, she loves to be around literate elements. She goes to the*

Figure 3.1 Tsehai Loves Learning © Whiz Kids Workshop P.L.C., Addis Ababa, Ethiopia

library. She has aspirations, you know, to one day – she wants to be a lawyer or an astronaut or whatever. She is there to model not only what girls can aspire to, but also to model for boys what girls can be. In Bangladesh, too, we have two female characters who are extremely strong that were specifically developed to be role models.

A more modest example comes from a fiction program in Kyrgyzstan telling the story of a strong girl character who struggles to lift a ban imposed by a king that denies all girls in the kingdom the right for schooling. As Farhad related the narrative in the interview, she wins the king over by exhibiting her intelligence and proving to him that girls are smart enough to go to school.

A unique example, one that faces the issue of girls' education in a direct manner, is the Egyptian docudrama *Fatma* (see Figure 3.2) that reenacts the true story of a girl living with her parents in an Egyptian village. Fatma's father has never allowed Fatma to attend school, since the family needs her to help them at the farm and at home. Now eleven, Fatma has demanded that she be allowed to do so, in order to realize her dream of becoming a lawyer. The program portrays her successful negotiations with her father; the terms of their agreement – she can attend school in the morning if she agrees to complete her chores in the evening and to succeed in school; her daily struggles and the work needed to overcome difficulties at home and in school; and her improved self-image as well as status in the family following her personal empowerment. The story of Fatma personifies a true-to-life TV model for capable girls around the world who have been denied an education due to traditional social arrangements and deeply entrenched gender inequalities. It highlights the complex difficulties facing the families who break with tradition, the special schools that have been established to educate the increasing number of older

Figure 3.2 Fatma © Egyptian TV Union

girls obtaining an education, and the girls themselves who undergo personal transformation in non-favorable circumstances.

Overall, while admittedly a very modest attempt to touch the surface of this basic premise of gender equity, producers in these countries have faith that personal stories that are real and honest can stir the hearts of their viewers, girls and parents alike.

Machismo Culture

The flip side of the liberal-feminist struggle for equality was found in producers' critiques of their own societies' "macho" cultures, to which young people are regularly exposed on their media screens, and their efforts to introduce a less patriarchal television viewing for children. The use of the words "macho" and "machismo" was almost exclusive to producers coming from Latin American countries, although those who live in other countries also expressed its connotations. Roberto (Argentina), for example, explained: *We are a very male-oriented society, machismo, although many women are ministers, and we have a big feminist movement, lots of women get access to decision-making jobs and power jobs, but anyway, there is still the men's culture the old fashioned way ... advertising still reflects this surrounding reality that the male should have the role of leading the family, feeding the family, and the female more indoor kind of world.*

Telenovelas, the popular Latin American serial dramas, were targeted by interviewees in particular as conveyers of such traditional values. Carlos (Uruguay) said: *In Latin America we are the machismo societies ... the problem of watching telenovelas with mothers – Brazilian, Argentinean, Venezuela ... all the time the same story ... the woman without parents, she works in one house cleaning and then she meets the father who is the great man in the story ... and she falls in love.*

Elaine (Brazil) added an additional dimension regarding gay characters: *And there are lots of jokes about gays. To be a macho you have to have the muscles, physical strength, use the kind of shirts that are very tight ... Mexico, they are even more stereotypically macho. In Brazil it is less, but the whole Latin America is a machismo society, you can see it in the telenovelas, very famous in the whole Latin America, it is all related to that ... but some [telenovelas] are bringing ,up some issues that are very interesting, like social issues and they are dealing sometimes with gay situations and women's situations in an interesting way. But, mainly on commercial TV, there is a bad view of women, like they are still in the second place ...* While critiquing telenovelas, Elaine also acknowledged their potential as well as the actual practice of positive social intervention in relation to gender, such as gay and women rights. Thus, she illustrates one clear axis of thought assumed by most of the interviewees: If television has social power and thus can be criticized for cultivating negative perceptions, it means that it also can have the potential to change such attitudes. This assumption will be the focus of later discussion.

The popularity of soap operas, the equivalent of the telenovelas in other parts of the world, among young audiences in countries such as India and its neighbours, was also a focus of such claims, given the general absence of locally produced programming for children. Amita (India), a freelance journalist, emphasized the role of this genre in legitimizing traditional ways of life: *Very conservative soap operas, glorifying women at home in traditional roles, are viewed by generations of women and girls. The stories are within homes. Women are central characters but upholders of tradition – women's roles and stereotypes, the bad woman who has a career ... women and self sacrifice ... The men are manipulated by bad women and rescued by good women ...*

From a different part of the world, Milan (Serbia) offered a similar argument: *What is also a big problem in my country is the soap operas which are really the very simple stereotypes when you talk about the characters, feeding the culture with some very dangerous stereotypes ... the women are just very good or very mean, they are very poor and sad ... on the other side are the men who are very rich but not happy because they are mean and this is it. And the men are always dirty business men or some losers that have our sympathy. So this is the kind of roles that I think people in underdeveloped countries believe in ...*

Machismo values were referred to by the interviewees as related to male violence, and particularly to the domestic violence that producers wanted television for children to tackle. One such example comes from Adriana (Colombia) who described her team's production efforts in this area: *We did this series about reading promotion where the father, the leading role is a male who is reading to kids, sewing, knitting, being tender, because our society is very macho, machismo oriented, and one has to watch how one is portraying gender roles – male and female – how boys treat girls and vice versa – in the program. And how we depict specific roles and our characters, we were very careful about discriminatory language, slang that may be offensive, very careful about including minority girls and boys ... and specifically we did this series about masculinity ... it was basically tenderness and men ... all about affection in treating children ... it was trying to reduce violent behavior at home, sharing ...*

Efforts at providing audiences with different portrayals of parenting, the division of labor at home and breaking with traditions associated with masculinity in productions for children were perceived by Adriana as part of the struggle to combat domestic violence through offering an alternative vision for manhood, in general, and fatherhood, more specifically. Providing positive male role models for children was discussed also by producers from other parts of the world, but from a different angle, as will be discussed shortly within the "neglected boys" theme.

The Western Beauty Myth

Another theme dominant in interviews with producers throughout the non-Western world, one that exemplifies the intertwining of gender and post-colonial theories, relates to these interviewees' critique of the Western "Beauty Myth"[17] (discussed in Chapter One). In particular, they expressed a concern for the homogenization of the desired female "look" as mostly young, thin, attractive, heterosexual, wealthy – as well as predominantly white. Producers (much like scholars[18]) were very critical of the priority given to selected images of Whiteness on television viewed by children, which they felt conveyed the message that Western beauty is superior to their own. The ethnic subordination of non-Western people was discussed in terms of disempowerment. Producers speculated about the impact these images have on self-identity, national pride, and behavior (including the purchase of products and plastic surgery that imitates Caucasian features). Many expressed an open longing to see on the screen their own society's children, with their own ethnic characteristics.

Eliane (Brazil), for example, conveyed this concern: *There are many commercial stations that use girls as hosts, in order to bring more attention, like beautiful girls. Even in Brazil, we are much more brown than blond, but you will always have a blonde girl, with blue eyes. So, in the commercial side, there is the stereotype of a female host that will attract more viewers. Including, in the past, there was a very important hostess for a very long time on the commercial main television, and she used to sing and dance with children and in some way she started a kind of model of this blonde beautiful woman, with a skirt like this [pointing up at her thigh] ... and then there is a cartoon, and then you come back to the studio and then they sing and then they show merchandizing ... very commercial. And she was a role model. It is a really typical Latin program. Being blonde is an expression that she is something special, but not like us. It was heavily criticized for a while by the intelligentsia ... they used to say also that fathers used to watch with the children because of her [laughs] ...*

Emma (Bolivia) made a similar point about discrepancies between Western and local beauty values when she complained about blonde models on TV: *... like the idol of women, for example, in the indigenous people is a full woman, not a thin woman, because if she looks thin she looks sick ... And for example the very, very black hair is very important for the indigenous people in Bolivia ...* Beatriz (Ecuador) said: *... when they get presenters, they try to look always like the typical American pop stars ... they make the girls look beautiful and very sexy and things like this ...* And Elenora (Argentina) also pinpointed the imported media when she said *there is a lot of pressure from the media to be thin, with big breasts and perfect skin ... the perfection of the body.*

While the above quotes demonstrate the centrality of this theme in interviews with Latin producers, similar concerns were raised in other cultures as well, where children have very little locally produced television fare. Margaret (Kenya), for example, explained: ... *We are a hip-hop nation, and we have taken up on television the wrong, superficial meaning of hip-hop, with the cursing and the tight clothes, and the make-up and the models and the looks and everything ... and our boys and girls are picking up on that a lot ... and, sadly, I don't really think they realize that their heroes are white. They identify and wish to be like them, like Britney Spears[19] for example. Yeah, they would. And this is exactly my point. They have not been brought up to appreciate who they are, to appreciate that they have values and cultures and things they need to be proud of as Black Africans and Black Kenyans. They have been brought up with all these programs that we have seen now. And they try to look like Britney Spears, they put blue contact lenses, and gray contact lenses, because that's what they have grown up with. They do not have anything better to see on television ... I would like to show them African beauty, authentic. And, you know, it is very interesting, because we have beauty pageants, and African bodies are not small, we are big people, but the people who win have stick figures. So, we have girls starving themselves. We have anorexia, so they can stay thin ... because we all want to stay thin and fashionable ...*

Concern over the desire of young people to forsake their identity, and even their distinct racial physical characteristics, was also a source of producer grievance from other parts of the world. In the Philippines, according to Leona, girls have been so desperately striving to achieve the Western look that it has fueled an industry of skin-whitening cosmetic products, as well as plastic surgery to open slotted eyes and to create, artificially, a Caucasian "nose-bridge." She shared the following views: *For a European coming over it will probably look strange – in every drug store and grocery store you can find skin whitening products, every lotion, soap, etcetera, are being made with papayas for whitening the skin, being fair, to be White, because the enzyme of the papaya is whitening. They want to be fair. The half-breed is the definition of beauty, also more Western good looking, Phil-Americans or Euro-Asian Filipinos coming home and becoming stars, you know, children of interracial marriages, Philippines and Europeans, they look very good, really attractive, and they can make a living back home* [laughs].

It's a colonial mentality, that you look to what the colonizers brought as superior and what is indigenous to us as inferior, so you combine it with gender, that merges in the definitions of beauty ... even for young children ... And some dark skin like myself, Morena, that's the more exotic version. Women want to have their noses repaired. The Chinese Filippina women want to have the operation that makes them more European. In our programs we are confronting the concept of beauty, what does it mean to be beautiful? ... slim, big breasted with a nose ... most noses here are flat but they want the one with the bridge. They want rounded eyes not slit eyes. In the last five years there have been a lot of cases of malpractice ... it is such a business.

Translated into the language of theory, Leona, Margaret, Beatriz, and Emma critiqued the "internal colonization" that occurs, according to Stuart Hall, when the adoption of dominant representations succeeds in having a person see and experience themselves as Other.[20] Black, Filippina, or Latina girls, for example, learn to see themselves through the White-masculine perspective that represents and speaks for them, thus internalizing an oppressive point of view of themselves and participating in a "process of whitening that attempts to modernize these identities while bleaching ethnicities."[21] More specifically, these quotations also refer to, indeed manifest, internalized "colorism,"[22] a form of discrimination based on skin color: Skin tone may determine different "shades" of racism and create status hierarchies and inequalities within the colored community itself.[23] Leona's discussion of the social capital of light-skin Filipinos is a clear demonstration of such colorism.

While the pressure of the Western beauty models targets girls for the most part, boys have not escaped its power, as Beatriz (Ecuador) illustrates: *Boys ... their looks is very, very modern with their hair, earring, like boys are used to wear right now on TV, with this kind of things like piercing, with their shirts and the blue jeans, very modern ... up to date and so and so, they try to represent the modern image that we have a lot in the programs from US.*

Clearly, as Beatriz and the other interviewees suggested, the struggle to attain the "Western look" also imposes an economic strain on children and their families, and economically it fuels production and consumption of products, clothing, fashion accessories, costly surgeries, as well as access to Western popular culture. Studies on girlhood have suggested that traditional conceptions tying girls to the domestic sphere and to restrictions on sexuality have been transformed to a large degree into an illusory freedom: "Girl-power" essentially means the power to freely consume and revive traditional feminine pleasures of fashion, cosmetics, and bodily display. Angela McRobbie, among others, has suggested that the media have a central role in positioning girls in our cultures as subjects of consumption.[24] Valentina (Chile) pointed this out directly, while trying to position her culture within the general Latin America scene: *The main goal in South America [is] the appearances, so they [girls and young women] go to clinics, they put on lip gloss for the day, lip gloss for the night. They spend a lot of money. Chile, not as much as Argentina and Brazil, but Mexico, the upper class, they spend a lot of money on their appearance. Chile a little bit less than that, but they are getting there ...*

Remarks by some Western producers demonstrated that they were cognizant of this issue. Indeed, those who did so also expressed a strong desire to see change in the beauty models offered to children. However, in this regard, they expressed mainly anxiety over physical and mental health, and so differed from the identity and colonization concerns that dominated discussion about the beauty myth by producers working outside the US and European countries. Caroline (USA) referred specifically to the concern over obesity and body-image among children: *... a lot of broadcasters are focusing now on issues of* *obesity and, because, you know, obesity is a huge, huge issue in the States, and fitness ... and so, you know, struggling with both making overweight kids feel like they're being represented on the screen 'cause there's such a huge population of kids who are struggling with weight. So, it's kind of both helping them not be overweight and also feel like they're being represented on television ... you don't see a lot of realistic body portrayals. I think this is particularly so with girls ... and I think the anorexic way is how they are portrayed, I think that most popular characters are thin and have large breasts ...* Indeed, Caroline is right in pointing out that the potential contribution of television to the current trend of growing obesity has become a major focus of public and scholarly attention in the US.[25] At the same time she is also pinpointing two seemingly contradictory forces that seem to be in operation here: On the one hand the argument that viewing TV in general is related to obesity (i.e. through lack of activity and heavy exposure to food commercials), yet at the same time the images viewed themselves of unhealthily thin characters suggest a glorification of thinning eating disorders.

Birgit (Germany) was more concerned with children's psychological well-being: *I think that the question of your looks is very important. What I mean is that, here in Germany, a very, very popular topic at the moment is all this plastic surgery ... and this question of having to be perfect, having to look good. This is something that really worries me because I think you should tell the girls ... or try to have the girls accept themselves, I mean, besides all that question of equal rights there are many psychological questions or so. This is something that has a strong impact on the girls. And if you go around and look at the girls, what they look like, it's horrible – things they have on and piercing here and they want to look attractive and sexy ... I feel terrible and so you must find role models nowadays on television that help girls, I think, to accept the fact that they are not perfect, cannot be perfect, and that looks are not everything.*

Abby (USA) carried this argument forward when she extended the theme of beauty as a perceived key "for everything:" *And there is a promiscuity about young girls and their expectations of what the world owes them. And, I think that when you think of the talent that has developed and the role models that young girls see, it's very dangerous. So you look at Britney Spears or you look at Hillary Duff[26] and you look at the clothing lines that they have, that there's this rather dangerous female stereotyping that girls can have everything, and they can have everything by being pretty, and by being blonde, and by being charming and being seductive, and I think that's very dangerous to our daughters, and it's everywhere.* Abby seems to be echoing the idea of the "Lolita Effect" (described in Chapter One) in suggesting that tying sexuality and attractiveness with "having everything" is cultivating a particular world-view among girls.

Hand in hand with the assertion by producers that unrealistic body images can be harmful to children both physically and psychologically goes the belief that appropriate images would have a positive impact. Indeed, Caroline (US) described just such a process on American TV: *And you know, it's interesting, the one thing that has changed in character portrayal, and as crazy as this sounds, is like with a couple of pop icons in American culture ... J.Lo [Jennifer Lopez],[27] a very popular Latina actress and singer, and Beyoncé [Knowles][28] who is Black, and because more ethnic music has become a bigger part of general pop culture they have become icons of beauty. They don't have bodies like typical White people, and so the notion of a more voluptuous figure has actually seeped into popular culture and so boys want to be graphic now, boys want girls with big asses now and that was never, you never heard them talking like that before. So there's a little bit more of a kind of acceptance and a more of a voluptuous figure that has direct connection to ethnicity.* It is interesting to note that it is through a form of "othering" of the two non-White cultural icons that Caroline was able to offer a critique of, as well as a direction for possible change in, television beauty models. However, in doing so, she accepts the category of ethnic difference as being the core of this process, rather than, for example, White models who represent alternative body images. Thus, Caroline's example serves to point out that "Latinas fall beyond the margins of socially acceptable femininity and beauty."[29]

It is interesting to note that none of the 135 interviewees mentioned the physical characteristics of male television heroes – including grossly exaggerated muscular shoulders and arms, and bulky chests that taper down to narrow waists – as problematic models for boys in their societies or a reason for concern over their health and psychological wellbeing. This suggests that producers themselves associate concerns about "looks" and body image with femininity. This finding is interesting given the growing scholarly work over the constructed nature of masculinity (discussed in Chapter One), and a need for a reminder that "gender" is as much about boys as it is about girls ...

HIV/AIDS

While the fact that HIV/AIDS surfaced as a major existential issue for African nations, as well as other regions in the world, was not surprising, what was striking is the finding that so many producers across the world cited it among the most urgent, important gender issues that need to be dealt with in television for children. Part of the explanation for this finding lies in the fact that HIV/AIDS is a sexually transmitted disease and many of the interviewees used the concepts of gender and sex interchangeably. For example, in response to my question about the concept of gender, Nicole (Hong Kong) discussed, immediately, their television's sex education campaign. However, as the interviews unfolded, it became clear that producers' views about the spread of HIV/AIDS were related to patriarchal structures, traditional gender power relationships, and the disadvantageous position of girls in their societies.

In detailing the nature of the problem, African interviewees related examples of common occurrences of rapes of virgin girls by men inflicted with HIV/AIDS, the result of a superstitious belief that such a sexual act can cure the disease. And, as well, the pervasive number of cases of subservient married women who feel they are unable to demand the use of condoms by husbands who are infected with HIV as a result of their frequent, normalized, extra-marital sexual encounters. Indeed, data provided by the UN estimates that, globally, young people aged 15–24 account for 45 percent of all new HIV infections in adults, and within sub-Saharan Africa, 75 percent of the infections are among young women.[30]

Part of the sense of mission that some of the interviewees conveyed was driven by their aim to use television's treatment of the HIV/AIDS crisis in their societies as an opportunity to empower girls and women. Paradise (South Africa) provided the following explanation: [...] *in fiction and non fiction ... both produced locally and imported ... we were very careful in the HIV series to really look at the issue of HIV and women, to begin to find a break in the stereotyping of women. For example, how women as sex workers are empowered so they can negotiate the terms of the sexual relations and the way they are perceived and the way they are projected ... Even with the issue of AIDS, it is a lot about men's views and condoms and men taking the role ... Women don't feel empowered and they don't feel like they can say "Hey, you use a condom." In every message that goes out there it is about the men. And, I think it is about time that we start saying to women that you have to take power ...*

Similarly, Virender (Canada), working in South Africa, described attempts to promote use of the female condom to protect girls and young women from the consequences of rape and to empower them to take control of some aspects of their lives, even in situations of terrible oppression: *There is actually one famous spot on 3 AMIGOS that we created on the female condom ... up to that point nobody in South Africa mentioned the existence of the female condom ... we reached a lot of young girls this way ... because there is high incidence of rape especially walking to and from school in some townships ... we played them on the air a lot and what we started finding out was that they were really good icebreakers for AIDS educators, for NGOs, for house clinics ... So if you have a young couple, they're watching television before having sex. And the spot comes on and the woman especially gets empowered, because she has the ability to talk about the spot. ... especially talking about the condoms; especially female condoms, which is very difficult for women to talk about ...*

Now, when you consider that it's sex, then you have to consider the empowerment of women, because this isn't a disease like malaria which is transmitted by mosquitoes ... you get AIDS through your own personal actions. It is not like cancer that you don't do anything and somehow you get the disease. And then when you talk about sex, so many societies around the world, including South Africa, where a man feels very often that he has a right to sex and that if his girlfriend is not available, he's gonna have sex with somebody else. And multiple partners are very common in South Africa at a very young age ... I think that culture is the main factor and this is a preventable disease, that's what gets to me – we know what to do; it has everything, everything, to do with gender and equality. So it is mainly a communication problem, it is mainly an education problem, and because it is an education problem, what we really need to do is educate girls, because they are the ones who ultimately are going to be out of control with this disease, until the doctors come up with the vaccine.

Not only were producers concerned with ways to creatively use television to educate children on how to protect themselves from HIV/AIDS, they were also thoroughly frustrated with their inability to find ways to counter prevailing images coming from the Western world that transmit counterproductive messages to their audiences, making it doubly difficult to deal with the disease in culturally relevant ways.

Paradise (South Africa) provided a detailed discussion of this problem in an especially rich interview worth quoting at length: *We are looking at AIDS in different areas: AIDS and orphans, AIDS and the region, AIDS and spirituality, how are we coping with HIV. We are also looking at alternative medication and alternative healing, as the reality is that we don't have the drugs and the money to cope with the damage. [... in the] discussion of young people engaged in sex, instead of making it a taboo, [they] may be offering them condoms [...] Uganda is a different example – "A B C" – Abstain, Be faithful and finally Condomize – use a condom. I think it turned it around, that it is going back to family values.*

And, oh, not everybody is engaged in sex ... I think it is the thing that there must be lots of young people that are engaged in sex but there are a lot who aren't, so there is this perspective that some young people are saying that "you assume that we are having sex and you give us condoms so we might as well use them."

[...] so it is different ways of dealing with it and sometimes the way that the media haven't really taken cognizance of the culture around and for whom it is supposed to be doing this, and this is what I mean by contextualizing it. For some of the young people it was an act of bravado of "I am having sex and who is going to tell me to use a condom, it won't happen to me" and there were others saying that "we have been pressured, the media are portraying one thing and you are saying something else;" and "everybody is telling me be careful of HIV, but everybody is having sex on television."

So women in our series have been much, much stronger and much, more profoundly discussant in their interviews because the fact of the matter is that they infected AIDS from their husbands, that is how it is contacted in most of the cases ... We had extreme situations of babies who have been raped and eighty-year-old grandmothers raped ... the superstition that comes out that if you have sex with a virgin you will be cured and we had a lot of different media trying to deal with that and say that actually you will not be cured ... When you are working on a subject like AIDS ... it changes your whole world ... when you come, the day of the filming, and the people you are making the program about have died ... priorities become clearer ... issues of gender and race and class and culture and everything else is so related to death and dying and loss of dignity, as AIDS is such an awful killer ... I think in children's media we are able to communicate that because ... it has no boundaries, it is not between Black and White and rich and poor and those kind of boundaries, it is just everywhere. So, how do we begin to communicate those kind of things to our young people? ... To take control of your dignity all by yourself? And, children suffer from it because children are embarrassed to say my parents have died from it ...

Paradise clearly connected gender with race and class and emphasized the need to contextualize discussions of gender to her society's particular cultural needs. The last point she made in the quotation above relates to the social acceptance of children who are victims of the disease, either as being infected with HIV and/or as orphans who have lost one or both parents to this killer. Attempts to face this issue head on have been incorporated, for example, in the South African coproduction of *Sesame Street* called *Takalani Sesame* (see Figure 3.3). It features a Muppet named Kami, who represents a five-year-old

Figure 3.3 Takalani Sesame. Sesame Street photos provided courtesy of Sesame Workshop (New York). Sesame Workshop®, Sesame Street®, Takalani Sesame®, Sesame Tree® and associated characters, trademarks, and design elements are owned and licensed by Sesame Workshop. © 2009 Sesame Workshop. All Rights Reserved

girl who was orphaned after her mother died of an AIDS-related illness. She is intelligent, resilient, affectionate, and empathetic. She is well informed about HIV and AIDS, openly expresses her feelings, models coping mechanisms, and is featured in contexts to which children can relate, such as playing with friends or going to the doctor. Kami (whose name is derived from "Kamogelo," which means acceptance and/or welcome in several traditional South African languages) was designed to promote age-appropriate messages concerning the humanization, destigmatization, and acceptance of people living with HIV/AIDS. The program attempted to encourage open discussion about issues such as coping with illness and loss. Thus Kami serves a role model for "Africa's Orphaned Generation" (as it is referred to by UNICEF).[31]

Caroline (USA) who supervised the *Takalani Sesame* coproduction recalled: *In South Africa we have this character, Kami, who is a Muppet, who is HIV positive. When the team was deciding her characteristics it was actively decided that she would be female because of the disproportionate number of women who have HIV ... There were all sorts of characteristics that came into play. She's healthy looking in terms of her persona, because there's a stereotype that people with HIV are sickly. She's vibrant. She knows a lot about HIV and AIDS. Just as with gender, the messages are implicit and explicit. The same thing with this HIV/AIDS character. Sometimes HIV/AIDS is not even part of the discussion or the activities that she's involved in. And just the very act that she's with friends and engaged in play is an implicit message that you can play with somebody who's HIV positive. And, sometimes, there are specific messages related to HIV/AIDS on the program where something might happen to Kami. Somebody doesn't wanna play with her because she's HIV positive. And, it'll come out that "oh, you can play with people who are HIV positive, you can't get AIDS just from playing with somebody." ... so gender ends up being presented in this way.*

These extensive selections are from interviews with producers working in South Africa, where they are experiencing one of the most severe AIDS epidemics in the world. By the end of 2007, there were 33.2 million people around the world estimated to be living with HIV (including 2.5 million children); of them, an estimated five-and-a-half million people in South Africa alone, with almost 1,000 AIDS deaths occurring there every day.[32] However, HIV/AIDS was also referred to by other African and North African interviewees (from Botswana, Ethiopia, Ghana, Kenya, Tunisia) as well as Asian ones (from Bangladesh, Bhutan, India, Nepal) in the framework of gendered issues of concern. For example, an episode of a low-budget Ethiopian puppet series (with animated and live-action inserts) entitled *Tsehai Loves Learning* (see Figure 3.1), featured Tsehai, a giraffe, trying to cheer up her friend Tsinat, a turtle, whose mother has died from HIV/AIDS. The episode deals with providing friends with emotional support as Tsehai tells Tsinat a heartwarming story about keeping lost loved ones alive in the heart. In Kenya, producers overcame resource limitations as well as restrictions on approaching children directly with discussion of HIV/AIDS in a creative way by broadcasting video coverage of the various public performing arts (drama, poetry, and music festivals) which dealt with HIV/AIDS issues.

The underlying logic behind most of the views expressed in the interviews included an acceptance of popular conceptions of AIDS as "a disease of improper acts" (mostly of non-procreative or extramarital sex, or sexual violence, with the occasional mention of drug abuse) as well as "a disease of poverty, and especially mismanaged global development." A third common conception of AIDS as a disease of "improper bodies" (bodies representing homosexuality or prostitution) was rarely expressed by the interviewees.[33] At the same time, producers challenged the all-too-frequent, generalized Northern portrayal of African countries, and specifically women within them, as passive victims. They recounted efforts to mobilize girls and women to take their fates in their own hands. In this sense they followed the 2001 UN Declaration of Commitment that "the people in developing countries are the most affected and that women, young adults, and children, in particular girls, are the most vulnerable (Article 4)," and "stressing that gender equality and the empowerment of women are fundamental elements in the reduction of the vulnerability of women and girls to HIV/AIDS (Article 14)."[34]

Thus, in summary of the four theme issues discussed so far, the primary gender focus of the producers interviewed in this study was on the wellbeing of girls and women, in the context of their relationships with the men in their lives. They have sought to address these issues in their productions and, in doing so, aimed to provide viewers with tools that empower and enable them to take control of their lives.

The Neglected Boys

The final local theme to be presented in this chapter has been referred to as the "neglected boys" problem, and serves to remind us that gender refers to masculinities as well as femininities. This theme was clearly evident in discussions with producers from the northern part of the world, mostly those from the Nordic countries, the UK, Canada, and a few in the US. In general, the producers from these societies shared much in common: They perceived their societies to be the ones reaping the benefits of the feminist revolution and as having moved to a post-feminist[35] era of equality. As in academic and public debates, interviewees used the term "post-feminism" in various, sometimes contradictory, ways. Most seemed to have adopted a positive approach according to which post-feminism is understood to be a new form of feminism; a feminism updated in the twenty-first century in which the supposed achievements of the feminist movements have been incorporated into social life and are moving forward. As such, they argued that in their societies, equality for girls has been achieved and is therefore a non-issue in their workplaces.

Concern for gender equity, according to them, has been mostly replaced by issues of ethnicities and diversity.

Given this view, these producers were concerned primarily with dealing with their perception that boys were falling behind. Four key phenomena were cited in descriptions of this conclusion: First, today, boys are failing in schools and not continuing on to higher education. Second, there is a rise in risk behaviors among boys – including violence, drugs, alcoholism, depression, suicide, unprotected and violent sex. Third, aggression, in all its forms – including dealing with one's own aggressive energies, deferred sexuality, and the pressure to be "man enough" – presents boys with mounting challenges. Finally, girls' accelerated development and the fact that many are more eloquent and verbally aggressive than boys and ahead of them in school sets boys on alternative routes of antisocial competencies that are deemed masculine.

Indeed, studies of the "crisis of hegemonic masculinity"[36] (see Chapter One) discuss the existence of fundamental changes taking place in the reality of patriarchal societies in general, and in the conceptions of hegemonic masculinity in particular. Some scholars argue that the crisis is mainly in the media's constructions of men and masculinities and the academic discourse that surrounds them, rather than in the reality of male lives or views. Furthermore, it has been theorized that portrayals of this crisis are intertwined with a "White crisis," as these men live for the most part in working-class Western subcultures.[37] Yet, the changing nature of masculinity in media images, the reality they claim exists, as well as the emergence of new types of representations struggling for acceptance and naturalization were perceived by interviewees to constitute a worrying social reality that requires active intervention on behalf of boys growing up in these societies.

Producers addressed the problem of the "neglected boys" in a variety of ways, though they applied two main social explanations. First, producers argued that this situation was due to the disintegration of the traditional family structure and the absence of male figures in children's lives – real and on screens. For example, Julie (UK) explained: *I think this is probably an issue in Western cultures where there has been higher incidence of divorce and separation; and, where fathers have sometimes stayed very involved with their children. But, sometimes this is not the case, as they go on to make new families and they pay less attention. So, I think, for boys, the absence of fathers is a huge issue and ... maybe for girls as well actually ... so, we do not do enough in our dramas to address the issue of good male role models.* And Silvia (Germany) said: *I think ... in the first place it's good to have them in the show, that boys see boys, and see men. I think you must have like role models for boys on television, of course.*

Carla (Canada), too, was concerned about the absence of male figures in children's lives these days, particularly for boys, and its impact on family portrayals on television: *The problem is with the presentation of adults around children that also reflect a reality – broken families, absent fathers.*

Either the father is drunk or he is crazy. You rarely see a father coming in and picking up the baby and hugging him, you know. It's like, rarely done on TV, and for me that's a pity ... In the professional films made for children, you know, we, because we try to make serious movies, then we have to add drama somewhere, which for me it shouldn't be necessary to include that [absent father themes] and we should show more of these present parents, you know. Because we see a lot of stories on TV with grandparents raising children, for example. But the actual parents have less positive influence in children's lives ... in popular commercial television you always have a happy family, happy parents and you know, in most of children's films there is a problem, and children, and an animal ... and at the end the problem is solved ... happy ever after. So in some way it's nice that we're showing different, more realistic situations, but it's a balancing act you know. We've gone from one extreme to the other. So now we're not showing happy families anymore ... we have to be careful, because there are consequences to that. Right?

Indeed, research findings support Carla's arguments, as they demonstrate that while portrayals on American commercial television increasingly depict dysfunctional families as well as alternative family configurations, television produced for younger children remains more conservative and tends on the whole to reinforce traditional family structures with two legally married parents in the home who are involved and competent in their parenting styles and roles.[38] Children, who regularly view general family programs and films, as well as those directed specifically at them, are receiving confusing messages about families in general and the role of men in particular.

In some societies, a proactive effort is being considered to introduce stronger male characters on TV who are involved in child care and yet maintain their distinct characteristics as strong and positive role models for boys. Hildegard (Austria), for example, discussed the attempts to develop strategies to get fathers more involved with raising their children by examining TV portrayals. She claimed that given the absence of male figures in children's lives – at home and in the school system – the main role models they have are the young "new-man" type moderators on children's programs, who are often openly gay, or the violent, muscular "real-man" type actors of action series.

Steven (US) also referred specifically to male role models available for boys in popular TV and films, and went a step further by suggesting what effects it might have on them: *In terms of media imagery in the US in general, men are depicted as buffoonish or violent, so you get heroes like Adam Sandler or Will Ferrell.[39] And when they're not being depicted as buffoonish or violent, they're being depicted as overburdened, overworked. They're either presented as not taking responsibility in the home or trying to take responsibility in the home, but not being able to juggle everything all at once and really being incompetent, as opposed to women, who are presented as super-people.*

So boys get all these different images of what it's going to be like to be a man ... And then if you add the fact that boys are given limited opportunity to express their feelings about anything in any kind of a public way; and to the extent that boys do express their feelings, the methods by which they express their feelings aren't necessarily recognized by adults, or appreciated by adults, or there's a fear that straight boys might be gay, because they're expressing their feelings in some way. There's just an awful lot of pressure on boys. My intuition is that, in their media choices, boys deal with that pressure by just blocking it out, watching sports, watching wrestling ... in kind of more evolved cases, they might watch slightly macho "how-to" shows, like Pimp My Ride *or the show about building motorcycles. But there aren't really shows that speak to their daily experience in a way that they can talk about afterwards and save face. It can't be like a really touchy-feely kind of things.*

What these producers share is a strong critique of the various male characters presented on TV – the gay "new" man, the violent Rambo-type, the buffoon, the incompetent father – as offering negative role models as well as not serving the wellbeing of boys who are in desperate need of strong, positive male characters in their lives to help them imagine and aspire to a healthy and happy masculine identity. These producers' arguments echo much popular analysis of the reasons for "boys adrift;"[40] which includes the feminization of education and the lack of heroic role models, as well as over exposure to negative ones in violent media fare.

A second, related, post-feminist-like explanation embedded in the interviews includes a form of anti-feminist reaction to the feminist movement, a "backlash,"[41] that undermines its important achievements. For example, some interviewees perceived the strengthening of girls to be at the expense of boys in their societies. Abby (US) argued for a need for additional role models for boys, as suggested above, but framed it differently: *I do believe that boys are left behind and that girls have so many strong role models now ... our female children are becoming so assertive that the boys are left in quite a terrified state by girls ...* Vicky (Canada) reinforced the argument of too many female role models: *Pre-schoolers need male figures because they have so many female characters.*

In her interview, Karolina (Sweden) reflected on the wrong turn the process of gender equity has taken, in her opinion, and the implication it might have on gender representations on television: *You mustn't take strength away from boys by promoting girls. You mustn't make the boys ashamed of themselves for being who they are. I want to change the system, not to make it as difficult for a boy as it is for a girl. I don't want to change the way a boy feels, as we need to understand each other and the differences between boys themselves are as wide as between boys and girls.*

This theme of a need for diversity within portrayals of each gender will be developed farther in Chapter Six.

In addition to these complementary and competing interpretations of post-feminist arguments, some producers ascribed the absence of male role models to the complexities of television production. For example, Julie (UK) argued that it was a casting constraint: *Because boys are hard to cast at this age. They are self-conscious ... they don't want to stand out and be laughed at. So, when you have auditions and open casting, there are always more girls than boys. It is much easier to cast a girl. They want to be the center of attention, while the boys of that age are self-conscious of their looks and their bodies and they don't want to stand out in that way.* Similarly, Vicky (Canada) argued that it is difficult to obtain men who are willing to be in pre-schooler programs. Therefore, despite their efforts to recruit more male figures in young children's programs, they are still heavily dominated by women.

Whatever the reason for the absence of male figures in children's lives on and off the screen in the northern part of the world (but not only!), producers point to this void as a contributing factor to boys falling behind in their societies. And they rank television interventions dedicated to changing this situation high on their list of priorities of gender-related issues. In so doing they are responding, albeit unknowingly, to a theoretical argument put forth by psychoanalytical feminist theorists[42] who claim that the fact that women mother in all societies and are the main caregivers of early childhood has lasting implications for the development of female and male personalities. Implied is the expectation that greater gender equality could be achieved if mothering were to become less exclusively female, and children had dependable and constant strong relationships with male caregivers as well. That television can serve as an important resource for fathering images in societies where real flesh-and-blood fathers are absent, is something that these producers believe in and seek to make happen.

It is important to note that while this theme was mostly evident in the northern part of the Northern Hemisphere, as stated above, it was occasionally mentioned in other interviews as well, even if as incidental remarks. Such, for example, was the case when Fundi (Kenya) discussed the cultural expectations that boys be the protectors and providers of their families at a time of global economic crisis. Suzzy (Ghana) emphasized the need to present male role models who stay away from criminal activities. Leona (Philippines) argued that *sometimes inadvertently we pay attention to the girls and we leave out those who will be the oppressors when they grow old.* And Larizza (Brazil) raised a concern for the high percentage of single mothers deserted by fathers and street-boys who are involved in violence. All of these are issues that TV is trying to confront head on.

Concluding Notes

As we have seen in this chapter, what gender means for producers around the world differs greatly, as gender is culturally constructed, practiced, and represented. One of the advantages of a study that looks at gender across so many cultures is that it enables us to better understand its local complexity as well as its global characteristics. The issues that producers prioritized were very different and obviously reflected their societies' many unique and complex characteristics: traditions, religions, régimes, economic development, education, democratization status, among others. Clearly, gender differences and visions for gender equity are not viewed in a monolithic manner throughout the world and thus cannot be treated uniformly through a single form of intervention, including the production of quality television for children. Indeed, as has been recognized in scholarly work: "being, becoming, practicing, and doing femininity [and – we might add – masculinity] are very different things for women of different classes, 'races,' and nations."[43]

At the risk of gross overgeneralization and oversimplification, one conclusion seems to be that beyond a universal, general concern for gender inequality on television, producers from different regions of the world are preoccupied with vastly different concerns and challenges related to gender for the television industry. Summarizing the themes that emerged from this set of interviews, it appears that areas of the world where Islam is strong are struggling with the universal right for education; in Asia and Latin America attempts are advanced to change macho stereotypes and to resist the American "Beauty Myth;" producers in Africa recruit television in the struggle against HIV/AIDS; and in the northern part of the Northern Hemisphere attempts are being made to recreate a new, balanced sense of masculinity. This heavy list of challenges sets a political agenda for major social change that is well beyond the capabilities of any social institution, let alone the institution of television, which is highly dependent on political, economical, and cultural forces.

In addition, it is important to recall that these producers related to gender through the discourse of Americanization and cultural imperialism, reflecting broader concerns regarding globalization that dominated social life and intellectual discourse at the beginning of the twenty-first century. Coming from a producer involved in coproductions with southern societies, Caroline's (US) observations capture the essence of this conclusion: *Now, the question is how you define gender equity, that's going to be different, culturally, since we are coming in with a value judgment, so to speak ... you know, every day I think about that, because I think ... we are so oriented towards trying in every possible way not to be cultural imperialists and we try to do it by providing a structure for engaging in a project but letting our partner* [from the developing world] *decide how to adapt that structure ... to make choices. However, having said that, nothing is culturally neutral, there's no such thing as culture neutrality and so, whenever you're engaged in a project like this, everybody's bringing something to the table and then I think in the end you neither end up with something American or something totally of the culture that you're in, it's a hybrid of sorts, and hopefully it's a hybrid that's enriching both sides.*

Interestingly, reference to the processes referred to through the concept of "hybrid cultures," a contested notion that has elicited much intellectual controversy, was alluded to by one of the interviewees, an American involved in empowerment-oriented educational efforts around the developing parts of the globe. As construed by Homi Bhabha,[44] "hybridity" refers to the dynamics involved in the encounter between the colonizing West and the colonized "Rest," in which a negotiation takes place that creates a new "third space." In this third space, neither the traditional colonizer (and/or the cultural one), nor the occupied, oppressed, and/or exploited in a variety of cultural and economical ways, is independent of each other. Instead, hybrid cultures are created through a process of reciprocity and exchange. This view of the dynamic interaction of cultural processes is different from the frequently advocated form of multiculturalism that perceives the preferred form of cultural interaction to be the coexistence of diverse ethnicities in which each maintains independent identities, cultural forms, and contents.

Again, most producers interviewed in this project made no reference to, nor expressed any interest in or awareness of, processes referred to as hybridist. Rather, in accordance with multiculturalism, each focused on his or her own cultural group's needs and characteristics, prioritizing local traditions and worldviews. The kind of cosmopolitan dialogue they were having in practice at the events they participated in was not translated in their interview reflections into a desire for dialogue between cultures and assigning space to other cultures on their screens. North American interviewees were oblivious to the possibility that their television screens are enriched by encounters with other cultures from within or outside their political borders (with the exception of Caroline's statement above). At most, they acknowledged the occasional commercial success of "hits" such as *Pokémon*, which is an example of the "megaphone effect" discussed above, as advanced by commercial forces in American society. Europeans made clear efforts in the interviews to disassociate themselves from the US, but at the same time showed limited interest in other cultures around the world. Interviewees from the southern parts of the world were occupied with distinguishing themselves not only from the West but also from other societies in their own region. While they were envious of the budgets and infrastructures at the disposal of Western producers, they distanced themselves from the West's cultural capital.

Thus, interviewees did not mention cultural processes such as reciprocity and exchange within their own productions that would refer to hybridity. Rather, exchange, when used by them, meant the purchase or acquisition of broadcasting rights of good quality programs from each other: In Western countries, as a way of educating their children about "other" children's lives; and in the non-Western countries, as a way of upgrading the quality of productions offered on their screens, since they cannot afford to produce such programs themselves.

The above discussion of the cultural meanings assigned to gender by the interviewees revealed to us some of the major lines of thought developing around the world, as well as unveiling the spectrum of feminist thought being developed in various ways by producers throughout the world. The next chapter analyzes one central theme that was a focus of major cultural controversies – the portrayal of sex and sexuality in children's television.

Chapter 4

The Big No-No

Sex and Sexualities

Television portrayals of bodily functions, human sexuality, and sexual identities were the most polarized sites of cultural differences in the interviews. Discussion of these phenomena was almost always initiated by reference to programs produced in The Netherlands and the Nordic countries screened during Prix Jeunesse events. In their comments, interviewees were in agreement that a distinctive characteristic of these programs was their surprisingly open, direct treatment of such issues, irrespective of the age of the target audience. Among the programs and instances cited were: *Dancing* (The Netherlands), a program directed to an audience of pre-schoolers in which there was full-frontal body nudity of a mature man and woman dancing; a discussion of male puberty, including the experience of first erections and wet dreams in *Ready Steady Grow!* (Sweden), a program for the 7–11-year-old audience; *Invisible Wounds* (Sweden) (see Figure 4.1) which dealt with sexual abuse of children in a program intended for 7–11-year-olds; *Odd One Out* and *The Day I Decided to be Nina* (The Netherlands) (see Figure 4.2) which followed a child born male who experienced herself as a girl and wished for a gender reassignment operation, as she went through the process of a female identity formation (with a target audience of 7–11-year-olds); the kiss between two gay teenagers in *Danny's Parade* (The Netherlands) (see Figure 4.3), intended for 12–15-year-olds. Of particular interest was *Girls* (The Netherlands) (see Figure 4.4), about the inner worlds of coming-of-age teenage boys, a program to which we will return later for in-depth discussion. Yet, interviewees failed to note that what was also particularly striking, in comparison, was the absolute absence of such issues in other programs screened at all of the events I visited in the course of my research, and concomitantly the silence in dealing with these issues in productions from other global regions.

Sex and the Media

The scope and nature of television's engagement with sex is debated frequently and often heatedly, and is undoubtedly a much contested terrain of public concern in most societies. The media, in general, are often harshly criticized

Figure 4.1 Invisible Wounds © UR, Sweden

Figure 4.2 The Day I Decided to be Nina © Lemming Film and VPRO (producers),
Ingeborg Jansen (director), The Netherlands

Figure 4.3 Danny's Parade © NPO and Netherlands Public Broadcasting (NPS)

Figure 4.4 Girls © IKON / The Netherlands

for making public the private domain of sex. In addition, debates over freedom of expression and censorship,[1] child protection from sexual abuse, and social moralities are frequently elicited by the appearance of sexual images. Furthermore, exposure to sex in the media has been blamed for many social ills: fostering premature sexual activity, promiscuity, teenage pregnancies, the spread of infectious diseases, and general erosion of morality and normative family values. Images of sexual children, in particular, have been targeted as encouraging adults to perceive children as sexually alluring and a stimulus for the activities of pedophiles.[2]

Scholarly examinations of sex and the media have tackled multiple issues beyond the effects on young people of exposure to sex, including evaluation of the amount and kind of sex presented, public attitudes towards such portrayals, and the effectiveness of advertising strategies employing sex. Researchers from different feminist perspectives focused their analyses on concerns over the sexual objectification of women, on the one hand, and the empowerment of female sexuality, on the other.[3]

Clearly, discussion of sex in the media is a complex area, laden with conflicts of interest, cultural traditions, ideological and moral perspectives. It involves contested terms such as "decency," "obscenity," and "taste." These debates include moralistic discourses of "protection," be it protection of society's traditions and normative values towards sex and sexuality, on the one hand; or the protection of society's free speech and individual right for sexual fulfillment, on the other hand. Indeed, an interesting shift in the principles of media regulation applied in these discourses is from debates over "taste" and "decency" toward a risk-based public health model with concerns for "harm" and "offense."[4]

Two seemingly contradictory, centrifugal social phenomena can be detected in these discourses: The sexualization of culture and the persistent traditional silencing of healthy discussions of sex and sexuality. On one hand, leading cultural analysts from a variety of theoretical traditions, as well as populist and conservative discourses, agree that media content circulating around the world today feeds a rapidly growing hypersexual culture, a "pornosphere," flourishing through "pornographication" of mainstream culture.[5] Sexual images seem to be everywhere: in revealing fictional episodes that push the boundaries of audiences' receptivity; in excessive "dirty talk" and a preoccupation with sexual satisfaction on popular television series and situation comedies; in the exploitation of sex as commodity on advertising billboards and in commercials; in confessional talk shows that openly discuss sexual fantasies and deviations; in reality shows that are granted permission to invade participants' private sexual lives; in variety shows that glorify liberated sexual talk; and in reporting of public scandals in televised news involving well-known personalities that include a variety of sex-related topics such as: sexual harassment (e.g. Anita Hill versus Clarence Thomas, Supreme Court nominee hearings); "dirty talk" (e.g. the revealing transcripts of phone calls made by the UK's Prince Charles to his extramarital lover, while he was still married to Princess Diana); oral sex performed on the President of the most powerful nation (Bill Clinton's affair with Monica Lewinsky), and so forth.

Furthermore, the market for legal and illegal sexual products, including pornography, is a booming business worldwide whose gross net worth has exceeded the mainstream movie and popular music market in the US.[6] This growth has been spurred by technological advents (e.g. development of videos, DVDs, the Internet and the availability of cyberporn, and more recently through sexting on mobile phones) that deliver explicit sexual content and pornography into the private sphere and away from possible social sanctions on consumption. Sexualization of the public sphere, conflated with the commodification of sex, seems resistant to the objections and protest of conservative, right-wing religious/political forces that use moralistic discourse in discussions of sex to preach maintenance of traditional views of sex, restricted to procreation. This view is perpetuated despite reproductive bio-technological innovations that allow for a complete separation between sex and procreation (e.g. different forms of birth control, *in-vitro* fertilization [IVF], surrogate motherhood).[7]

The expansion of sexual consumerism continues despite public debate and critique as well as efforts by activists and anti-pornography feminists who perceive pornography to be a mechanism of violent subordination of women on and off the screen (with consequences for both women employed in this industry and women in general, who are affected through the general degradation of women in society).[8] Yet, the success of this "striptease culture" demonstrates a number of clear facts: There is an eager voyeuristic audience that seems to thrive on pleasures obtained by peeking into other people's sexual lives, fictitious or real; there are participants who are willing and/or are pressured out of economic, social, or psychological needs to perform for the camera; and the industry thrives due to a regulatory environment that condones or at least permits exhibition of persons engaged in stripping, physically and/or emotionally, for their audience. Indeed, sexual exhibitionism in the media, it has been argued, "make[s] up a culture in which public nakedness, voyeurism, and sexualized glaring are permitted, indeed encouraged, as never before."[9] However, as several critics have pointed out, while the commodification of sexuality and sexual exhibitionism in the media is pervasive and carries with it the promise of endless pleasures for marketing goods and generating profits in a capitalistic society, this is not at all the same as eroticism or sexual liberation and freedom.[10]

Yet, on the other hand, researchers found that the vast majority of societies around the world have yet to develop comprehensive, age-appropriate sex education and/or socialization processes for younger generations, whether through formal school systems, professional counseling, or informal parenting and mentoring. In the few cases where sex education does take place, such as school-based curricula in the US and UK, the main tendency is to reinforce sexual conservatism and the stigmatization of non-heterosexual expressions of sexuality. Furthermore, most prescriptive discussions of sex education apply a medical, scientific frame of reference. In doing so, sex is referred to in three principal ways: First and foremost as a mechanism for procreation; second, in relation to the risks and consequences of sex, in particular HIV/AIDS infection and other sexually transmitted diseases, as well as unplanned pregnancies; and, third, following on from these two messages, in terms that allow the preaching of abstinence. Thus, the normative values driving sex education are exemplary of what Foucault claims in his "history of sexuality:"[11] Sex is constructed as a natural, straightforward form of "making love" practiced exclusively by married, heterosexual adults. Practices deviating from such norms are potentially inappropriate, risky, and immoral.

As a result, investigations of sex-education programs have found that few touch upon central issues of healthy sexual development, such as aspects related to relationships and interpersonal intimacy, sexual identity, or desire, playfulness, and pleasure. Furthermore, according to a popular truism, parents are too embarrassed and uncomfortable to engage in sex education with their children, and hope this task will be attended to by other socializing agents. As a result, children receive mixed messages: They are aware, perhaps baffled, as they develop physically into active sexual subjects while surrounded by cultural sexual stimulation. However, at the same time, they are being told directly that they are not supposed to be sexual and that they are expected to practice "abstinence."[12] Girls, in particular, are allocated the roles of maintaining a "good" reputation by suppressing their sexual desires, are assigned the role of controlling the "unleashed" sexuality of their young male partners, and are taught to feel guilty if this does not occur.[13]

Overall, then, it would appear to be the case that since neither formal nor informal educators offer what many observers consider to be effective sex education, addressing the needs of pre-adolescents and adolescents as they grow up, the media fill this vacuum and become the most central socializing force. Thus, sex is a realm of life that is initially encountered by many children through the media, rather than in non-mediated reality. Their familiarity with it develops through years of consuming media content amidst the absence of competing sources of information and models, well before engaging in their own real-life sexual experiences. Given this analysis, it is not surprising that studies conducted through the Cultural Studies school of research, which involve listening to children and adolescents, found that teenagers relate to the media as their preferred source of information and guidance about sex. They use television's portrayals of sex and sexuality as a basis for conversations about its relevancy in their lives. Researchers found that pre-adolescents and adolescents reported having frequent encounters with sexual material in the media, including popular texts such as soap operas and teen magazines, valued the information received from them, and used them as a learning resource.

Participants in these studies demonstrated a range of critical skills in interpreting sexual content and evaluated such content through what they perceived
to be sexual morality. Furthermore, teens' views were heavily influenced by
their cultural background and gender, and they also used media content to
resist sexual conservatism as well as to challenge like-minded messages advocated in formal sex education.[14]

In contrast to the Cultural Studies approach, research conducted through
the media-effects tradition implies that childhood is a sexually innocent
period[15] and that sexual knowledge is potentially dangerous. Adolescents'
budding sexuality is considered to be of great importance and is, accordingly,
framed as a social problem, particularly with regard to girls.[16] Media-effects
studies found that popular teen stories are organized around the central theme
of the "troubled girl" who is usually also the "sexual girl." "One of the ways
that such social anxiety is mapped on to the 'troubled girl' of soap is through
the troubling of her sexual pleasure and desire so that indulgence in sex has
negative consequences for her emotionally (e.g. turmoil, anxiety, depression,
self-doubt), physically (e.g. unwanted pregnancy, sexually transmitted infection, abortion) or socially (e.g. rejection, derogation)."[17] One consequence of
"troubled girls'" behavior is of course unwanted pregnancies. Accordingly,
teen mothers are assumed to be sexually promiscuous and immature, "children
having children."[18]

As a result, research in the effects tradition emphasizes the risks involved in
heavy exposure to media sex, rather than the potential learning or pleasures
that can be achieved through sexual portrayals. Accumulative effects research
suggests that children and young people internalize sexual attitudes and behaviors from distorted portrayals of sex and sexuality on commercial media.[19]
Based on research with college students (since studies of pornography consumption by underage teens are rare), media critics infer with reference to
younger audiences – that the pornography easily available today on the Internet, in magazines, and on DVDs has serious implications for the development
of a healthy sexual being: It models various sexual practices; prescribes promiscuous attitudes and beliefs about the role of sex in human relationships;
establishes expectations about self-performance; objectifies women and dis-
perses negative attitudes towards them; underplays the severity of sexual
crimes and their consequences, and the like.[20]

However, irrespective of research tradition, methodology, and assumptions regarding childhood applied in these studies, scholars are in agreement
that media portrayals of sex have a central role in the development of young
people's sexuality and, thus, should be looked at carefully. Furthermore, it is
also clear that there are interrelationships between sex and many other
central realms of life – such as violence, emotions, commitment, family,
childbearing, and homosexuality – that require special attention by those
concerned for the role of the media in advancing the healthy development of
young people.

Discussing Sex and Sexualities

Many opinions have been offered regarding the types of sexual relationships and practices appropriate for children to watch and at what age. These views vary not only from one society to another, but also between subcultures, as there are many ways in which race, ethnicity, class, tradition, religion, and history, among others things, affect sexual beliefs and practices. While studying television programs for children and interviewing their producers, it became obvious that what is sexually relevant for cultures of advanced capitalist societies, at this particular point in time of late modernity, is not necessarily relevant to other societies around the world. For example, as noted earlier in this chapter, there is an unparalleled, relaxed, and permissive approach in Nordic countries regarding the inclusion of nudity, erotic behaviors, scatological humor, as well as free talk about sex and bodily functions in programs intended for young viewers. In contrast, according to my interviewees, US television is as a whole much more conservative and less permissive. Yet it too is perceived as overly revealing, indeed indecent, by those from many developing countries in Africa, Asia, and South America. Needless to say, when interviewing producers on this topic, one confronts considerable difficulties given the many sensitivities involved regarding young people's own sexuality, questions of morals, values, and religion, as well as personal inhibitions of the interviewees (and interviewer) themselves.

Discussion of these issues was stimulated either spontaneously by the interviewees or in response to my direct questions regarding specific programs that attracted their attention; in particular, programs that they could not take back with them to air in their own countries and/or would not like to do so even if they could. Indeed, discussion of these programs itself caused occasional embarrassment, often requiring dancing around blushes. An interesting observation about the strength of some societies' taboos on this topic is that many interviewees lacked the vocabulary – at least in English – that would enable them to engage in such discussion. The three distinct topics that emerged in analyzing interviewees' reflections on these issues, detailed below, are – sex on television as a taboo, homo/lesbian sexualities, and sexual abuse.

Sex on Television as a Taboo

The most common reference to queries about sex and sexuality was an unequivocal statement that such programs could never be produced and/or aired in one's respective country. Statements such as: *That's a taboo* (Chan-ho, Korea); *You don't talk about sex on television* (Obinna, Nigeria); *I think our parents – they will stop that broadcast, they would not allow it* (Sumita, Bangladesh); *They can talk about many things, but not sex* (Amer, Jordan); *Sex is one of the main NOs* (Maria, Quatar); *In Iranian festivals, if you even have a children's film where a boy and a girl are holding hands, they have to cut that scene out* (Carla, Canada, discussing working in Iran); *Sex, we cannot talk about sex* (Bounnhang, Laos); *I saw one production on sex, when they were teaching about love and kissing ... Nope, no way ... in Ghana that would be taken off, it would not even see the light of day* (Suzzy, Ghana); *We are sexually less liberal. ... we don't speak about sex* (Augustine, Portugal); *When we saw this program we were really shocked, we were totally shocked, because we never show such programs to children on our TV. Parents would never, never agree to show it* (Katherine, Ukraine).

Most interviewees explained this taboo in terms of cultural inappropriateness. Talking about sex or exhibiting sexual behavior is just not part of their culture; indeed it transgresses many deeply engrained values and traditions. Katherine (Ukraine) explained her statement above by saying: *Sex was never a topic of discussion in the Soviet Union*. Indeed, scholarship about Soviet Union culture argues that sex was regarded as indecent and unmentionable, and the régime as a whole demonstrated a lack of interest in questions of personal pleasure and sexual fulfillment. "Sex profaned the revolution by lowering it, by making it commonplace, and thereby open to question. The revolution, many believed, was above and beyond such speculation ... The revolution and sex was distinct, one high, one low."[21] Since social mores were dictated by the state, they crippled sexual expression and disabled support for sex education.[22]

Cultural explanations were particularly evident in the Asian interviews. Edmund (Sri Lanka), for example, explained: *Because of our culture and our religion ... we are Buddhist, we don't like to show issues like homosexuality and sex. That is secretive*. Similarly, Mai (China) talked about Asian culture more generally: *Sex is kind of a taboo in our region, in our beliefs, our culture ... You cannot be open about it, it's quite sensitive for the audience because of our cultural background ... It is very normal in Chinese programs to talk about the girl who is secretly in love with somebody, but not actually the doing of sex*.

The legitimacy of choosing romance over sex by presenting it to children as clearly distinguishable is evident in Mai's quote, and was repeated by several other participants as evidence of them making the right moral choice. This choice illustrates very vividly arguments made by some feminist scholars who suggest that girls and women are taught to experience sexual arousal and desire as romantic love and by so doing continue to relegate sex to the realm of procreation and family, thus maintaining the traditional social order. In romantic-love attachments, the notion of sublime love breaks away from earthly sexuality as it elevates the spirit above the constraints of everyday reality and physical desires and needs. Rather than focusing on the body, romantic love channels the energies to experiencing the other as a special person with whom deep connection is made instantly through "love at first sight;" who serves as the piece "missing" to feeling complete; and without whom life has no meaning.[23]

Overall, research suggests that different cultures influence how we codify sexual arousal as romantic love and how we will experience those sensations – be it "love at first sight" or "sexual passion;" the meaning and significance we attach to the experience as well as the various ways sanctioned for expressing and representing it; whether it will fall under accepted norms of sexual conducts. For example, Western societies, in particular, have constructed romantic love as part of consumer culture and capitalist ideology expressed via the purchase of luxurious commodities (e.g. flowers, jewelry, perfume, wine, greeting cards, chocolates) and staging its expression in particular settings (e.g. candlelight dinners; sunsets on the beach) that help elevate the emotional experience above and beyond routine existence. Thus, in Western societies, the media serve a central role in disseminating this capitalist ideology, as well as distributing it further to non-capitalist societies.[24]

This interpretation seems to be particularly relevant to the views related by interviewees from more traditional and nation-building societies where ideologies of sex are strongly bound to the procreation perspective, and so serve the goals of the collective to preserve itself. In particular, communist countries such as the former Soviet Union and China, where they are experiencing unprecedented, rapid capitalist influence yet trying to resist the values attached to it, silence discourses of sexual freedom, according to the two interviewees cited above, among others. Given Western representations of leisure culture that glorify personal liberties and individual pursuit of pleasure and happiness, sex is perceived to be hedonistic according to this view and, as such, a threat to national ideologies and goals of solidifying a collective identity.[25]

Of course, this process is not unique to communist or traditional societies alone. Sexual attachment and "passionate love" have been perceived, historically, as disruptive and dangerous since they threaten rational thought and the social order based on it: "It uproots the individual from the mundane and generates a preparedness to consider radical options as well as sacrifices."[26] Puritanical discourse, in particular, denies all sensual pleasures and views them as distractions from spiritual engagements and religious moralities. As Foucault and his followers argued, such ideology represses and controls sex through discourses that are formal, institutional, and scientific (as noted in the earlier discussion of sex education). Such social organization of sexual desire, they argued, subverts and redirects it to productivity; a mechanism that guarantees continuation of labor and support of the economic system and/or the nation.

Many other interviewees acknowledged that their cultural backgrounds serve as a form of explanation for the taboo approach to sex on television, particularly for children. Some also pointed out what they perceived to be related consequences, as did Mi-Jung (South Korea) when she said: *Korean society is very conservative. People don't talk about sex really, but under the ground there are problems, like sexual abuse, rape of children. Nobody teaches children about sex.*

The striking differences between many Asian cultures and the Nordic ones were noted by interviewees when commenting on the variety of programs viewed during the festivals, as Salma (Pakistan) explained: *I find a lot of the programs from the Western world, like the Scandinavians, are very dominant, as usual, more based on the fact that there is more sexuality in them … I presume it is a way of life there, because they are very free. Maybe, for those of us from Asia, that is something that we don't talk about and don't discuss. We dream it, fantasize, I am sure we enjoy it, I do, but I think it is something we would like to make private, so that's something that is my cultural bias, where I come from.*

Nassing's (Malaysia) sense of relativism encapsulated in a cultural context is conveyed in her own self-analysis: *You won't see a lot of intimate scenes on Asian television. They are much more conservative in that regard. But on Western cable you see a lot of things, nothing is left for the imagination. So it is about culture, what you are exposed to and what you are expecting. For example, when I watch a Hindi movie now, in comparison to like a few years ago, now they have some movies where they kiss on the lips, which they never used to do before. So that's shocking to me, although all the while I watch English movies that do more than just kissing … I am consciously bound by what I have seen and what I have been exposed to in regards to what I expect and accept.* So while a kiss on the lips in a Hindi program is perceived as perhaps too much sex, an intimate sex scene in a Scandinavian program is acceptable for the very same viewer as it presupposes a different cultural context.

Indeed, while most of the reasons provided by interviewees for their discomfort with sexual openness in some Western children's TV were grounded in cultural inappropriateness, some chose to distance themselves from this view by stating clearly that they were not taking a position on the issue. Omar (Syria), for example, said it very directly: *I am not saying that this is good or bad. I'm saying that it would not be appropriate for Syrian viewers.* Manisha (Nepal) expressed similar sentiments: *I don't say it is the wrong thing. It is OK with me, but my society, my tradition, my people cannot accept sex on TV.*

However, other producers framed their statements through a moralistic "good or bad" discourse in which they expressed concern for television's bad influence on children, as the following quotations demonstrate. *We don't talk about sex. I think it is not good not to have some limits, because they copy what they see on TV … we have another culture* (Amina, Tunisia). Though impressed by the program on gender dysphoria,[27] *The Day I Decided to be Nina* (see Figure 4.2), Ibrahim (Turkey) was unequivocal in stating that this program would be perceived as immoral in his society. And, even if deemed possible to broadcast, it would require, in his view, extensive background preparation and discussion forums in order to enable his culture to open up to receive such images: *You cannot show something unethical and turn your back … they'll be shocked!* Suzana (Kenya) related that in her country: *The girl would have been locked in a hut at best and maybe thrown in the lake with a stone tied to her head. They can't begin to deal with such issues.*

Discussing a constipation scene in a Swedish program, Cindy (US) said: *It was very well done, very matter of fact, straightforward. It was very informative, but I could never show that in the US ... It's just that bodily functions are a taboo subject for TV. The other one that we wouldn't show would be* Dancing. *We wouldn't show naked people like that.*

Taylor (Tanzania) was truly annoyed when discussing scenes in a program from The Netherlands that presented scatological humor, including a scene of a person peeing on himself and farting. He exclaimed, rhetorically, in real disgust: *Why are they doing this?!* His response was deeply grounded in joint social internalization of what scholars refer to as "pollution:" everything that is related to substances entering and leaving the body exposes the instability of the body's borders – which distinguish between its inside and outside – and suggests that the body is penetrable and potentially polluted.[28] Therefore, it is not surprising that discussion – let alone exposure – of feces, urine, semen, menstrual blood, mucus, vomit, passing gas, and the like, are great inhibitors and are perceived to be either shameful and/or disgusting in many societies (although there are cultural varieties regarding these phenomena).

Thus, in summary, the notion that threats to the purity of the body's stable boundaries should be presented on television for children was unthinkable for most interviewees, as demonstrated in the quotation above. A related notion is that some parts of the body are considered penetrable and even erotic by different cultures, while others are considered dangerous or polluted. We will return to this notion when discussing producers' reactions to homosexual identities and sexuality.

A twist in moralistic concern was shared by some producers who agreed that discussion of sex was appropriate when there was a moral lesson to be learned, as in programs highlighting teen pregnancy (Emma, Bolivia). Thus, tying sexuality with improper behaviors and negative consequences was permissible, while discussion of other aspects was dismissed. Emma, like many of the interviewees from the South, brought up the contradiction inherent in completely different approaches to sex and sexuality in TV fare their children are exposed to from both local and global-commercial channels. *It's a hypocritical situation,* proclaimed Leona (Philippines). *On one hand, local TV was being over protective of children: You are not supposed to see this or, you are not supposed to know that. But, on the other hand, they are flooded with these images and sounds from movies and TV programs from outside the Philippines.*

Yegor (Kazakhtan) described the situation in his culture in a similar manner: *We have a different mentality. We can't discuss it like that. But "thanks" to American movies they know everything. I don't think it's good because they know more about sex than they need to at this age. They come*

*home from school and they sit with their mothers and they see the soap opera;
and they are talking about this one that divorced her husband, and this one who
had sex with that man or with another man … it is not good, sex all the time.*
And Eleonora (Argentina) was even more blunt in pointing out the double
standard: *We don't talk about sex or we don't talk about our fears about it … it
is a very religious country and we can't talk about it to children on TV. But in
the soap operas they are always fucking, and they're almost nude. So sex is
everywhere, all the time, all through the day, for children and adults.*

Critiques regarding the excessive preoccupation of commercial (and mostly
Western) TV with sex came from other countries as well. For example, Sarah
(Australia) was critical of much of this TV fare for young teens in the Prix
Jeunesse festival: *They presume that the only thing in the programs for 12–15
is sex, yet there is a lot more in their lives than just that … part is the
dawning interest in the opposite sex, but I think there has been a tendency in
the programs to just deal with that – girls in love, proliferation of those issues.
I think that kids are interested in other things and I think we should be
showing them that it is cool to do other things at that age group, not only sex.*

Salma (Pakistan) agreed with Sarah's observation: *I found the programs this
year of any age group except the younger group, extremely focused on sex. Is
that all Westerners think about? If it is, then I am very sorry, I wish it wasn't
so. There must be other things they want to talk about. Almost everything had
a sexual connotation to it. I found that embarrassing, actually. And I find it
almost pathetic that we are depicting children that that's all they are thinking,
when this is not true. Children think about so many other things: fantasies,
they want to go places, they want to see people, they want to be people, they
want to jump up trees like superman, why aren't we looking for such things?
We need to do that.*

So while Western programs and movies, particularly those traveling globally, were pinpointed as exhibiting a lot of sex, it is important to emphasize
that many producers from Western countries choose to disassociate themselves
from the sexual openness exhibited by the Nordic style, arguing that their own
societies would not be receptive to such content: Natalie (France) explained,
*We are not allowed to speak about sex on public TV … and no kissing and no
acting like American teenagers …* And Sally (US) added: *American culture is one
where sex is all around, but we never talk about it. So especially for kids, I feel
like it's really important … We would never have something like that … it's not
OK to talk about sex, it wouldn't be something that was really addressed on
Nickelodeon in a real way.*

A somewhat different twist on the same argument was the emphasis put on
sexual content not being age appropriate. Sarah (Australia), for example, presented this rationale: *There have been a few programs that there is no way we
can screen in Australia for a child audience … we have standards that don't
allow us. There were things like a girl going to buy condoms. I wouldn't show
that in Australia. We can deal with a relationship to a point, but the program*

needs to be suitable for a child to watch. Surprisingly, age-specific concerns did not surface very often in interviewees' comments. This finding may be further evidence that the taboo over sex is so broad and universal that nuanced, age-appropriate discussion of sex did not have to be raised in making the counter argument.

Akiko (Japan) also discussed the presence of condoms in programs for adolescents and in doing so echoed the media-effects tradition described above when expressing her concern that the presentation of sexual practices on TV encourages premature sexual activities. She described her public broadcasting station, NHK, as quite open to discussion of issues such as homosexuality and sexual abuse, yet she asked: *Is it really necessary to teach growing up people about using condoms? If we do too much of it, are we also suggesting that you accept having sexual intercourse among the really young ages.* The notion that open discussion of sex – whether in sex-education curricula or on TV – legitimizes and encourages early initiation of sexual activities is clearly a central argument employed in discourses that object to such interventions in the lives of adolescents.

On the other hand, it was impossible to tell whether some producers' statements were framed as critiques or as expressions of admiration and envy of the Nordic programs, wishing they could be involved in such open programming as well. Indeed, only a few – some American interviewees – expressed this envy openly: *You know, we've been trying for years to find a way to do a show like this for boys and girls ... to figure out a way to take away the taboo ... and we also have to be thinking about what they are able to watch and not feel embarrassed to watch around other people. So it's very complicated, but I wish I could put that program on the air, it's just doing such a service* (Lori, USA). Similarly, Laura (USA) stated: *Americans are squeamish about the issue of sex, in any form. Yes, they probably think about sex all the time, guys in particular. And, pornography is enormously huge. At Cartoon Network I learned pretty quickly that I could show a show where people are killed and no one would call to complain. But one sexual comment and people would go absolutely crazy. And it's because of this whole refusal to acknowledge sex. Maybe if they kind of ran shows about sexuality and sex for 10- or 11-year-old kids and didn't make sex a taboo subject it would be better.*

An interesting exception was presented by Jamal (Palestine), who also wished he could be more open about sexuality on TV: *I wish that we could show some of these programs, but we don't want to push the borders of our society too much. When we do a talk show about sex education for children we get a lot of phone calls, and even when we touch in a mild way, we get complaints that we are a porno TV station. So every time, we try to push the border a little bit further. This is how you try to introduce change in your society. But some of the material here I can't put on because it is like jumping to the other side.* Jamal brings up a central thread in discussion of introducing

Figure 4.5 Mortified © Australian Children's Television Foundation

change in TV for children, which is the need to progress in small steps rather than through "shock-treatment." This is a discussion we will return to in Chapter Six.

The distinct difference between the direct Nordic approach and avoidance strategies employed by other Western countries was strongly evident in discussion of *Mortified* (see Figure 4.5) – an Australian program about a young girl dealing with "the talk" about sex with her parents. The program won a special theme prize for gender sensitivity during the Prix Jeunesse 2008 for the following reasons, as worded by the Selection Committee and read at the closing ceremony:

> *Mortified* is based on a strong girl character Taylor who plays a role that is commonly reserved for boys – the comic hero. She breaks girls' stereotypes by expressing her individuality in a fresh, determined, and believable way. Even when the object of her "crush" falls for her older sister, she doesn't allow the rejection to disempower her and erode self-esteem. The young male lead of the series, though often bullied, isn't cast as a stereotypical "wimp," but as a very nurturing, mutually supportive, and authentically nuanced relationship with Taylor. Despite its positive portrayal of gender roles, *Mortified* is not a typical festival winner but a sitcom series that really hits the target audiences. Fortunately it manages to avoid the common pitfalls of this popular genre (overly simplified character, cynical one-liner humor, etc.), and has the choice to make a difference for children of both sexes in a far-reaching way.

While the audience is presumed to know what "the talk" is all about and so be capable of empathizing with the protagonist's anxiety, the program dwells on talking about "the talk" rather than actually discussing the content of "the talk" itself. As a result, it remains an embarrassing secret that is not exposed clearly nor talked about openly. Sally (US) was wondering about this "avoidance" solution: *The whole episode is about "the talk," "the talk," "the talk" ... and then you don't get to hear "the talk." It's humorous, she has a good relationship with the parents, it's very real, and the girl is smart and is certainly inspirational. But I wonder if the intended audience is relieved that they don't have to hear that part? Or do they really want to hear exactly what it is about? It must have been a clear decision ... that tells you how our culture is kind of similar to Australian culture, because this would have been how we would have handled it too.*

Thus, sex and sexuality itself is reinforced as a private secret in these discussions, one resonating with anxiety – perhaps even fear and shame – that should not need to be shared with others (represented by potential viewers here); a secret that talking about with parents is "mortifying" for a maturing middle-class girl in an educated family. The message to the audience of such a moralistic lesson seems quite clear: there are limited chances that teens will engage in a frank dialogue about sexuality and sexual options; that is, one in which teenagers will be able to talk about their knowledge, experiences, anxieties, and so forth without being lectured to by knowing adults.[29]

Nordic and Dutch producers were very much aware of their prominent stance in the festivals and of being the object of a spectrum of reactions, from admiration to shock. Therefore, I was interested to understand the sentiments such reactions aroused among them. Many of these interviewees dismissed the allegation that what they are doing is so outstanding or problematic, but insisted that it is much in line with their lives. Hanne (Norway), for example, said: *I don't really think that we do a lot of things that are considered controversial or challenging* per se. And Karolina (Sweden) explained: *It is true that the issues around sex are much more openly discussed in the Nordic countries than other parts of the world. Children today are quite open about it, they are not shy, they know that they are allowed to ask about things and no grownup will be shocked.* Famke (The Netherlands) also tied it to her own cultural values: *In our society there is a strong belief that it's better to deal with some issues like prostitution, homosexuality, drugs; to keep it open, rather than to try to cover and hide it. So we are often surprised that some topics are an issue abroad.*

All of the interviewees from these countries dismissed the notion that they are being purposefully provocative, testing the limits or challenging other societies. Instead, they believed they were only reacting to what they consider to be the appropriate needs of their own cultures. At the same time, they were also aware that their societies are changing with the growing nature of European multiculturalism and that they, too, are now facing new challenges in broadcasting to children. Kim (The Netherlands) explained the dilemma she finds herself confronting: *Children are starting their period of pre-adolescence earlier. And, you know, they are watching two hours of TV a day and are behind their computer screen for an hour every day, and there are lots of influence from the media. You have to take them seriously. You don't hide things about sexuality from them. But, on the other hand, you have sixteen-and-half percent of people from abroad in your country, and we all know that people from the background of Turkey and Morocco don't want their children to see a kiss on television, that it will drive them away from your station to commercial stations with violent content. So that's why we are looking for a balance of being honest: What are your emotions? What's happening with your body? etc. So being honest and telling them about everything. But what is everything? How far should you go? And I know when we showed the naked clip again, we got a lot of phone calls from people that don't want to see it.*

So sex is a clear "NO" for some countries in the world, while for others the question is "How far should we go?" – whether it is in consideration of age appropriateness or adjusting to the multicultural changing nature of their society.

Homo/Lesbian Sexualities[30]

While discussion of the presentation of sex on children's TV elicited a broad span of views, often expressed with strong emotion, two related themes received more specific endorsement by interviewees, albeit of differing natures: portrayals of homosexual and lesbian characters, and sexual abuse. Discussion of these issues was stimulated by programs screened at the events and reactions were very different. Many scholars would argue that neither of these themes is about sex *per se*, and indeed, it is clear that the positions elicited are embedded in much more general ideological issues about identity, gender, human relationships, and social power structures. Yet they are treated under this theme since most interviewees reduced them to a discussion of sex-related issues. In this regard, it is also interesting to note that while the discourse surrounding gay images was sexualized and highly controversial, the one focusing on sexual abuse was de-sexualized and quite consensual.

Danny's Parade (see Figure 4.3), a Dutch program presenting a gay teenager and more specifically a gay kiss, triggered comments shared by many interviewees. Most framed the program in sexual terms and stated, in a manner very similar to their discussion of other images of sex, that showing the program would be inappropriate in their cultures, in general, and on TV for children more specifically. Laura (US) said she regretted that the TV scene in the US has regressed dramatically since 2000 with growing and widespread anti-gay sentiments: *We wouldn't even be able to mention that someone is gay on PBS kids.* Similarly, Augustine (Portugal) observed: *I cannot broadcast it unless it is at 2 o'clock in the morning, which is not appropriate for children. I can't show this during family time, because we are not as open to homosexuality in public. The majority of the audience is not open to see this kind of show*. And, Suzzy (Ghana) said: *I am a bit worried about this issue of homosexuality, like* Danny's Parade. *I can't show it in Ghana. Such things are considered taboo even when you know that people are doing it underground. It's not an issue that we discuss openly.*

Homosexuality, so it seems, causes quite a bit of anxiety in all the societies represented by my interviewees. Indeed, if there was a topic in my interviews that was a "red flag" across all cultures, including the Nordic ones, this was certainly it. This was the case despite the fact that gay youth are featured, occasionally, in popular Western teen soaps (e.g. *Degrassi High* [see Figure 4.6]). Several interviewees related formative incidents in their professional lives that clearly set the boundaries for them in regard to their daring to touch upon the topic. One such experience was referred to by several US interviewees, from their various perspectives. Laura (US) recalled in detail an incident with an animated program on PBS that depicted the protagonist visiting a friend who, in a scene incidental to the main plotline (which focused on maple syrup production in Vermont), presented him with a photo saying: "There are my two moms." *Without even seeing the episode, the mere mention that there were two moms in an episode, and that government money funded some of it ... people went absolutely crazy ... it became this huge issue ... We didn't even run the show because it got so much negative attention that the head of PBS at the time chickened out and pulled it off. All the producers were trying to do was show different kinds of families. And without even seeing the episode, people were energetically damning us to Hell.*

Similarly, Jerome (US) recalled the reference to two lesbian mothers in this very episode as a landmark negative experience that set clear boundaries for what is not permitted by his station. *There are issues for kids' television, such as sexuality ... it's a very protective place. They don't really talk about it, especially like transgender stuff, or homosexuality ... no way. You cannot present it. We had a show pulled from PBS, the only show that's ever been pulled in the entire history of our station, because there were two mothers in the background, same-sex household, two lesbian moms. And it wasn't even what the story was about ... It wasn't a program about sexuality. I mean, a show where there is a mom and a dad is not about heterosexuality ... and there was a sense that we had an agenda, which we didn't, other than helping all kids feel affirmed in seeing their household on television.*

The representation (or absence) of homosexuality in children's TV can be seen as a form of hegemonic regulation, an informal control mechanism that reinforces the taken-for-granted nature of heterosexuality. It assumes that the binary distinction between heterosexuality and homosexuality is natural, total, and universal. It also demonstrates the limited impact of much of queer theory's problematizing of these conceptions. Furthermore, these perspectives seem to support the view that there is limited evidence that rethinking social categories has advanced our understanding of heterosexuality itself, including legitimization of a variety of sexual practices and the pleasure derived from

Figure 4.6 Degrassi High   © 2009 courtesy of Playing With Time Inc. / Epitome
Pictures Inc, Canada

them (and, note, as a result, the appreciable rise in their media portrayals, as
pointed out earlier, in television series such as *Sex and the City*).

The specific example of the program on PBS discussed by several interviewees, independently, can be understood as a struggle between social and
political forces that, on the one hand, are driven to preserve the normative social
order and, on the other hand, those challenging and seeking to break away
from these compulsive forces that naturalize heterosexuality as the only natural,
normal, and – most of all – moral form of human sexuality.[31] No wonder that
images of alternative conceptions of sex, gender, and sexuality – such as presentations of various activities of gay youth – pose a major threat to most
social orders around the world.

Indeed, examples of attempts to normalize heterosexuality and to omit any
traces of alternative sexualities, were provided by many interviewees. Noga

(Israel) created her own rules about the presentation of homosexuality: *There was this scene that felt like it is approaching something lesbian, so we kind of softened it to become a friendship between girls but without the sexual issues, because it was for ten-year-old kids and I wasn't sure they needed that.* This "cleansing" tactic employed against what are perceived as social deviance and aberrations, speaks to the fantasy view of a "hygienic," gay-free world and a purely heterosexual régime.[32]

Noga continued her discussion of the potential lesbian scene by sharing the following strategy: *But we did approach the issue through the mediation of a presenter in a program we did a couple years ago for Gay Pride day about a boy who has two mothers. The presenter interviewed the mother and he was able to ask her the kinds of questions the child viewer at home would have asked, something you can't do in a drama.*

Indeed, distinguishing between fiction and non-fiction genres was a central strategy presented in the discussion of sex and sexuality in general. What was perceived to be an unacceptable form of normalization within dramatic narrative was treated with more tolerance when it was highlighted as a "topic" in news or special programming, cushioned by a protective environment of discussion, commentary, and adult mediation. While obviously such presentations are informative and potentially educational, they can also be viewed as a form of "othering;" that is, a special discussion of special children in special kinds of families – clearly marked as "different from" the normal majority.

How "far" the audience would permit the producers to go was cast quite differently in the Nordic countries. Hanne (Norway), for example, recalled an incidence that caused a controversy in Norway: *We had an episode not so long ago that was in fact a kissing lesson – how to start kissing ... we have this series where we use Barbie dolls to show different things and Yetti, the female host, used two Barbie dolls to show how to get into a kissing situation. And one journalist contacted this really orthodox Christian organization and it became quite a big, big issue in the media. You know, two Barbie girls with Barbie dolls with long blonde hair. But what they all forgot is that girls start kissing each other, they try, I mean, they have to try kissing, they have to rehearse; and this part of childhood is sexualized by adults and it really makes me angry.*

Discussion of explicit gay kissing on children's TV was a very emotionally laden issue. In reacting to the homosexual kiss between two teenagers on *Danny's Parade,* Pamke (The Netherlands), an interviewee who identified herself as an open lesbian, said: *It's so important to show this kiss. I have two gay colleagues who said: "It wouldn't have taken me until my twenty-eighth year if I would have seen more kisses before." I, myself, was unhappy for quite a long time because I didn't want to admit that I wanted to kiss a girl. And now children can see it and I don't believe that it stimulates them, but I do respect that these programs cannot be shown in many cultures.*

The desperate need to have one's identity affirmed in mainstream media as well as the fundamental right for visibility of all human experiences is a central issue in much of the writing on the representation of sexual minorities in the media.[33] This is particularly the case for sexual minorities, many of whom grow up in secrecy and shame in a heterosexual environment since they are perceived as deviant in many societies today, invisible to others, and isolated from support systems. The exhibitionist nature of events such as Gay Pride parades, featured in *Danny's Parade*, speaks exactly to the needs, argued for by proponents of this view – for visibility and pride, which are generally absent on TV directed to young viewers (despite changes in representations of homosexuality visible in Western TV, both on prime-time as well as in ghettoized programming).[34] Other, perhaps more commonly prevalent views, claim that homosexuality is a learned abnormal practice. Therefore, portrayals of homosexuality encourage viewers to experiment with homosexual activities and provide them with immoral "ideas" and role models. The more radical view claims that in presenting homosexuality children's TV can serve as a site of resistance to subjugation of sexual activity to procreation, and thus pose a threat to the normative sexual ideologies described above. However one perceives the discourses in conflict, the vast majority of the interviewees in this study, from all countries, believed that their audiences are not receptive to such images and therefore chose to refrain from their inclusion. This position illustrates Foucault's notion of ideological self-regulation of sexuality.

In contrast, relative tolerance was displayed by the same interviewees who expressed strong objections to the presentation of homosexuality to such programs as *The Odd One Out* and *The Day I Decided to be Nina* (see Figure 4.2) that focus on gender dysphoria. The influence of theories that seek to undermine the binary model of sexual differences (male and female) and to challenge the certainties of clear and stable heterosexual or homosexual identities (such as the prominent theoretical perspective offered by Butler[35]) are entirely invisible on TV in general and on TV for children more specifically. Yet, at the same time, we find that the occasional presentation of sex-reassignment surgery is deemed acceptable even in the festivals where this study was conducted. It seems that such a discussion falls neatly within both the medicalized and normative discourse of sex: A mistake of nature can be fixed medically, restoring the normative alignment between the biological sex organs and the gendered identity, rather than challenging it.

Sexual Abuse

Quite a different approach was evident in producers' discussion of *Invisible Wounds* (see Figure 4.1), a program from Sweden that discussed the sexual abuse of a girl, the help she received, as well as her road to healing. Here no opposing views were expressed by interviewees about whether such a program is valuable or "moral," but only a discussion of what would be a suitable format for presenting the topic. As with other topics deemed sensitive, this one in particular was cast in terms of a need for a protective broadcasting environment. For example, Laura (USA) explained that her network would not be able to present a program on the sexual abuse of children during regular broadcasting hours, rather only in a setting specifically designed to touch upon such a topic during prime time, with *a whole lot of protection* in the form of advanced warnings, promos, and follow-up discussions to protect PBS's reputation with parents as a safe haven for children: *People put their kids down in front of the TV and they walk away. They go make dinner and they do the wash, and they don't want to know that there's going to be anything on PBS that they have to worry about or explain, or that their kid is going to be confused about or surprised by ... they don't want anything controversial.*

Sally (US) noted that such a topic would fit well into the format of an "after-school special," but not something that was broadcast during regular Nickelodeon hours for the 6–11 age group. Dominique (Nigeria) suggested that while it was not appropriate to screen any explicit sexual-abuse program on TV, it was possible to address the specific target audience in schools via screening and guided discussions.

The need to culturally contextualize the discussion of sexual abuse in a manner that is credible and relevant was raised by Erika (Mexico) in her discussion of *Invisible Wounds*: *It is very remote ... it's Swedish. I mean the whole aesthetic and the policewoman have nothing to do with our police. I would like to buy the rights and do exactly the same thing, but within a Mexican context. Because then children won't think "Oh, it's Swedish, it's for Swedish children ... these are things that happen to them."* It really has to feel close to them.

These differing references to the topic of sexual abuse engage in a desexualized discussion that has been transformed by circumventing cultural taboos about sex to become a "proper" issue for quality TV. On the face of it, these reactions could be interpreted as an advanced reading of sexual abuse and incest, not solely as an act of sex and uncontrolled desire. Further, it could be considered to be a case of patriarchal power enforced on the vulnerable segments of society (mainly children and women). Such an interpretation would echo feminist readings of sexual violence against women and children that are viewed as a form of terror designed to preserve subordination, limit freedoms in the public sphere, and erode their basic human rights.[36] Another interpretation of the interviews that could be offered suggests that removing sexual connotations from these cases of sexual abuse was a strategy employed by producers to circumvent broadcast restrictions, and more specifically, the public unease and "embarrassment" involved in explicit discussions of sexual deviances and crime. The broader strategy employed here claims that children should be protected from the world's dangers and atrocities. Thus, according to this latter interpretation, discussion of sexual abuse was a legitimate protectionist topic when the framing employed avoided discussion of homosexuality, as it served a similar function of "protecting" children's naïveté and wellbeing. The consequence of such actions is that it comes at the expense of contributing to the development of an empowered sexual subjectivity.

Girls: An Integrated Case Study in the Representation of Sex

To illustrate many of the issues discussed above in a more integrated manner, let us consider *Girls* (see Figure 4.4), a Prix Jeunesse winner of 2004. Aimed at 12–15-year-old teens, this program from The Netherlands is a documentary in which three boys (aged fourteen and fifteen) talk about their preoccupation with girls' bodies and sex, and gradually reveal their insecurities and vulnerabilities. The innovative aspect of the program was constructing a format that facilitated boys' talk about their inner world, something rarely done on TV. This fact is explained, partially, by some interviewees who claimed boys often feel inadequate and put down by girls' more eloquent verbalization.

The screening of *Girls* created quite a commotion at the 2004 Prix Jeunesse Festival and interviewees were quite animated when discussing the program, well beyond 2004. For example, Karoline (Sweden) stated: *I loved it. They were allowed to say that they often talk about girls ... but when they got deeper they really got emotional ... like when he said: "I told them I have done that"* [had sex] *... being open about it* [...] *I don't think the program objectified women, because I think it went on and revealed boys' real feelings, that it's the way they talk about it* [sex]. According to this view, letting boys talk about sex in their own way, in their own voice, sharing their sexual fantasies, as well as their fears and vulnerabilities was innovative and valuable. Doing so speaks directly to the need for producers to address the "neglected boys" crisis discussed above.

A similar line of support came from Sylvia (Germany) who spoke about the critique of the program's imbalance: *It was quite controversial because a lot of the participants at the Prix Jeunesse argued that it was done only from the boys' perspective, which I found to be very good, because this is not usually done. You always have the idea that you have to be balanced between the sexes, and in that case I found it especially very, very interesting and revealing to have only the boys, and they presented it with a very nice development; from the beginning, where the boys were self-confident "oh yes, I like the butt of the girls and the big breasts the best;" and then throughout the program you learn that they do not have much experience with girls and that they're very afraid of sexual encounters ... It was very well done. I think it is very good for the viewers to see how those boys have fears, but where they are also very strong and funny. So this impressed me.*

When confronted with the view presented by an African interviewee who argued that the program legitimizes sexual objectification of girls, Sylvia continued: *I disagree. At a certain age girls are sex objects for boys; I mean, this is what they think about, a lot. Of course there are also classmates and friends, but in their mind they are girls physically, and this is something perfectly normal and OK. What is important is how they are in their relationships later; how they treat girls; how they spend their lives together. But at a certain age girls are sexual objects because they are girls, physically. I think this program had a very nice development because at the beginning they behaved in this very clichéd way and they talked like that because they tried to show off a little. But then it became very clear that they were all even afraid of girls, you know, and they didn't know how to talk to them, and how to contact them, and how to act when they came close, and when it comes even to having sex ... those are things that concern boys [...] Maybe in Africa it's not a good thing to have a program like that. Programs are always part of the culture and background where they are made. I can understand the criticism ... but here in Europe I found that a very good program.*

As Karoline and Sylvia pointed out, the program gradually unveils the expected norms of "performing" masculinity in youth culture (to use Butler's term discussed in Chapter One), by sharing the process of "manning-up" that can include objectifying women, exhibiting sexual lust, and bragging about sexual experience. Yet, at the same time, the program reveals the inner world of emotions and sensibilities of these male adolescents, and their deep insecurities in their masculine identities. The freshness of this approach and its revealing of boys' world was greatly admired by many (mostly European) interviewees, especially because it presented alternative views to traditional stereotypes, in a somewhat risky and unconventional manner.

However, other participants were passionate in objecting to and expressing their harsh criticism of *Girls*. Some criticism of the overt sexuality was similar to previous discussion about sex as a social taboo. There were many examples of this kind of criticism, such as the one offered by Manisha (Nepal): *There are programs that are not acceptable in our society; like when they are talking openly about sex, like* Girls. *Boys there* [in this program] *are just looking to undress every girl. That kind of thing is not accepted in our society. We do tell them about all these things, but in a different way, not openly through the TV. Not in a vulgar way, but in a different way. There is a large gap between Asian children and specifically children in Nepal and foreign children.* Similarly, Obinna (Nigeria) said: *Some things, like the program* Girls, *you cannot show on TV because of moral values. If we air something like this the producer might lose his job. It could better be used as workshop material when you are talking about sex education. You don't talk about sex on public television.*

A different line of critique, argued particularly by African interviewees, moved away from the discussion of sex as a taboo to a concern for gender equity, and more specifically, to the issue of sexual objectification of women. For example, Samora (South Africa) said: *The program* Girls – *if you look at it, it is technically well done, and the program to my shock and disappointment was about three boys, three young boys that look like they are under fifteen talking about girls. It is called* Girls *but it has nothing to do with girls, and the boys talk about girls with whatever language they want to use; like calling them bitch, that it is OK. And it looks like reality, that that's what happens, producers' voice through the camera shots, focusing on sexual parts of the girls' bodies, so the boys are saying "I like a woman with big tits and nice ass; that has to be a body like a bottle." And I am thinking, what does this have to do to a girl? Thinking that the boys who are being socialized this way. That I have to look this way and dress this way and behave this way, because it was on TV.*

The producers fail to bring in the voice of girls. What do girls think about this? How do they feel about boys saying these things? It is one thing letting fifteen-year-old boys talk openly and endlessly about girls and about their sexual fantasies and how many girls they would like to sleep with. But if you don't ask them about the effect of what they are saying and what does it mean, aren't we perpetuating the way men are treating women? Saying to them that it is OK. Because as TV producers, I think they have a duty to get people to reflect on what they are doing, what they are saying, think about how it affects people around them.

Interestingly, Samora's wish for a program that balances *Girls* with a sequel – *Boys*, one that presents girls' talk about boys, was actually fulfilled since such a program was presented in a subsequent Prix Jeunesse event. However, it was not considered by some interviewees to be a satisfactory response, as reflected in these comments by Mpule (Botswana): *I particularly didn't like the* Girls' *story, you know, where boys were just talking about girls as objects of their sexual fantasy. And don't tell me you're gonna be running another program where you put girls ... you have to have a balance from the beginning. You have to have all the voices in each program for kids. That's what you call balance. That's why you say equal time, equal opportunities, because whatever somebody sees and hears for the first time maybe the only time they'll see that episode with boys talking ... they may not see it again.*

Clearly these producers believe that such TV texts can cultivate youth viewers' worldviews and that as creators and disseminators of these texts producers have a responsibility to promote gender equality.

A related, third line of argument introduced the issue of race into the mix of arguments about too much sex, the sexual objectification of girls, and the lack of a balanced picture. Sarah (Australia), for example, mentioned this theme in passing: *I thought it encapsulated the myth that all boys are interested in is sex. I would have had less of a problem if that was half a boy's perspective and the other half a girl's perspective, if it was balanced ... but it was just the boys' view. It was only the images of girls that were shown ... it was all white girls and the lead characters were black kids. It objectified the girls. They were solely sex objects for those boys. I didn't think it gave a very balanced view of anything. It wouldn't be aired in Australia for children.*

Julie (UK), too, mentioned the issue of race without pursuing it any further: *I was absolutely appalled by this documentary. It's about two Dutch black kids and an Indian boy. All boys who talk about girls, and that's all they do – talk about girls and sex. I couldn't show this film, I wouldn't get permission. I wouldn't put it on the air, because it just reinforces objectification of girls. People have argued that by the time you get to the end of the film the boys are exposed as phonies and really closet romantics, and that they were just showing off and had no idea what they were talking about when they talked about sex. That it actually serves to undo the image of the "Angro."*[37] *That's a valid argument. But you have to watch the whole thing to get that and I enjoyed it and I admired it and I think it is really a lot true, what boys think. But I wouldn't put it on my airtime.*

The mixed emotional reaction to this program evident in the above quotation moves from "*I was absolutely appalled*" at the beginning to "*I admired it*" only several lines below. However, the introduction of the racial characteristic of the program was not pursued despite the fact that the program could elicit some interesting questions. This was pointed out by Salma (Pakistan): *I was a little irritated, because the skin color – why are they all black? They should have been white. Don't white boys feel the same? I find this to be so condescending. And, it has been coming out more since 9/11. I am sure that boys talk about girls, but girls talk about boys, too. So, where is the other part of it? And why is it only breasts that are important? Or how much skin we show? Why aren't the boys saying, "I'd like to talk to a girl and see what happens and what makes her tick." I thought it was extremely gender biased, and all of us thought so.*

It seems that the selection of three minority boys in the double role – being unrestrained sexually and at the same time revealing such non-traditional masculine vulnerability – was uncomfortable for several interviewees, although they had difficulty expressing the reasons for their objections and did not pursue their arguments. From a more theoretical point of view, the decision to cast minority youths, the "others," in the role of non-conventional masculinity may not have challenged white hegemonic masculinity since they might seem to be less threatening or deviant due to their inherent marginality. Yet the choice of three minority boys lusting over white girls, too, might be thought to touch upon and arouse some deeply held, latent fears ingrained in white societies of the stereotypical black man who poses a danger to the purity of white girls. Black men have been systematically represented in literature, popular culture, legal courts, and general racist beliefs in the US as dangerous others, uncivilized, uncontrollable sexual and physical beings, and a threat to Western civilization. In particular, they have been historically framed as having unusually large penises and sexual appetites. The fear of black sexuality and the protection of white women from bestial black men was often the justification for lynching black men in the US (along with the common act of castration). Indeed, even today it is common to find a disproportionate number of black men cast in Hollywood movies as rapists.[38] The argument has been made that the hypersexual closeness to nature attributed to black people works to secure the belief in white people as restrained, rational, and civilized.[39] The lack of awareness of this deep-rooted history of anxieties and prejudice in the casting choices of the main characters in *Girls* seems worthy of special notice and may provide a partial explanation for the strong emotional objections elicited by the program.

In conclusion, we can say that the case study of *Girls* demonstrates how deeply issues of sex, gender, and race were entangled in interviewees' observations and shows the difficulties involved in analyzing producers' reactions to presentations of sex on quality television for children.

Concluding Notes

There is no doubt that we are witnessing a proliferation of sex in contemporary media, including an excessive preoccupation with sexual pleasure and display, open discussion of sex, flourishing commodifcation of sex, along with many new ways of interacting and acting out sexuality in interactive media (e.g. posting and sharing naked photos of oneself; sexual talk on instant messaging). Furthermore, some adult TV dramas now present women as "desiring" sexual subjects, rather than solely objects of male desire (most notable for our purposes, is the hit HBO series *Sex and the City*, which is often referred to as exemplifying "post-feminist" women).[40] Undoubtedly, the representation of sexual conduct in popular media has become bolder, more confident, and more diverse.[41] However, the findings presented here suggest, in contrast, that global agreement remains steadfast: Sex and sexuality are inappropriate topics for children, tweens, and even teens. This overarching finding tells us a great deal about the construction of childhood as a naïve pre-sex time that needs to be preserved by clear limits on the "sayable" and "unsayable." Accordingly, productions from The Netherlands and the Nordic countries are the exceptions that prove this rule. Programs from these countries serve as "chaotic" gale-force winds amidst a waveless ocean, which attempt to transgress the hegemonic sex order. In contrast, most non-Northern European producers refrained from incorporating such themes in what they perceived as quality television for children, nor did they advance age-appropriate engagement with sex-related issues. The exception to this rule can be found in programs whose aim is HIV/AIDS prevention, and in which sex is treated mainly as a risk-related behavior. However, there are exceptions to this generalization, such as the short animation *Sexteens* from Argentina. *Sexteens* addresses young teenagers through direct, bold, humorous, and non-judgmental references to sex (e.g. including sounds of sexual moans and groans, featuring male erection and female pleasure).

This overall finding stands in sharp contrast with the well-documented trend to increasing frequency and explicitness of sexual portrayals in popular media consumed by young audiences (movies, popular music, music videos, prime-time television, soap operas, and Internet).[42] Indeed, commercial media continue to send very ambiguous messages about teen sexuality: "We want teens to 'wait' but often expect that they will, nevertheless, engage in sexual activity. Parents and educators promote abstinence, and yet teens' peer culture often suggests that only nerds and prudes abstain. On the other hand, teens, especially girls, learn quickly that having sex might hurt their reputation. Adults often approach the topic of sexuality with discomfort and alarm, and teens have come to expect that 'sex talks' with adults will be awkward, if not intolerable."[43]

This dual stance is particularly intriguing, given the rising levels of sexual activity engaged in by adolescent populations with significant consequences that include rising rates of teen pregnancy, the spread of HIV/AIDS and other sexually transmitted diseases, recognition by medical authorities of a mental state of "sex addiction," moral panic over the Internet as a social space where sexual predators lurk, as well as growing evidence of the prevalence of sexual abuse of children.[44] Furthermore, the global context of the sex industry and sex tourism – including modern forms of female and child slavery – have long been transferred from the private to the public sphere. At the same time, sexual violence in all its forms – rape, battery, sexual harassment, sexual abuse of children, pedophiles, prostitution, pornography, sexual slavery, "honor" murders, genital mutilation, mass rapes as war crimes, as well as the pervasive forms of sexual violence perpetuated in all societies on the personal and domestic levels – have become a major social ill of global proportions, reported widely in the global media. For example, a 2006 UN report estimated the following: 150 million girls under 18 have experienced forced sexual intercourse or other forms of sexual violence involving physical contact; among every 10 women, one to four have experienced physical violence before the age of sixteen; the first experience of sexual intercourse in adolescence is unwanted and even coerced for a large number of girls; and so forth.[45]

This seeming contradiction can perhaps be understood by reference to well-ensconced, largely unquestioned views rooted deeply in ideologies and traditions that perceive children as asexual and the construction of childhood as devoid of sexual feelings and experiences and in need of protection from the influences of sexual adults. Here, the discussion of sex and sexuality, even through the paradigm of the healthy maturing process, seems to threaten two competing conceptions of childhood – the child as primitive and untamed as well as the child as pure and innocent,[46] both of which require – according to their rationale – adult supervision and protection. Thus, according to these dominant perceptions, children's socialization includes the association of sexuality with the shameful and unspeakable and the traditional silencing of discussion of sexual drives and behaviors.[47]

When Foucault addressed this issue, he observed that the open talk about sexuality that characterized the eighteenth and early nineteenth centuries in Europe was repressed later as a result of a preoccupation with anxiety over evidence of boys' masturbation and the need to manage it in both public (e.g. school) and private (e.g. home) realms of life. Of particular relevance for the purposes of our discussion is Foucault's general argument: Discourses and practices of repression and silencing regarding sex produce diametrically opposed results – endless preoccupation and discussion: "The seeming repression of sexual discussion and sexuality itself had an unintended effect, that is to increase the desire to speak about sexuality and increase the pleasure gained from violating these taboos."[48] Following this line of argument, we may have a better understanding of the apparent contradiction between the silence surrounding the development of healthy sexuality in children and adolescents, and the hypersexualization of our culture. That is, both views reflect the same societal discomfort experienced with this central aspect of our humanity, and human life. And, despite its innovation in so many other realms of life, quality television for children seems to have barely engaged this challenge – at least on the basis of these global findings.

This conclusion reminds us of the fact that sex is not a mere personal choice and private form of behavior, but it is also a political arena where ideological and practical battles over issues such as abortion, pornography, prostitution, sex education, and gay marriage are being fought regularly. Sex on TV, too, is related to all forms of power: political, economical, and cultural as it depends on those who control the discourse surrounding it and the practices deemed legitimate, and those who make money out of them.[49] In this regard, we can apply the questions posed in regard to the heterosexual dominance of the media: "Which sexual stories ... get told and re-told, by whom and how?"[50] and add to this list – "to whom?" Clearly, these stories are neither told nor re-told in television aimed at young people.

Control of the representations of sex takes a variety of forms: Through state interventions, such as obscenity laws and censorship of content deemed to be indecent, corrupting, or offensive to the audience; through market self-regulation by broadcasters who respond to perceived audiences' values and tastes by avoiding offensive contents and so protect and garner profits,[51] or, in the case of public broadcasters, to retain their license and viewership. Children have had a symbolic role in debates over censorship and the regulation of media content. They are framed as a weak, vulnerable segment of the audience in need of protection[52] as well as constructed as the "others" of adults. In this, they are a preventive social-change tool used by adults to preserve the dominance of hegemonic conservative approaches to sexuality in adulthood and childhood. This process was evident in the interviews in producers beliefs that they were responding to dominant ideologies in their societies regarding sex and children and serving as guardians of normative discourse. Interviewees were also very aware and demonstrative in explaining their perception that any deviation from such expectations would be sanctioned immediately by disciplinary practices (e.g. angry audience reactions, pulling programs off, employment threats, etc.).

While criteria for determining what is inappropriate or too explicit in portrayals of sex and sexuality on television are historical and cultural (and thus change over time and across cultures), in contrast, many scholars agree that sexuality is central in modern societies and is at the heart of personal identity.[53] The capacity to give and to experience sexual satisfaction is now recognized to be a central task that should be cultivated through many sources of sexual information and advice, as well as through a variety of options for training and medical support, including the use of medication and aphrodisiacs. Thus, originating in a variety of sources, it does seem clear that adult-oriented media – across all genres – have aroused political and cultural debates over the last several decades about how alternative understandings of our sexual selves as well as a variety of sexual tastes and practices should be represented in appropriate ways.

Yet children and adolescences remain outside of any of these discourses, as neither sex education nor television programs addressing them dare to talk to them directly about any of these issues. Rather than being offered representations of democratic and emancipatory sexuality, as called for by Giddens and others,[54] they continue to depend on the unreal, romanticized, stereotyped, stigmatized, and often unhealthy exploitive images of sexual relationships they often encounter in pornography and popular culture. This process stands in dramatic contrast to an approach that requires an understanding of the complex meaning of sexuality for adolescents, grounded in their cultures and traditions, and aimed at cultivating healthy sexual subjects.

In this regard, it is interesting to note that while women's rights for access to sexual representations that are respectful of their humanity and catering to their emotional, social, and physical needs have been largely accepted in Western societies as legitimate, adolescents' rights in these same domains have remained for the most part outside of this debate. Instead, the prevailing discourse remains protectionist: protecting perceived-to-be-vulnerable children from the perceived harm of sex (and at the same time protecting parents from the possible embarrassment involved in dealing with this issue) by placing restrictions on scheduling hours for various television contents and developing criteria for rating films and video games deemed inappropriate. As is the case with all forms of censorship, this one can be seen as the result of cultural and political tensions; as well as limitations imposed by the powerful (in this case – adults) on those lacking power (in this case – children). According to this form of prophylactic, preventive approach to social change, "weaker" segments of society – be they women, minorities, lower social classes, or children – are perceived as impressionable and controlled by their emotions. "The belief that children are sexual innocents who can be harmed by exposure to sexually explicit materials is so deeply engrained in our society that it is difficult to gain a hearing for a contrary view."[55]

The irony is that all this is occurring while at the same time children's culture is highly hypersexualized, with tremendous pressure placed on sexual appearance (particularly for girls) and on the exhibition of a strong sexual drive (particularly for boys). The result is driving children into premature sexual adulthood without providing them with appropriate tools, knowledge, and role models for healthy sexual development.[56]

The void left by quality television and edutainment genres for young audiences in regard to healthy development of their sexuality strongly echoes the absences of careful engagement with issues related to gender and sexuality evident in school curricula, as both socializing agents seem to share the same worldview toward sex and sexuality. In doing so, both fail to address a central aspect of children and youth development, thus leaving the field of socialization and education to profit-driven market forces, on the one hand, and to right wing anti-sex moralists on the other. In short, both fail to promote sexual health in young people by incorporating themes that introduce the three Cs: commitment, contraceptives, and consequences.[57] While one might argue, following our discussion so far, that the definition of "sexual health" in itself is open for discussion, there is a consensus among sex educators: First, sexual relationships are part of committed relationships; second, the proper use of contraceptives can avoid undesired pregnancies and sexually transmitted diseases; and, third, being knowledgeable and taking responsibility for the consequences of sexual relationships are central ingredients in developing into being a mature, responsible adult.

The challenge "that we gain and exercise the right to find, articulate and celebrate our own sexualities, while showing due respect for the tastes, desires and sensitivities of others"[58] does not embrace the young people who probably need it most as they are introduced to the world of sexualities. Similarly, Giddens' call for a democratization of sexuality, where it serves as a medium of emancipation, according to which "A non-repressive society ... would be one in which sexuality is increasingly freed from compulsiveness ... it is separate from permissiveness in so far as it creates an ethics of personal life which makes possible a conjunction of happiness, love and respect for others,"[59] remains, too, outside of the realm of reference of most producers of quality television for children.

Chapter 5

The Segregated Workplace and the Implied Audience

This chapter attends to an unanticipated but important theme that emerged from the interviews – the political economy of gendered television production. This theme was manifest in the interviews in relation to two central aspects of the interviewees' professional lives: First is the fact that children's television is a professional territory inhabited mostly by women, or as Augustine (Portugal) put it: *It's a womans world*. The second relates to these professionals' perceptions of the implied audience of children's television and the implications these perceptions have for their work. While seemingly unrelated, both themes have significant implications; first, for the gender representations constructed by producers and available to young viewers; and, second, both aspects are deeply rooted in and shaped by the institutional aspects of media systems, including the complex interrelationships between professional employment, audiences, production processes, policymakers, advertisers, and market forces.

Gendered Workplace

No matter where in the world the producers called home, all agreed that children's TV is a feminized profession. A quick glance at the meeting halls of the events where I conducted this study provided first-hand evidence that the majority of the participants were female, as was reflected in the composition of the sample of interviewees (two-thirds female). Thus, the global trend for feminization of media professions (i.e. the growing proportion of women in them[1]) is apparent, as well, in the more narrowly defined world of children's TV. Interviewees' various explanations for why this professional niche was particularly appropriate for women recall many scholars' research findings and theorizing about this phenomenon.

One line of explanation suggested by interviewees is that caring for children is more of a female concern, as stated by Hanne (Norway): *Women choose caring jobs and children's television is more caring than economics, news, or sports. So, you can see the same pattern: Most of the people involved in children's television are women.* A similar argument was put forward by Eric (Canada): *I think it is a way to balance the fact that there are so many men working in media and other fields, and women are caring, and they are good in nurturing children, so it's a good thing.* The above two quotations suggest the argument that, first, the definition of femininity includes a capacity for caring, apparently lacking in masculinity, and that children's television is an extension of the private sphere of child rearing and nurturing, as is evident in many professions dominated by women (e.g. education, nursing, social work). Many other interviewees provided evidence of having internalized this position as well. This was particularly evident among female Asian interviewees (e.g. from Pakistan, Malaysia, Nepal, Iran) who explained how children's television was perceived as a legitimate professional area for women's employment in societies were women's presence in the work force was not necessarily always deemed to be acceptable.

Another explanation offered for the dominant female presence in this domain relates to the political economy of media employment. Hope (US), for example, provided a structural argument in addition to the nurturing one: [It] *started coming about twenty-five years ago when it was a fairly young industry, so women who came in at the bottom as I did, as somebody's secretary, were able to move up in the ranks.* This explanation too, is not unique to the television industry: Women find it much easier to move up the ladder in young organizations with a yet-to-be established tradition of male domination.

Thus, based on evidence gathered from this global collection of media professionals, the relegation of women to specific areas of employment – a process known as "horizontal segregation" – is much more evident in the area of children's TV, in comparison with other departments of television such as news or prime-time programming. This phenomenon has its consequences, as Silvia (Germany) indicated: *The Children's Department is heavily dominated by women ... [this is]not the same in the other departments; entertainment for example. I think this is because it's easier for women to get access to that group, because it is considered a female area ... they would not say so, but we have lower status ... the budget, the wages for salaries, especially for freelancers ...*

That the feminization of media professions is associated with lower status and income, as well as less permanent contracts, has been documented before (as is the case in the feminization of other professions – such as education, administration, or family medicine), and its discussion is not within the scope of the present book. Yet evidence of this significant phenomenon leads to more general political-economy concerns related to the interlocking relations of gender and money,[2] including their impact on the field of television for children more generally (e.g. global phenomena of limited governmental support and low budgets) as well as to the material conditions of women working in this domain of media practice.

Furthermore, there is additional employment segregation along some marked lines within the children's TV world. Interviewees agreed that while women occupy most of the roles of producers, developers of content, and consultants, they remain a minority among those who actually convert these ideas into television programs; that is, those in the technological and production professions – such as directors, camera and sound professionals, as well as program directors. Megan (Canada) related her personal employment history: *There are more women producers than men producers, but there are far less women directors. When I was a multi-camera director, I was one of the only three across the country. At the same time there were probably twenty-five, thirty men ...* In trying to account for this difference, she continued: *I think that it's easier for women to get into producing because it's the organizational part, for the most part, and women are perceived to be great organizationally. When you are a multi-camera director, you're in charge of the whole crew and the crew is quite often mainly men. The camera guys are still men; the sound people are still men; all the technicians, yeah, so you have to be a strong woman in order to have them listen and respect what you do. And so women, for whatever reason, don't even want to go down that path, they don't want to fight those fights.* Thus, while organizational and content-oriented roles are more "women friendly" and deemed more in line with feminine traits and skills, the technical ones have been historically male dominated and thus more difficult to infiltrate and flourish in. Most notably, argued many interviewees, the world of animation, which dominates the industry and perpetuates many of the problematic stereotypes, remains mostly a male world, as very few animation artists are women. Indeed, the animation guild reports that women represent only 10 percent of its membership.[3]

In addition to the various aspects of horizontal segregation, many interviewees brought up issues related to vertical segregation, i.e. the hierarchal authority structure within each workplace. Despite the fact that children's TV is a "woman's world," in many places this world is still managed by men at the executive levels of decision making. While this situation was changing dramatically, according to North American and European interviewees, it remained particularly true in many other countries in the rest of the world.

What Difference Does Employment Make?

The discussion of the gendered aspects of employment in children's TV brings us back to the focus of this study's mission: the influence this situation may have on the content produced in such an environment. Clearly, television production is not an individual creative activity, but is part of a contextualized cultural process situated in a particular institutional setting. However, specific reference to the people involved in the "moment" of production "in which cultural objects or texts are brought into being"[4] deserve our attention. This line of thinking leads us to a series of questions, such as: Do women produce different types of programs than men? Do they prioritize different issues? Do they bring to the screen different perspectives? Do they choose more female characters? Do they develop different narratives? Similar questions have been debated, for example, in the area of news journalism (e.g. do women journalists define news values in a manner different from men? Do they advance a different social agenda? Use a different language and style? Interview more women and present them in a less stereotypical manner?).[5] However, to date, there have been very few academic studies of media production for children in general,[6] and even less with a concern for the feminization of the profession.

Overall, it is interesting to note that few interviewees evidenced awareness that the gender of people involved in the TV world makes a difference to the kind of television content produced for children. Among the few who reflected on this connection, Nathalie (France) declared passionately: *It must have an influence, yes, we are a majority of women and we chose things that we deeply like.* Maggie (Ireland) said: *I think women will show more the complexity of both roles;* and Noga (Israel) explained more generally that *we think about what we want our own children to see on TV.*

Julie (UK) provided a more reflexive perspective that explained actions being taken in her department with regard to this issue: *[...] it's interesting. I have a lot of women in my department and ... they've definitely pushed the agenda of the heroine, you know, we need to have more girls leading drama series; we need to have them take charge and be competent ... And now we've added more men back into the department since we noticed that we actually have quite a few programs that feature girls in our leading roles and we need to actually readdress that balance and bring more boys back just as we did in the department for girls ... it's more about ... making people aware of asking the question: Who are we presenting? What are we saying about these characters? Is this what we want to be saying, and so on ...*

Interestingly, the more salient gender perspective was raised by producers, such as Julie, whose reflections seem to have been driven by the flip side of the argument: that children's TV is dominated by a female perspective, and it needs to be balanced by reintroducing more men. Eric (Canada) said: *I would like to see maybe a little bit more men ... it is always one person making the final decision of what children will see across the country, and it is mostly women in these positions, for me it is problematic ... it is another issue of decision making and gatekeepers.* Similarly, Hanne (Norway) viewed this situation as problematic and as one in need of action: *What we have to do to get a gender balance is to recruit men.* Similar to our previous discussion of the "neglected boys" discourse, these producers obviously believe that having more men in children's TV will lead to a qualitatively better "boys' perspective." Clearly, for these interviewees, the gender of the text's producer does make a difference to the content of the text.

Several interviewees refined this argument by explaining how this process might be working. The following exchange was recorded during a closed-door workshop in Los Angeles, among an audience composed of many leading Hollywood producers of children's programs. One participant observed: *A lot of the writers found it easier to write to boys, superheroes. They just don't know where to go with the girl characters; should she be perfect, etc? More recently there are more funny girl characters. In the past we struggled with finding someone to write a girl comedy.* A top female executive added: *They don't know how to write girls as funny.* To which a top female animator responded: *It is much harder to write a dynamic girl character, because there are very few animation writers that are women ... most of the animators who draw these characters are men and their fantasy of a perfect woman is the skinny waist, long hair, big bust. They are thinking of what's beautiful to them, assuming that then the boys will like it as well.* As the discussion unfolded, the arguments shifted to focus on the observation that popular male-based animation throughout the world today is heavily influenced by Japanese traditions of animation, originating in adult sexual fantasies in Japanese adult comics which flourished at the time that pornographic magazines such as *Playboy* were prohibited. Images employed there trickled down to children's *manga* (comics and cartoons) and from there distributed around the world.[7] The hypersexualization of girl characters in children's animation, according to this explanation, reflects an "evolution" of imagery that has its roots in male objectification of the female body.

One other, unique perspective that ties employment issues to contents was shared by Paradise (South Africa): *We are also seeing a new breed of young black producers, mainly women, who come from having been activists. So there is a struggle element in who they are as a people, and therefore what they convey in their programming.* Who producers "are as a people" seems to influence what they produce. It follows, of course, that if producers change, become more informed, more aware, and more oriented to social change, that will infuse the kind of television they make for children.

However, as many of my interviewees suggested, in one way or another, it is the survival impulse of making money that is much stronger among female industry leaders than their feminist conscience and therefore women in positions of power do not necessarily behave differently or make different choices than do their male colleagues in similar positions. As noted above, this argument has been made in reference to other realms of media production and suggests that the gender of the professional is no guarantee of gender blindness, nor does it provide them with sufficient motivation to struggle against institutional barriers and to take personal career risks.[8]

Directly related to this debate is the second political-economy-related theme: The multiple ways in which producers perceive their audiences and what they presume these audiences need, desire, and expect from their television screens; a matter to which we turn now.

The Implied Audience[9]

The children's television production and broadcasting community shares one assumption that seems to be used in an axiomatic fashion, as a non-debatable truism: Although girls will watch boys' shows, boys will not watch girls' shows. This central belief is shared throughout the industry and has been documented by the few researchers who have studied this phenomenon.[10] The implications of this truism are profound as it provides a rationale – both economic as well as "moral" – for the production of more programming aimed at boys' interests and needs, under the umbrella argument of serving children's tastes and pleasures; a matter to which we will return after presenting rich evidence of interviewees' perspectives of this truism.

Unsolicited and often raised spontaneously by interviewees, this "axiom" was hardly ever challenged and so seems to be a deeply rooted belief. Indeed, even when it was posed with a tone of reservation (such as: *I don't know if this is true or not, but the industry has it that ...*), it remained within the unreflected realm of general "wonderment." Also interesting were the few cases when contrasting evidence was raised by interviewees themselves (e.g. when discussing some of Nickelodeon's programs, with its innovative record of advancing female leads that proved to be successful among boys as well), as it was hardly used to counter-argue or undermine this basic premise. On the contrary, such programs (see discussion in Chapter One) seemed to be cited as the exceptions that prove the rule. Indeed, a male animator in the LA workshop, who was one of the few interviewees who criticized this truism, reaffirmed this interpretation in reflecting on his own experience: *I have been writing animation for twenty years now, and the mantra one always heard from the toy and production companies in the industry is that girls will watch boys' programs but boys will not watch girls' programs. And when you show another example, like* Kim Possible, *they'll say: "but that's an exception!"*

The gendered nature of producers' perspectives regarding their "implied audience" was deeply located within the dominant and current popular consumer-driven discourses of childhood. Other discourses include: the protectionist discourse of the vulnerable child that needs protection from the negative effects of the media; the child-centered discourse that emphasizes the implications of developmental differences on children's media use; and the discourse of the child as a potential citizen.[11] Whether uncritically accepting the arguments or being critical of them, most interviewees combined elements of different discourses and so seemed to be entangled within the internal logic that frames the overarching constructivist view of children as active media consumers who choose the programs they view in response to their personal needs and interests.

The "rule," then, has two basic components: First, boys and girls live in entirely different cultural worlds and are interested in very different television contents, genres, and audio-visual appeals. And the corollary rule of thumb, with very important policy and fiscal implications: While girls watch both boys' and girls' programming, boys will not watch programs aimed at the audience of girls. The rationale, degree of detail, and sophistication in approaching this belief varied greatly among interviewees, but it seemed to be most developed in the US where the wide variety of available programs and the competition over the child TV market apparently foster even stronger gender segregation.

Segregated Gendered Tastes

In order to understand interviewees' extension of this axiomatic argument from a global perspective, I have selected a mosaic of voices that share this binary, gendered view of the television world:

From Asia:

Nasing (Malasia): *I think it is very much a segmented audience ... I think boys want to have more action and reality programming. The new trend, though that seems to have captured a wide profile of the audience, from young to old, appeals to both genders. But you didn't see a guy going to a program or a movie that is very emotional, chick flick, they don't like that.*

Jigme (Buthan): *The girls love to watch college movies, teenage movies, where there is a clash over a boy, and parties ...*

From Australia:

Sarah: *There are programs that are very girl-skewed that boys won't watch. I don't think boys will watch this Australian–Canadian coproduction about girls and horses [...] And girls are not interested in packmen and boys' animation, certainly if it is sort of boys' action stuff. I know from my experience of an eleven-year-old who for a period of time liked* The PowerPuff Girls, *but by the time she was nine she was beyond that and she watches very little animation if any. And boys at this age still watch animation.*

From the Middle East:

Jamal (Palestine): *Boys prefer violent programs like* Power Rangers *and girls like* Cinderella. *This is generalizing, but this is the impression.*

Dikla (Israel): *We know that girls stay with us [a pre-school channel] longer than boys ... we feel the pressure on boys, already in kindergarten, to watch more violent programs is such that boys do not feel comfortable admitting that they are watching us because it is not masculine enough ... and since we are a channel that is not willing to introduce aggressive content or competitions with prizes, we are perceived as a channel that is not so attractive to boys ...*

... it is a matter that bothers us a lot and we try to balance it to attract more boys, but motor noises of cars is the most "manly" thing we can purchase ... I look at the line-ups and I just know that I can't put a program about buses

and then a program about mechanics one after the other, because girls won't watch it ... or for example, we are planning a program about dance and movement, but in order for it to attract boys as well, we had to call it Yes, Commander. *So to "cover up" the fact that the main character is a woman, we gave her a militaristic name so we can claim that it is also an active program for boys ... part of it is that it is hard to find good male characters – when women and men come for auditions – they always tend to behave childishly. It is difficult to find a male character that feels comfortable talking to children.*

I admit that when pushed to the wall and I have to make a decision, I usually prefer the option of a boys' program, because we are trying to balance our audience.

When we prepare our line-ups, there are clearly programs that are girls' programs, and others that are boys' programs, but we assume that the girls would want to watch those as well. Even the issue of the colors ... If the general look is more "pastel" or more contrasted, or the general features we don't usually think about ... like active and passive, fast and slow ... the contrasted, fast and active – I associate in my gut feeling with boys, and then the logo, or the opening song, or the promo, will be directed more to boys. One has to make a decision how to attract the audience.

From Europe:

Silvia (Germany): *We try to attract both boys and girls and we have formats that are targeted more to boys than to girls, or more to girls than to boys [...] we know that science is something that attracts the boys more, and sports is generally more attractive to boys than to girls ... but it's not only a question of topic, it's also a question of what the format looks like, the design of the program, and of course, the question of who is hosting it [...].*

It is not only the content but also the way it looks [...] We try to get the boys, but we don't want to lose the girls. So for example, we don't use too much pink and too much girls' stuff in a show. In the boys' programs we have more like metallic look, and quite a different lighting. And the girls – you know girls – they love glitter, they love pink, and orange, and yellow, and more, you know, playful staff. So we have that in mind.

Famke (Netherlands): *We do have a problem getting "cool" boys, because we have the problem that public television is more appreciated and watched by girls than by boys. Nowadays, almost with every format we have a real discussion about how do we attract the boys. So that's the big thing. To attract the boys we always have to have some real physical things in it, and some real competition [...] as soon as it is a cultural program – we have a problem with the boys.*

Mitja (Slovenia): *Everything for girls seems the same – fashionable cloths, interested in boys ... we don't plan it, it is quite spontaneous ...*

From the Americas:

Grazielle (Brazil) *Boys won't watch programs with only female characters.*

José (Cuba) *Girls prefer romantic things, boys more action ... boys more sports [...] going away from the house. Girls more in the house.*

Roberto (Argentina): *I assume that girls are more likely to connect to a male protagonist than a boy will connect to a girl one.*

Beatriz (Ecudaor): *If you place more girls than boys in the program, boys will not be interested in it ... that's one of the reasons that I put an emphasis on a majority of male characters.*

Tina (US): *What we often do is look at the top hundred shows for teen girls and teen boys to see how many of them are the same ... and you look at the top twenty – almost none of them tend to be the same [...] They watch completely different things. Boys still like animation, and moving to more adult-type animation like on Cartoon Network [...] Ours is more drama, but we want to be sure that our channel is not boys-repellent. We don't want to drive them away [...] On Valentine's Day, we did a stunt called Hurt Love, its basic ... the girls love – love; and also it's a whole weekend celebrating love. This year was basically the hunks of the channel, so it's all the hottest boys. It's difficult to have a boy come in and watch that. He is not going to be comfortable in that environment with lots of hearts. It's all really about cute boys and to me that's boy-repellent.*

Kate (US): *... and then I saw more and more, that boys, for whatever reason at the age of four, five, six really wanted very male leads, you know, more and more, action-oriented programming. And girls went just like insipidly sweet and there's this theory in the kids business that boys won't watch girl shows but girls will watch boys' shows. I don't know if it's true or not, you know. I don't know that. But I do know that even at four-and-a-half my son is saying "I don't like to watch that because it's a girl" and "do you have anything with police?" [...] In the boys' programming there's a lot of action adventure, not a lot of plot, a lot of special effects, lots of blowing up, you know, not a lot of deep emotion ... but if you think about the hits, you think about the things that are really engaging kids, I think they're pretty traditional [...]*

Eric (Canada): *Shows for girls ... in the casting of girls more often than boys, the content, the storytelling, the type of story they are telling ... it's more a girly show about love issues, what people think about you, the clothes you are wearing [...] shows about relationships between girls, having friends, and so I prefer that, because I am the kind of producer that targets more girls than boys ... I think the boys with more sensitivities will watch them too, like me ... as a boy I watched these shows ... but then you have the masculine type, the macho type who is into sports and that's about it. Boyish programs are space programs, some types of animated programs with big laughs and vulgar fights, and stuff like that.*

So how can we summarize what the interviewees believe are the tastes of their implied audience, what boys and girls like and dislike around the world? Above all else, the interviewees believe that boys want male lead figures. They like cartoons and stick with them a lot longer than do girls. They are attracted to action/adventure content, sports, and competitions. They shy away from educational/cultural programs that are slow paced, and particularly from anything with a girly touch to it in style and color (e.g. anything pink and glittery). Girls, on the other hand, prefer girl leads, and are attracted to displays of emotions, relationships and romance, and to narratives that are confined to the domestic world. They like princesses and fairies, dancing and music, and are drawn to pink, pastel colors, and all that is "girlish." They outgrow animation at a younger age than boys, and stay longer with educational and public television.

These very traditional observations have been substantiated by the review of theory and research about television fare available to children (presented in Chapter One), as well as by earlier research on children's media world. Indeed, studies have documented that, overall, boys prefer action/adventure and sports genres, while girls prefer human relationships and romance. At the risk of overgeneralizing, scholars have argued that boys' culture is game-dominated, while girls' culture is composed of relationships and communication.[12] At the same time, many interviewees also agreed that both boys and girls are attracted to strong personalities who are engaged in interesting stories. We will return to this premise in greater detail in Chapter Six.

The absence, in the above collage, of quotations from countries with an underdeveloped television industry – most notably from African participants – is neither accidental nor an oversight. African interviewees made it clear that when the selection of programs available to children is restricted, everyone will watch whatever is on and there is hardly any gender segregation. This situation has implications for the age-old question of whether the television industry is indeed catering to existing tastes and desires or whether it is actually creating them by constructing particular types of expectations. It is especially striking to note the inherent contradiction in this situation: Societies with limited resources to produce their own television programs or to purchase them from overseas are for the most part resource-poor societies with indigenous worldviews regarding gender and social equality. Yet their children are the ones who are not (yet?) under tremendous popular-culture pressure to maintain the stereotypical old-fashioned views on gendered childhood. While at the same time, the overwhelming choice of television programs available to children in wealthier societies – those generally concerned with and seeking to advance gender equality – are being driven, to a large degree, to maintain a hegemonic, traditional view of gender as binary and segregated. A feminist political-economy perspective would suggest that this is a fine illustration of the intersection and collaboration of capitalism and patriarchy, as mutual interests build off one another in maintaining the construction of childhood as segregated and thus profitable.[13]

Thus, what was absent in the interviewees' views of gendered tastes was a willingness to question and to discuss the constructed nature of "choice" offered to children and the seemingly independent development of "taste," as has been voiced in the scholarly literature: "We can collaborate with our children in resisting the branding of our imaginations by refusing the most fantastic market-produced myth of all, the myth of choice, that it is we who produce the products the market offers us."[14] This argument claims that what we think of as children's own viewing choices are adults' constructions of what they know, what they have become accustomed to, and not necessarily what they would have chosen under different circumstances. An alternative approach would ask such questions as:

- Would boys be interested in romantic relationships if they were not so heavily construed as "feminine" and did not involve social sanctioning?
- Would they be still so interested in aggressive content if it was not constructed as a "cool" exhibition of masculinity?
- Would girls be interested in science and technology if they did not think it threatens their sense of feminine identity and is unattractive to boys?
- Would they be playing more sports if they did not think competition and physical hardship is "unbecoming" for girls?

These are, of course, difficult questions to tackle for those who assume that none of our gendered behaviors and identities are independent of social life. Yet they are important to bring up in challenging the industry: Whose choices is the ratings system measuring? Would children be making other choices given other available possibilities to choose from that are not gender segregated?

Political Economy Driving Contents

Many interviewees, particularly the North Americans, were cognizant of the economic mechanism behind the logic that "boys will not watch girls' shows, but girls will watch boys' shows." Matt (US) expressed it in this manner: *You know, there's a theory over the years espoused by broadcasters and their advertisers, and what not, and it can be borne out in tests, focus-group tests, etcetera, that boys will watch boy shows and not girl shows, but girls will watch boy shows. Yeah. So therefore if you are gonna target your program at an audience, it's better to target skewed more boys than girls. And from an audience rating and share prospective, which is how television is measured and therefore how advertising is sold ... that theory has a long history of support behind it.*

Similarly, Cindy (US) illustrated the decision-making process at her own station: *I don't know whether it's research or myth that girls will watch boys' programming but boys will not watch girls' programming. So therefore you see a lot more boy programming on TV currently being aired and even within the company, the programs, the properties that are being developed are more strongly boy properties.*

Well, for example, Bob the Builder; *the construction industry is a more male-oriented industry. Bob is the main character so it's a boy lead. We have* Thomas the Tank Engine, *so Thomas of course is a boy's name. He is a boy engine, the narrator is male, there are more male elements within the show, and traditionally I think more boys are more apt to be playing with trains than are girls, although I know that's not exclusive but more traditional probably. We have one show called* Angelina Ballerina *which is based on a series of books, very girly you know, it's a girl mouse who is a ballerina and so it's ballet, it's dance, she's a girl, her best friend is a girl. There are a lot more girls and it is not doing nearly as well. And it sort of reinforces the fact within the company that it's boys' properties that have more potential. Because if you have a show that appeals to boys, but you know girls will watch it too, isn't that better than having a girl property that boys won't watch? So you're serving a larger audience.*

Vicky (Canada) added another angle to the reasons behind the industry's preference for boys, namely the insight that girls "watch up;" that is, they are willing to join an adult audience at a much earlier age than are boys: *In Canada there is gender and diversity awareness, for a long time, behind the camera as well as in front of the camera. These issues are commonplace for public TV. However, there is the assumption that girls still will watch boys' programs and not the other way around. So we are producing more for boys and girls are neglected. There is also the assumption that they [girls] watch adult drama/romance anyway, so there's no need to produce for them.*

While producers transferred responsibility for the situation to higher echelons in the decision-making hierarchy, interviewees holding higher policy positions assigned the main responsibility for this situation to toy and merchandizing industries, as suggested in Hope's (US) analysis: *The general feeling in the US is – and something that we have been working hard to break – if you make a show for boys, the girls will watch it, but if you make a show for girls, the boys won't watch it [...] I find that when kids are little, when presented with a strong interesting character, it doesn't matter what gender it is. Dora, for example, there is an equal number of boys and girls watching the show. But there isn't an equal balance in the toy market, the licensees decided that Dora is a girl product so it is in the girls aisles with the pink ... and you can't battle it because it is so entrenched in America ... because Nick tried to make boy and girl toys, but the stores won't buy them, they don't know where to place them ... I think it is easier to get a mix of kids to watch TV, than it is to deal with the toy market ... boys don't want to wear a T-shirt with a girl on their chest. But girls might wear a boy's, and might be more attracted to it ...*

Chris (US) presented the same argument from a different angle, including how the toy industry may be affecting production choices within a program: *If you have a show that's gonna be a toy line, you're probably gonna have more masculine features in it, like bigger shoulders, slanted to boys ... girls seem to mature quicker, so they aren't as active in animation as they get older, while boys still hold on to it.* Kate (US) provided another illustration of the same argument about the reciprocal relationship between programs and merchandizing in regards to gender portrayals: *I'll tell you something interesting. Their character – Zoe* [a female puppet on *Sesame Street*] *was not selling any books till they put a tutu on her. And, as soon as they put a tutu on her, they started selling books like you can't believe, so now she wears a tutu all the time.* It is important to note that whether this claim is factual and accurate is beside the point. What is significant, however, is the entrenched belief repeated in the interviews that this is indeed the reality of both children's and their parents' tastes.

One can argue endlessly over the nature/nurture debate, as undertaken in academic and public spheres, and discuss the degree to which differing tastes have biological roots, are entirely social constructions, or are a combination of both. However, there is little doubt that in keeping with the capitalist project, children have been targeted (and studied) for consumption directly and aggressively[15] and that in this process they have been constructed as knowing consumers with clear differing tastes that are gendered. In this process, for example, children's programs are often referred to as "program-length commercials." Such actions reinforce the codependency of the television, toy, and merchandizing industries, all of which continue to dwell on gender differences, play them up, and push them to the extreme as they carve out unparalleled audience segments for profit.

The degree to which much television programming is made compatible with commercial considerations that are linked to licensed merchandizing for children has been extensively studied and documented. From these studies we learn that, for example, the industry prefers programs with "toyetic" qualities (such as culturally neutral animated characters that can be sold around the world; teams of characters that generate "collectability;" backgrounds and props that can be marketed as playsets and toys; online applications that will increase brand loyalty; educational value that will appeal to parents, etc.).[16] However, such toyetic qualities do not necessarily have to be negative, as children may engage positively and creatively with television programs, beyond the viewing situations, in ways that can benefit their development. This having been noted, we cannot deny that the toy industry is one of the most significant players in the perpetuation of gender segregation of childhood, as toymakers exploit children's quest for gender identity by exaggerating and intensifying it.[17] Different packaging and different store aisles cultivate the impression that certain toys are only appropriate for boys and others only for girls, just like television programs. Boys are steered towards toys involving traditional masculine traits: action, machinery, weapons, construction, so that their play is designed to be exciting and adventurous. Girls, on the other hand, are directed towards traditional feminine interests such as caregiving and beautification activities with dolls, household toys, and fashion and decoration products.[18] Furthermore, as many of the interviewees argued, while boys may watch some of the girl-skewed programming, such as *Dora the Explorer* in their pre-school years or *High School Musical* in their tweens, they will not touch any related licensed product since they are perceived to be "girly."

The case of *Dora the Explorer* provides an eye-opening illustration of how the toy industry drives gender stereotyping to its extreme, much more than television programs themselves. As these lines were being written, a petition was circulating on the Internet against Nickelodeon and Mattel's plans to "makeover" Dora into a sexualized tween. It is worth quoting the full petition in order to appreciate all of the arguments employed:

> Don't give Dora a tween makeover. She is beloved by little girls and boys everywhere for her adventuresome spirit, curiosity, and bravery. If she is to grow up in doll form, please keep her true to herself rather than follow in the footsteps of the makers of *Strawberry Shortcake*, *Holly Hobby*, and *Trollz*. We don't need any more tween dolls teaching girls that growing up means turning into a fashionista, excited about secrets and crushes and going shopping. We don't need dolls that replicate the thin ideal. The APA Sexualization of Girls Task Force report shows that teens only rarely achieve this body type and when they don't they are vulnerable to depression and body image problems. Please don't push this version of what it means to be a teenager on young girls. It limits them, narrows their options, and leads them to think that what matters most about themselves is how they look and what they buy.
>
> If the Dora we knew grew up, she wouldn't be a fashion icon or a shopaholic. She'd develop her map reading skills and imagine the places she could go. She'd capitalize on those problem-solving skills to design new ways to bring fresh water to communities in need around the world. Maybe she'd become a world-class runner or follow her love of animals and become a wildlife preservationist or biologist. We'll never know because the only way a girl can grow up in tween town, is to narrow that symphony of choices to one note. It's such a sell out of Dora, of all girls.
>
> There are already too many dolls out there that limit the potential of girls. We ask you to reconsider your Dora makeover. We have a team of experts (including girls!) ready to help you re-design her to be a teen doll that parents will be pleased to bring home to their daughters, one with stories to tell, places to go, equipment to use, and knowledge to pass on. Don't underestimate parents of girls and girls themselves. Dora can be a new kind of teen doll and you can make it happen. Either "Let GO" of Dora and let her live on as her wonderful self, or create a pre-teen doll that is true to who she was as a child![19]

A follow-up update on the petition website (June 2009) suggested that by the time Mattel/Nickelodeon received 13,000 signatures a month later, "they started assuring parents that Dora would stay her feisty, environmentally aware self." While the outcome of this process has yet to be determined at the time these lines are being written, the initial impact of this grass-roots initiative demonstrates the potential power for social change of speaking to corporate powers through consumer pressure that builds on critical awareness.

Pressure on children to conform to normative gender stereotypes may be driven by an American toy industry that is itself tilted in favor of boys, according to some of the executives who spoke at the Los Angeles workshop. This well-calculated stance is due to market findings that boys play with toys longer than girls; the more expensive toys, such as electronic ones, are purchased for them; and there are hardly any toys for boys that are not media driven. Some suggested that boys buy more toys and their play follows television narratives more closely due to the fact that boys' programs are action-packed and thus lend themselves to imitation of action. Girls' programs, on the other hand, are more about inner psychological states and relationships, thus inspiring more creative play that is not bound by the specificities of imitating an action plot. As one presenter stated: *Most of the shows are driven by the economics of toys. That's the explanation for the gender imbalance on TV. Boys need more guidance in terms of play patterns; they need more stories delivered in TV and ads, especially three years old, while girls make up more their own stories of the figures. Girls are telling stories on their own, so a lot of the toy companies were selling toys for girls without TV shows, while TV shows were driving the selling for boys, so that's how it started. If the goal is to sell and at the same time have rating, than you want programming with boys because girls will also watch boys' programs, and they need less pushing of merchandizing.*

Thus, in summary, a number of factors are cited as the rationale for prioritizing boys' programs: girls will watch them too, so it is a better investment in terms of drawing a larger audience; the toy and merchandizing industries drive production since they claim that their products thrive better on boys' program tie-ins than on girls' programming; and girls abandon the child market at a younger age. As Laura (US) put it bluntly in her critique of the situation: *I am basically protesting the fact that everyone had sort of dropped the ball for girls, and then complained that girls stopped watching cartoons by age eight. And it's like, well, you know, you spend three years showing them where the door is, and then you get surprised that they take the exit!*

And one final comment in regard to the seeming contradiction between the prioritization of the boy audience and the theme of the "neglected boys" discussed in Chapter Three. How can boys be neglected if they are the target audience for the vast majority of content produced for kids? The answer lies in the difference between the amount (quantity of boy-centered programs) and the nature of the portrayal (quality of the portrayals): While some producers argue for an economic imperative that will justify providing more programming for boys than for girls, they neither offer nor make a claim that the narrow range of narratives and characters be altered. This is an issue to which we will return in Chapter Six.

Gendered Channels

The competition between television networks over the share of the children's market drives them to differentiate themselves from one another and to create brand identity and loyalty,[20] characterized, among other markers, by a specific gender appeal. And their global success suggests that they have succeeded in maximizing their appeal worldwide. While they seek to erase cultural traces as much as possible in order to create a common cultural denominator, such a process is apparently not needed in regard to gender differences, as they have been retained in a universal manner in order to attract all young audiences. The transparent motivation and operating mechanisms by which this is achieved were shared by some of the interviewees from North America, who are part of the system. They offered a kind of insider perspective based on first-hand experience with the workings of this self-regulated gender segregation, and thus served as very valuable informants.

One clear outcome of the analysis of these interviews was a mapping of the major players in children's television, with a clear distinction between educational television, in general, and commercial production houses. In regard to the latter, the Disney Channel is "girls oriented," while Cartoon Network, Fox Kids, Warner Brothers, and Jetix are "boys oriented." The fact that public television has been gradually losing the boy audience to commercial television due to its longstanding concern with more educationally oriented television that is aggression-free has resulted in a "twist" in this gender division as it is now actively investing in attracting boys. The following quotations demonstrate interviewees' mapping of the field: Kate (US) stated that *there are so many channels for kids […] and the audience is so fragmented […] and networks themselves have become so targeted so that Disney knows their audience is girls, and Jetix is for boys, and Cartoon Network for boys … so a little boy, like mine, isn't gonna turn on the Disney channel and watch it, as he could watch Jetix that is dealing with stuff just for boys […] As you get older and older you watch less and less together […] the older they get the less they have in common […].*

Matt's (US) long, detailed analysis of the TV industry is worth quoting at length due to the insights he shared: *It's been very interesting over the last six years to observe Nickelodeon being very dominant, and its audience very balanced between boys and girls. Their series are largely comedies, and there is almost no action/adventure. They have reemphasized animation and have less live-action dramas or comedies on their air. And they control probably 60–65 percent of all children's advertising dollars spent in the United States. Their two competitors, if you can call them that, because they're so far behind in popularity, are the Disney Channel, and the Cartoon Network. And the Disney Channel as a brand itself has historically been extremely, extremely powerful among girls, young girls. Whether it's* Mickey Mouse, Winnie the Pooh, *or you know, their greatest hits, you know,* The Little Mermaid ... *and the princess collections from the* Snow White, *and* Cinderella ... *Disney has long been directly associated with girls, and without girls the Disney empire is not an empire. Cartoon Network is on the other side,* Warner Brothers *and* Hanna Barbara, *those two have almost no girl shows in them. They consist of everything from* Bugs Bunny *to* Scooby Doo, Daffy Duck, *and* The Smurfs ... *And their boys' shows range from comedies to boys' hard-core action/adventure programs. And there you have it, the triangle. Nickelodeon, balanced boys/girls at the top, Disney Channel leaning far more towards girls than boys, Cartoon Network leaning more towards boys.*

Overall, there was general agreement among the interviewees, particularly those residing in the US, regarding the gender composition of the television audience and the fact that it is a result of a broadcasting strategy. A striking and very interesting exception to this finding is the industry leader, Nickelodeon, which while it was originally a somewhat gender-neutral channel has been involved in extensive gender experimentation. While it retains a more balanced approach in its programming than any of the other major networks, the analysis revealed that interviewees perceive it to be skewed towards girls.

An insightful view of the evolution of "gender brand identity" was shared by Lori (US): *Girls really, really like live-action dramas where there's a lot of dealing with relationships and, you know, because it's the thing they're struggling with in their lives, and they like to see it worked through on television. And our experience is that boys are much more attracted to sports programming and animation, they have a much higher toleration for violence ... The one thing that we found kind of cuts across both genders is comedy. So, you know, when we first realized we were just getting girls, we said "Well how can we get our boys back?" and, you know, we tried to look at comedies, we tried to look at things that could bridge the gap. And, then, we just realized, no one, no one, is really serving just girls so why not play to our strength? And so, we,* The N [21] *is a network for girls, now. We don't wanna alienate boys but we, we wanna, continue to attract girls.*

While gender characterization of the main global corporations was not a major concern in the interviews with producers outside the US, several were well aware of this aspect of corporate gender branding, as stated by Elaine (Brazil): *So, for example, if you see Fox Kids, it used to be much more for boys, having boy characters, much more the kind of animation ... I don't want to say that it is violent animation, but it is action animation, most of the Japanese animation, and the manga, is for boys. For girls in some way you have also adventure but it is somehow ... for example, the Disney Channel at that time was mostly girls, because for some way the stories and the action of the stories is not so speedy ... maybe it is a little bit stereotyped ... and even with Nickelodeon, we were always comparing* [ourselves] *to them as our competition, they used to have more shows for girls. An animation with a group of girls who are running together, dealing with the boys, or with their problems, this is something that maybe doesn't appeal to boys.*

The dynamics of the television industry in the US and the economic constraints within which they operate contribute to television's gender segregation worldwide in more than one way. For example, they continue to promote a worldview where boys and girls are encouraged to inhabit different electronic and cultural spaces. They do so through the contents offered as well as by serving as a model for younger, resource-poor television industries. Furthermore, even the exceptional transgressive border crossings, particularly by boys into girlish territories (e.g. a boy walking in the "pink aisles" in a toy store or enjoying a "chick flick") may be heavily stigmatized and sanctioned. Similar concerns can also be raised regarding other forms of audience fragmentation, particularly along race and sexuality lines (e.g. African-American programs, Hispanic programs, gay programs) and their intersection with gender identities in contributing to the identity project of individuals in this era of late modernity.

Turning the Tide?

A few interviewees observed that these trends are gradually shifting. Sally (US) discussed growing awareness at Nickelodeon and efforts to address the issue of channel segregation: *If we play up the action and adventure, we might attract the boys more. I'm not saying that girls are not interested in it, but obviously the promos where it's very prominent are aimed at boys, but we still hold on to the girls ... and our princess stories aren't typical princess stories. We do have Dora as a princess, but she's very active, adventurous, and she's the one who saves the day as the princess. But that still is more appealing to the girls. I mean, boys are watching it, but it still draws in more girls. It's very close, we're talking about not major numbers, but enough for us to talk about it and discuss and strategize.*

And, continuing on with Matt's extensive monologue quoted earlier about Cartoon Network and Disney Channel trying to compete with Nickelodeon's supremacy with the children's market, Matt (US) explained in detail: *But both second-place networks don't wanna be second place anymore. So they're both making aggressive pushes to try and have a more balanced schedule. What does this mean for each of them? Cartoon Network needs more girls. First thing they did is they dropped the Cartoon Network logo [...] What has been proven in this country and around the world is that when girls get older, they don't want to watch cartoons, in fact they are much more interested in live-action programs. So Cartoon Network, the name can potentially carry with it some baggage, so they've created CN as their name [...] As far as the programs are concerned, they're doing far more comedies, far less hard-core boys' action; they're putting far more programs on the air with girl leads, inspirational characters, as well. And they're starting a pre-school channel which is more gender neutral, if you will. Not a channel but a segment on their channel is gonna be dedicated to pre-scholars to try and introduce them to the Cartoon Network concept.*

What does it mean to the Disney Channel? A boy show for the Disney Channel means more comedy, more animation, less live action and, and putting some more boy-led live action dramas on the air [...] it is less social, and less about social communication and more about physical communication [...] You know, it is a complicated answer, because all genres can be attractive to boys and girls ... it's about the show. SpongeBob SquarePants *appeals to both boys and girls,* Rugrats *appeals to boys and girls,* Hey Arnold *appeals to boys and girls ... you can go down that Nickelodeon line-up and point to every single show on that network as having a very strong boy–girl appeal.*

Clearly, some of the strategies detailed by Matt are content changes – selecting lead characters from both genders, diversifying the genres of programs and the narrative styles. Others are packaging and marketing strategies that involve changing Cartoon Network's logo to CN, playing down the "cartoon" aspect, or developing a pre-school line-up to develop early brand loyalty. Matt concluded by pointing out that it is indeed possible to offer programming that attracts both genders and still be (or perhaps even – as a result of it – be) the number one player in children's television. Indeed, evidence supporting Matt's claim came from news about Disney's efforts to attract 6–14-year-old boy viewers to the new Disney XD cable channel and website.[22] One scholar reflected on these initiatives in a particularly vivid manner: "As part of such efforts, Disney has enlisted the help of educators, anthropologists, and a former researcher with 'a background in the casino industry' to not only study all aspects of the culture and intimate lives of young boys, but to do so in a way that allows Disney to produce 'emotional hooks' that lure young boys into the wonderful world of corporate Disney in order to turn them into enthusiastic consumers."[23] Expanding the audience to include boys is clearly understood as a marketing strategy that is not aimed at blurring gender segregation or erasing stereotypes; rather, on the contrary, it is geared to offering a clearly defined "boys' world" – an X Disney – in addition to the existing girls' one.

Concluding Notes

The ways in which producers perceive and construct their young audiences as largely inhabiting two very different gendered cultural worlds draw heavily on developmental theories and existing evidence. Research suggests that the tendency for children to segregate themselves by gender and play more compatibly with same-sex partners is already evident in early childhood, around the third year, and it progressively strengthens by middle childhood. While boys and girls are intensely conscious of each other as future partners and spend a larger proportion of their time as they grow up in trying to satisfy their curiosity about the other group, they experience tremendous social pressure to remain separate during childhood. The causes and consequences of this segregation are a major topic of investigation in child psychology and education, and lie beyond the scope of our discussion here.[24] Suffice to say that gender-segregated childhoods provide different contexts for social development for children, which do not necessarily prepare them for mutual understanding and collaboration. This segregation runs parallel to the current popularity of the "Mars and Venus" metaphor,[25] according to which men and women are perceived as essentially different beings with opposing communication styles and emotional needs. This difference has been pinpointed as the main cause of problems between the sexes, suggesting that it may be resolved once we acknowledge it and learn to communicate properly. This perspective has recruited to its service key elements of the post-feminist sensibility, best represented by the slogan "different but equal." Some observers have suggested that this is a reassertion of sexual difference represented by the shift from a liberal feminist focus on "equality" to a third-wave feminism focus on "difference."[26]

Television and toy industries seem to be capitalizing quite successfully on this popular trend, pushing it to its extremes in their pursuit of ever-expanding markets and profits. It appears that their view of their "implied audiences" is based on their interpretations of findings aimed at identifying children's tastes, desires, and pleasures, as mechanisms serving these industries' goals. The dominance of such thinking is evident in the fact that none of the most well-intended and critical interviewees employed a competitive perspective; one that either is or has the potential to compete with or even cast doubts on the roots of the industry's "truisms" about what boys and girls will watch and the toys with which they will play.

Missing in interviewees' observations as well as in scholarly critiques is a clearer articulation of the mechanisms underlying and driving gender differences. Earlier research on the gendered nature of media consumption by children and youths has demonstrated that, overall, girls do develop an interest in traditional masculine genres whereas, on the whole, boys continue to show no interest in female ones.[27] While this descriptive evidence does provide empirical support for the popular axiom applied by children's entertainment industry and media professionals, we lack a critical analysis that is the result of unpacking and identifying the mechanisms creating this phenomenon. For example, according to the feminist analysis of social change, this process can be partly explained through the observation that girls as well as women, more generally, have learned to gradually incorporate typical male perspectives and values into their lives while not abandoning their traditional female responsibilities and interests. This echoes other situations where efforts at improving status and position are advanced through the process of subordinated social groups adjusting "up" socially. Perhaps the trend of girls' interest in boys' genres represents their growing sensitivity to the advantageous position that boys hold in our society and the higher value associated with their tastes and interests.

And, in all the extensive discussion by media professionals and scholars of girls' and boys' differing tastes, no one seems to be addressing the moral issue: Because something "works" (i.e. is profitable) does not necessarily mean that it is "right" or "just" (i.e. socially moral and good for boys and girls).

In applying questions raised in the field of critical audience studies, where the focus is on making the child audience visible, we can raise a host of questions presently absent, as well, in producers' global discourse: Does the contemporary television-(land)scape "permit them the opportunity to adjudicate on whether their [children's] rights (cultural recognition, freedom of expression, freedom from harm, plurality of view, privacy, freedom from commercial exploitation) are being met? If they can participate, is this as members of civil society or, more minimally, as complaining consumers?"[28] Challenging the construct of "the child audience" as developed by the TV industry seems to be the first step in changing the existing discourse and opening it up for debate.

An oversimplified political-economy model suggests that television as a business works according to three principles: "Keep the audience up," "keep the costs down," and "keep the regulators out." In considering how decisions are made in the children's entertainment world, a fourth principle has been added to the mix: "find someone else to pay the bills" – in this case, the toy industry.[29] Support for this fourth principle was strong and clear in my interviews, as the view held was that there is an intensifying role played by media corporations and the toy industry that is achieved through a deep reworking of children's culture into a completely segregated world. Segregation in of itself sends the message that gender differences are fundamental and non-reconcilable – a message that many scholars, media professionals, and parents dispute and argue is dangerous as well as false, as it continues to perpetuate stereotypes about gender and threatens equal opportunities. This ideology is being transported worldwide, above and beyond any specific cultural varieties of gender inequality, through the expansion of the television and toy industries into international markets, driven by their insatiable desire for exponential profits.

In summary, as I have argued elsewhere: "For huge entertainment corporations, children are not future citizens but first and foremost they are consumers. From such a point of view childhood is not a distinct period in the life cycle, one that should be attended to with compassion and responsibility. On the contrary, it is a distinct market opportunity."[30] According to the interviewees in this study, the development of a healthy gender identity that serves the wellbeing and needs of maturing boys and girls and, as well, promotes their mutual understanding and collaboration seems to be lacking in much of the strategizing going on in the leading television and toy industries.

The fact that the workplace in the field of children and television is heavily dominated by women, worldwide, does not seem to have made a major difference in the field – yet. There are many reasons for this: A lack of critical engagement with these issues; marginal presence in positions of policy and power; the influence of the professional socializing press; and/or processes of buying into the market game. Whatever the reason or mechanisms involved, progressive change in the television industry that works for the benefit of children's wellbeing and health is negligible, while preservative interventions that work to retain gender segregation advance rapidly and are driven primarily by profit motives. The evidence from this study alone suggests that there are many media professionals involved in the field of children's television production – women as well as men – guided by critical awareness, gender and cultural sensitivity, commitment to social change, and deep concern for children's wellbeing – who are attempting to advance a very different vision of gender and gender relations. We turn now to the guiding principles they employ in their unique efforts to break away from the existing television culture.

Chapter 6

Gender Representations in Children's Television

Eight Working Principles for Change

What have we learned from hearing the voices of so many professionals around the world devoted to producing better television for children? How do we make sense of close to two thousand pages of interview transcripts regarding their guiding values and recommendations for translating them into action? Can we recognize a forest among these many and diverse trees? Is there a bottom line to this inquiry?

The aim of this chapter is to provide a conceptual framework for producing better gender portrayals on television for children around the world. To do so, eight grounded main principles are presented that are at the heart of what the media professionals interviewed shared with me. While the concept of "principle" is commonly used in a variety of ways (e.g. as a statement of a basic truth, law or assumption; as a rule or standard; as a fixed policy or mode of action; as a basic or essential quality), I am using it here as an ideal, a vision to be achieved, and through which prescriptive statements for action by producers seeking to "repair" the world are derived (remember the Hebrew expression "Tikkun Olam" from the Preface). Accordingly, the details to be presented are framed as "working" principles that can serve as strategies for production practice and recommendations for advancing concrete change on television screens viewed by children and youths throughout the world.

The principles shared involve the following core concepts: Equality, diversity, complexity, similarity, unity, family, authenticity, and voicing. Indeed, concern for these principles seemed to be shared by many interviewees – despite differences in cultural and geographical location, gender, education, conditions of employment, professional expertise – and thus can be claimed to be universal in large degree. However, clearly, the interpretation of how the principles presented could, or should, be translated into media productions, as well as their social implications, vary culturally. For example, while most interviewees agreed that presenting children in television programs in the context of a nurturing family is a key to healthy development, they disagreed about what family structures might be appropriate for their culture: While some might celebrate single parents or mixed-race families, others may denounce same-sex parents and/or promote the extended three-generation family. Similarly, while all interviewees agreed that presenting racial diversity is a key to fostering a more humane, just social world, they had different ideas about what kind of diversity is relevant – and tolerable – in their own context. The same argument can be made in regard to each of the concepts. Indeed, at their core, each of them is open for critical debate. For example, not all interviewees would agree that "authenticity" is an ideal concept that lends itself to a desirable working principle; that "similarities" between the genders should be emphasized; or that "unity" is desirable or even achievable. This having been noted, when most interviewees referred to each of these conceptual ideals they did so with the intent, I submit, of stating that these are issues that concern them and are part of their decision-making process in conceptualizing and executing a programmatic idea for children's TV whose general vision remains within the general goal of engaging young viewers in a humane, just world.

As in any conceptual scheme, some of the boundaries between the principles are blurred occasionally, particularly when considering specific quotations that engage more than one category at a time. However, the purposes of this analytical summary are to highlight the main principles, without oversimplification, and to share some of the concrete strategies suggested by interviewees to progress toward greater realization of these ideals. Furthermore, there is no intention to suggest that these conceptual domains can be dissected independently of one another. For example, the issue of diversity calls for the presentation of diverse characters in terms of race and ethnicity as well as the need, first, for varied characters within each group; and, second, for a clearly integrated sense of authenticity presented by a program, such that all are, of course, closely intertwined with the goal of promoting gender equality, and so forth. Finally, the order of presentation of the working principles is not hierarchal and does not follow a self-evident inner logic, but rather the order is a matter of personal choice and convenience of style. And, with these provisos in mind, we turn to presentation and discussion of each of the eight principles for change in children's television, grounded in this study.

Equality

Equality is advanced when boys and girls are treated equally as well as offered equal roles and opportunities on television, all the while recognizing and respecting their differences.

The central, underlying assumption driving interviewees' observations was the need for gender equality in programming for children. While interpretation of what exactly "equality" means in different contexts varied significantly, as noted in Chapter Three, the value itself was never challenged, overtly or saliently. More specifically, in line with the spirit of the UN Convention on the Rights of the Child (November 20, 1989), interviewees seemed to hold the view that boys and girls should have equal rights, equal opportunities, and equal responsibilities; and that both genders should be given the same care and nourishment to promote their wellbeing and materialize their potentials, to live a dignified life of self-worth and fulfillment, and to become productive participants in their families and communities.

Head Counting

"Head counting" functions as the basic prerequisite of any discussion of equality in the interviewees' action perspective. According to the most salient view, males and females need to be on the screen in equal numbers, because their presence symbolizes the need for their actual, real presence on equal terms. Clearly some narratives lend themselves to one gender more than the other, and this golden rule of equal numbers was not suggested as a strict guideline for each and every episode or program. Rather, the "look" of the line-up of programming of a given station is expected to achieve basic numerical equality.

The most obvious active implementation of this value is for there to be equal numbers of males and females on the screen, in all manner of presentation and in the types of characters: boys and girls and men and women in fiction and non-fiction formats; as protagonists and antagonists of narratives, hosts of programs, celebrities, public figures, and news presenters; as background children in the school bus or on the benches in the stadium; speaking in voiceovers, promos, and opening-credit scenes; as front-stage or background animated animals in the forest, fish in the sea, aliens in outer space, or robots in underground factories.

For some participants, numbers were the only criteria of equality applied, as it seemed that they were still coming to terms with the concept of gender and with a basic liberal perspective on social inequalities. But clearly, equality is not reduced to the *quantity* of characters on television, but rather is about *quality* and contexts, as we have discussed in Chapter One. Accordingly, we can ask: What are the personality characteristics, roles, behaviors and appearances assigned to each gender? Who gets to say the "good" lines in the program? Who gets to have the better storylines? These were among the questions that many interviewees raised.

Role Reversal

For many interviewees, gender equality meant allowing both boys and girls to own the same personality characteristics, to occupy the same roles and professions, to have the same position in the story. More specifically, interviewees talked about "role reversal" where roles traditionally associated with one gender are portrayed by the other one: Boys aspiring to be ballet dancers, hospital nurses, or teachers and girls aspiring to be bus drivers, boxers, or

Figure 6.1 Boxing Beauty © Israeli Broadcasting Authority (IBA) and EBU

scientists; boys engaged in sewing, cooking, and taking care of young siblings while girls play sports, lead a group, and operate technology. For example, several interviewees brought up *Boxing Beauty* (see Figure 6.1), an Israeli program about a girl boxer who combines this unconventional sports interest with a traditional feminine interest in beauty. Amer (Jordan) wanted to present *women as doctors, lawyers, pilots, teachers, famous people.* Jamal (Palestine) suggested an affirmative action towards gender equality, since change, according to him, *doesn't happen on its own. We try not to be balanced, because it is an unfair situation in the first place. We try to enhance the other side, so we have more girl heroes than boys, purposefully. The situation in our society is that it is mainly a father society, where fathers control, so as educational TV we try to enhance and influence the role of women in the society. We started three years ago. We produced six films about gender role models, not necessarily only women, but also men supporting women. We try to show that women can do as much as any successful man, women can be political leaders, good managers; women can play an important role in any aspect of our lives.*

Strategies for role reversal can be both explicit and/or implicit, as Caroline (US) explained: *I think what they're trying to do is build implicit messages as well as explicit messages. So sometimes the characters are engaged in segments where they are actually describing what girls can do: "When I grow up I wanna be a lawyer, I wanna be a doctor, I wanna be whatever." Sometimes the messages are much more implicit. You might see a live-action film where there is a girl who is doing something that many people wouldn't assume a girl would do, like learning a particular skill that boys are usually more akin to. Or you might see a role reversal where there is a father who is participating in house chores, but the segment is not about that at all, that's just happening kind of in the background, so that's seen as both an implicit and explicit ways.*

Similarly, Karolina (Sweden) suggested: *If you make a good drama series, see to it that it is not only about what people say but what they actually do. Like you have a scene of washing the dishes, let the father do it, don't make an issue out of it, he is in the background and doing it. Or going to the nursery to pick up little sister, let the man do it. You can't make it look too obvious, you have to be smart about it, be very careful.*

The idea that professions, roles, and duties are not gender specific was echoed by many interviewees. Boys and girls should be able to engage in any activity and role they wish to on and off the screen (e.g. playing sports, developing hobbies, initiating projects, engaging in social activities); take similar responsibilities (e.g. household chores; assisting their parents; volunteering in their schools and communities); and grow up to be whatever they wish to be (e.g. all professions open to both). For example, Lori (US) discussed breaking traditional stereotypes: *We like to present the entire palate of types of people. We try very, very hard not to do stereotypical portrayals of kids of either gender. We avoid the bully, and the cute girl, and the cheerleader which are types that you see a lot in American television.* Similarly, Karoline (Sweden) said: *I would like to show girls that take responsibility for their own lives, not only relying on somebody else; girls being more active; but I would also like to show boys in more emotional situations, because boys are as emotional as girls but they are not allowed to show it.*

One comment repeated by many was the desire to be able to show girls in leadership roles and boys in nurturing ones. Leona (Philippines), for example, said: *[...] depicting boys and girls free to be who they are, making the presence of fathers and other men in the lives of children more visible in the show, being careful to cast characters and create stories that show the diversity of roles of men and women and girls and boys, that emphasize relationships of equals. We have storylines that would challenge stereotypes, for example, of what girls can and cannot do, or of boys being suppressed in expressing their emotions.* Caroline (US) introduced change in masculine roles as well: *We have a number of segments that feature boys in roles that might counter people's traditional thinking; boys helping with chores around the house, cooking, that kind of thing, but doing it just as part of their everyday activities.*

The desire to see more images of boys reflecting on their inner world and expressing emotions surfaced as a central theme for interviewees from diverse backgrounds, but particularly those concerned with the "neglected boys" theme described in Chapter Three. Lori (US), for example, elaborated on this issue: *[...] we wanna try and find a way to represent the inner life of boys a little better than I think is generally shown. You know, boys don't talk about how they feel, about things; they don't work through their problems out loud on television and often in life. So we're trying to figure out how to do that and still have a realistic portrayal of boys, you know, particularly boys in puberty [...] they don't have any kind of outlet. That's one of the things that we're learning about gender differences is that girls talk about their feelings with each other and they work things through with each other, and boys just don't have those outlets, they don't, that's not how they talk to each other. So I think that identity issues are even more pronounced for them because they don't have an outlet and so I would love to find a way to portray boy characters as thoughtful and sensitive and struggling without them being seen as soft; because I think that we still are hampered by those kind of things, you know, whether it's machismo, or homophobia. I don't know what it is, but I know that boys in our audience respond to characters who are very boy or manly or whatever, so finding a way to portray characters who talk about how they feel in a boy way, so that boys can see that there are safe places, that there's a safe way to work through their issues and still be able to have credible characters.*

Lori is very much aware of the difficulty of introducing such change as it challenges deeply ingrained gender perceptions that threaten her own audience's self-image, yet she is quite clear that it is a much needed prerequisite for any vision of gender equality on and off the screen. This vision includes the ability to present the entire range of emotions in both boys and girls without being restricted by social expectations that boys conceal their vulnerability and girls control their inner energies. Both cry when in pain and are sad in distress; both yell with excitement and express anger and rage; both display frustration and disappointment. It is not through the expression of emotion itself that the character is being evaluated as being a "strong" one (rather than a masculine or a feminine one), but through the way they choose to handle these emotions and channel them into reflection, behavior, and self-growth. Therefore, on the one hand, equality for boys meant, for interviewees, allowing them to express themselves and to display nurturing and caring qualities. On the other hand, equality for girls meant developing characters who are smart, independent, and assertive, who are allowed to be humorous and strong. Above all, producers want to see boys who have given up on aggression being their focal driving force; and girls who have given up on sexual flirtations as their perceived strength. They wanted to see boys and girls who empower themselves in other, more constructive and diverse ways.

Different presentations of characters were discussed in relation to their being deeply integrated into the kind of narratives they can drive. For example, freeing boys from the concept of relationships created in action and physical interaction (e.g. fights, sports) and freeing girls from relationships bound only by talk (some of it quite socially aggressive) allows exploration of different storylines that move away from traditional competitive action/adventure for boys and girls' involvement in romantic crush storylines. In regard to girls,

Abby (US), for example, stated: *I think that a girl's life needs to be a bit more about learning and a bit less about how you look and cosmetics and being thin, and all these issues that we deal with.* Caroline (US) addressed the concern for the wellbeing of boys in the pursuit of gender equity: *[...] what we're really trying to do is look at it in terms of both boys and girls, and in some ways they are seen as having different needs ... one element is to help boys understand girls' empowerment but also speak to boys who in some cultures are, increasingly, having problems.*

But aspiration for equality does not mean implementation at any price, certainly not at the expense of the quality of programming, as Meghan (Canada) noted: *When there's a tie it should go to the under-represented group. It should go to the woman. It should go to the multicultural. But when the dominant group has clearly the better stories, then I think those are the stories that should be told. I don't believe in artificially promoting when it's not nearly as good, but when it's close I give a nod to the under-represented.* Her position, also expressed by other interviewees, seems to be the proverbial – a society is perceived to be as strong as its weakest segments; and equality means, above all, caring for the disadvantaged and discriminated.

Different but Equal

Parallel to the discourse about equality was an occasional echo of the third-wave feminist slogan "different but equal," suggesting the legitimacy of presenting gender differences under the same umbrella of equality vision. The need to accept and respect gender differences and to give them a voice on children's television was expressed, for example, by Silvia (Germany): *[...] and I think you should accept that there are boys' topics and girls' topics, and you should care for what is interesting to boys and what are their needs and not think that you have to make them all the same, boys and girls, because they are not the same. They are physically different, and mentally also. You have to be aware of that I think. There are some programs that are quite attractive to boys and to girls, such as quiz and game shows. But there are other programs like special sports programs that are more attractive to boys and you have to accept that.* Similarly, Abby (US) stated: *The key to me is that there needs to be respect for differences because I believe that there are differences;* and Grazille (Brazil) reinforced: *[...] it is very important to be equal, but it is also very important to respect differences. There is no one way, just the same opportunities for both sexes.*

Recognizing the possibility of the intertwining of nature and nurture was a corollary to this theme that emerged often, as expressed in the following quotation from Leona (Philippines): *I'd like characters to be fit to be themselves, that they can transcend stereotypical expectations about boys being hard and macho and being dominant and not being concerned with nurturing. But, also, girls do not have to give up the nurturing role because there is a case to be made for biology also within us and the interaction with culture, and enabling children to explore the full range of the roles they wish to play. So, OK, I want to be a mother. But, it doesn't mean it has to be at the expense of wanting to be a policewoman. And there are also enough role models in our society. Or, if I want to be successful in my career, it doesn't mean I can't be a father too. So, boys* [can be] *fathers and whatever they want to be, and girls* [can be] *fieldworkers and individuals ... for me that's the idea ... It is just creating the space on children's TV that those things are talked about, making them part of the discourse, rather than before,* [when] *you just take ... for granted that girls are girls and they are meant to grow up, look pretty and be good mothers and good wives.*

However, recognizing gender differences seemed to raise more concern for boys' wellbeing, as it seems that they were perceived to have a much narrower range of legitimate possibilities for "manhood." Silvia (Germany), for example, expressed the dilemma she faced in this regard: *... this is difficult because, on one hand, I think that it is important to boys that they see role models that tell them it is good the way you are. It is good to be a boy; it is good if you love fighting, for example, it's good. And on the other hand you should have role models that show boys how they can get along in society by being not just very aggressive. For example, you have fathers that go on maternity leave, you know. They don't have to be softies ... for them it is something perfectly normal to cook dinner, for example.*

The means for recognizing the need to legitimize difference without taking away from a claim for equality was often expressed by suggesting that new competencies could be added without necessarily retracting existing ones. Kasper (Denmark) referred to this strategy: *Instead of putting boys' programs on the ground and stepping all over them, I think we need to show more complicated versions: Not only boys playing football, but also boys talking; boys who take care of their siblings; boys that are scared. It's OK to be scared. We should show that.* Another example related to the belief that since boys prefer action over reflection, it is important to offer them strong hero characters who are active and virile, yet not necessarily equating action with violence and aggression.

Stripping boys of their need for action and offering them only hyper-reflective gentle and emotional heroes may not serve as an authentic surrogate for their need for positive role models.[1] Currently, boys lack a positive vision of masculinity to which to orient themselves that respects their physicality and need for action, but is not violent and destructive. While it is permissible for girls to express difficulties, to be vulnerable and weak, and to seek help, there is no parallel leverage for boys. Socialization into hegemonic forms of masculinity emphasizes restraint, strength, and fearlessness, and rejects emotions perceived as feminine such as fear, weakness, tenderness, and softness. Deviation from these norms is mostly prohibited,socially as well as psychologically, as any departure is seen to be threatening to masculine identity and may result in a degrading homophobic framing.[2]

Kasper (Denmark) expressed his view of accepting gender differences while realizing they are not that central after all: *I would like to have it in such a way that it is all right to be different ... but I also would like them to know that they are not THAT different, it is not like they are from Mars or Venus as they say. I would like to show that girls can be strong and boys can be weak, that girls can take care of themselves and boys can cry because they are happy or they are sad. But I also like them to show that it is possible vice versa, it is all right to be whoever you are, and it is all right that we are different and boys sometimes like to fight and be the warriors, and girls sometimes like to be the ones that take care and also organize ... I would like to portray that smart children are good children.* Thus, according to this view, "courage" and strength can be defined in non-aggressive and non-physical ways: The courage to stand up for one's values and rights, for example. Presenting boys who are vulnerable, compassionate, and caring who refuse to be aggressive can contribute to a positive notion of being "a real man," and portraying girls who value boys who reject the "tough guise" and prefer different forms of social courage may be the track for positive alternatives.[3]

Language Sensitivity

Some interviewees raised the need to pay particular attention to gender-sensitive language. For example, one interviewee referred to the guidelines that *Sesame Workshop* developed for presenting segments about gender equity in their coproductions around the world. They recommended avoiding excessive verbal explanations of gender equity (e.g. "I had a difficult day at work today, so Dad cooked us dinner") because they can produce the negative effect of highlighting that this is an exception rather than a normal routine. Avoiding stereotyped labeling (e.g. "he is crying like a girl;" "she is as pretty as a princess") as well as linking gender with innate abilities (e.g. "she learned to embroider so quickly, you can tell she is a girl;" "look at those fists on this baby – he is going to be a great fighter!").

However, the recommendation to use gender-neutral language may take a different form in different languages, as different linguistic structures pose different barriers to gender equality. For example, in English, the use of mail-person instead of mailman opens up the possibility of breaking traditional stereotypes and facilitating more equal opportunities. In some languages (e.g. neo-Latin languages as well as Hebrew), plural as well as singular nouns and adjectives require gender agreement (e.g. both children and child will have a gender denotation) since nouns are marked by gender (e.g. there is a girl-child or a boy-child, but no general term that stands for a gender-neutral "child"). Using a gender-balanced language thus requires high sensitivity and creative linguistic choices.

Summary

The principle of equality requires that boys and girls be treated equally, and offered equal roles and opportunities on television, while recognizing and respecting their differences.

The major strategies offered for following this principle were:

- Show equal numbers of boys and girls
- Present role reversals
- Break stereotypes
- Expand competencies and skills
- Use gender-sensitive language
- Present equality in both explicit and implicit ways
- Depart from gendered audio-visual styles of production

Diversity

Diversity is achieved when children are represented through a wide range and variety of characters, both within each social category of gender, race, ethnicity etc. as well as across all possible groups.

The requirement for a variety of characters within each gender was raised frequently. The position was clear: When there is only one girl (or boy) in the program, she or he is expected to stand for all girls, or for all boys. In this situation, being female or male is their most striking feature, a fact that lends itself to stereotyping. In contrast, when there are many girls (and boys), characters can exhibit a variety of characteristics and qualities: you can have the pink "girly-girl," the adventurous girl, the tomboy girl, or the intellectual girl. They can appear in different forms and shapes and as a combination of many possibilities. When producers create just one female character, she has to be the "perfect" fit for all viewers, an impossible goal. When many characters are present, some can be good and kind, others do not necessarily have to be so. Scriptwriters can experiment with all possibilities without the sense that one character bears the responsibility of representing her entire gender. Thus, the presence of a variety of characters is a creative opportunity because it makes it possible to tell different kinds of stories with more interesting plots.

The pressure of casting just one girl in a program was related to me in a conversation with Diklah (Israel). During negotiation over a coproduction with *Sesame Workshop*, she was offered the opportunity to add a new, Israeli Muppet to the permanent Sesame collection. Since all of the Muppets were male (a historical fact much regretted by current professionals at *Sesame*

Workshop), her team was eager to incorporate a female Muppet. However, as they brainstormed about the profile for this girl Muppet, they discovered that each foray led to the same conclusion: Any idea for a personality trait and characteristic of appearance that they proposed resulted in the creation of a potential stereotype: Should she be a red-haired tomboy? Should she wear a dress? Should she be smart and assertive? Should she be the younger or the older sister? Whatever route was selected, so they felt, it would lead them to casting that one Muppet as a female stereotype. They concluded that one female character would not work for them; rather they needed the possibility of adding variety within gender.

Leonora (Mexico) simplified the discussion by the following illustration regarding girl characters: *You can have a princess, and she can wear all the clothes she wants, with high heels and polished nails and walk around … that is one way to be a girl; and then you can have a girl who wears glasses and reads in the library – and that is another way to be a girl. There are so many ways to be a girl – so what is your way?* This binary presentation does not take into account the post-feminist possibility discussed in Chapter One of combining traditional femininities with "Girl Power," but it speaks to the choices that producers are forced to make when they have a limited number of girl characters to design. Similarly, Kim (The Netherlands) illustrated the point with regards to boy characters: *Don't always have to have powerful boys. We also need shy children in the program – children who want to do something, to dream, to be creative […] that's why I'm against the animation stations, since they only have strong boys as role models and they are always so powerful. You can see it through the camera's point of view and the use of music and the dialogue. In my opinion children are viewing these kinds of programs and they think that's the way the world is; you have to be strong, you have to be clever, you have to win. And I want balance in my programming, to show that this is how children really are, and they are all different. I want to see all the differences too. I don't have one ideal person.*

The principle of diversity also calls for attention to be directed to the intersections between gender and all other central human circumstances and characteristics that interact to construct identities: race, ethnicity, class, religion, language, geography, history, abilities, age, sexuality, and family. The argument that gender cannot be considered independently from concerns about social inequalities, nor understood independent of cultural contexts, has been stressed throughout the pages of this book.

It is important to note that references to diversity were raised spontaneously by interviewees, in response to my questions regarding gender, and were mainly in one of two forms: Concern for gender equality as one aspect of a general sensitivity to issues of diversity; and a form of "post-feminist" argument, according to which gender equality is taken for granted and the more burning issue is other forms of social inequality.

Either way, diversity was a major concern expressed by many producers. Abby (US) for example said: *I think diversity is a huge issue in this country […] African Americans, Hispanics, Asians […] there is very little diversity in children's television […]. Race, religion, culture – trying to become a united country, we need to also recognize that we are a diversified country, we are different, we respect people who are different. We need to say to children that we are human beings, and at the same time we are a man or a woman.*

Svein (Norway), described diversity issues related to recent immigration waves from around the world, a concern expressed by many north-European interviewees: *We try to raise the status of children coming from other countries, especially in Oslo, as there are a lot of immigrant children, nearly half of the children born in Oslo are from immigrant families. We have to reflect that in all of our programs, both in terms of the percentage, whether adults or children, but also in the way we are dealing with the programs. We have to show children from Turkey and Pakistan, and also from Asia – Korea, Vietnam. A lot of the children have been born here and they are mixed in the Norwegian society more than their parents, and that's where some of the conflicts are. And we have to deal with it on television.*

Elaine (Brazil) framed the discussion of diversity in terms of presenting to children a society of inclusion: *An issue for us is much more the issue of inclusion, so the issue of boys and girls is also about inclusion, because they used to be excluded. When we talk about inclusion we are talking about the blacks, and the poor, the disabled, the Indians. So, in this moment in Brazil, we are much more concerned about inclusion as a whole, and that's what my television is trying to do, for example, a show about disabled people.*

A number of interviewees made the argument that a diverse screen provides more realistic, humane portrayals of societies around the world and is also central to the wellbeing of the children growing within them. Kate (US) argued, for example: *You know, the truth is that most of the writers who work in the business are white, most of the stories are white […] I think it's important for kids at home to see people who look like them on the screen. I think that if you're a Hispanic kid growing up and there is one Hispanic show on television, you don't have any role models or anything else to sort of relate to and see. I think television has the power to do a lot of good in this regard. And I think that as an industry we need to be sensitive and responsive to that, especially with children […] I think we have some work to do there in terms of getting some diversity, in terms of the voices.*

Clearly, a white child's experience is not necessarily a black child's experience or that of a Hispanic child, and many producers claimed that the assumption that a white child's experience speaks for all children is a false one and needs to be challenged. Furthermore, the principle of diversity refers not only to inter-group relations but also to intra-group relations. For example, there is a wide diversity of groups among Latinos, that is, between Mexicans, Brazilians, and Cubans, for example. Dora might be a wonderful Latina

Figure 6.2 Peace Intiatives Institute: Media Initiatives for Children © The Peace Initiatives
       Institute

girl, but she does not stand for all Latinas' experiences. The same argument
can be made in relation to other races. The requirement for diversity thus
relates to the need to have a wide range of characters, beyond "token" representation, as Todd (US) commented: *But you can't have just one character
carrying the load. It's not enough to have just one black character or one
Hispanic character. You can't do justice to it ... you really need to find multiple models that children could learn from.* Thus, the presentation of a "palette" of races and ethnicities as discussed in Chapter One,[4] which includes one
of each (e.g. in *Barney & Friends*, which includes children of different races; or
in the Peace Initiatives Institute's "Media Initiatives for Children" (see Figure
6.2) featuring a wide variety of physical, ethnic, cultural, and behavioral differences) is certainly a major step forward, but only a first step toward
implementing a much more inclusive vision, across and within our richly
diverse societies.

The interviewees' recommendation in this regard is to have diversified characters who are central to and not only "sidekicks" of the mainstream characters.
When searching for illustration of this point, they had some difficulties pinpointing positive examples, and ended up referring to a limited number of
examples: Dora for pre-school; Gabriella, the main female character of the pre-
teen movies *High School Musical*; and the composition of characters in the
various series of *Degrassi* (see Figure 4.6) for pre-teens and teens.

A related recommendation is producers' warning against "hyper-correction," when a minority character is introduced as excessively talented, unusually benevolent or successful, etcetera. Such unrealistic portrayals within the program's larger social context, are a form of over-compensation that can be perceived by some to be condescending and offensive. Instead, each character needs to be presented as just another character in the group, defined by personality and behavior rather than by racial, ethnic, disability, or any other limiting identity. Lori (US) spoke of this issue: *The freeing thing about this show, because the three main characters happen to be black, is that we are able to show the whole range of personalities ... types ... interests ... backgrounds, and so, so when you only have one Latino or one Asian, or you know, one Jew, it's just too easy to wrap who that character is around their ethnicity, but when you have many, you have an opportunity to show the variety [...]. I think there's something in the Cosby model where your blackness or the ethnicity is in the texture and it's not the point, and I think that, often, when we talk about ethnicity it has to be hammered over your head. I think it's finding subtle ways to reflect culture and ethnicity without people feeling like they're getting a lesson.*

This argument was also made in regard to other forms of diversity, such as disabilities, as in the following quotation from Matt (US): *We put Pelswick on the air which was the first animated series about a boy in a wheelchair. And the series wasn't about, you know, teary-eyed moment of feeling sorry for a child who is in a wheelchair, but rather about a kid who was in a wheelchair and who acted like any other kid, and even sometimes used his wheelchair to get to front row seats at a Kids Concert because he could.* Normalizing and mainstreaming diversity was presented as a preferred strategy, rather than dwelling on the differences and disadvantages that comes with it.

Overall, participants' framing of diversity assumed a general liberal position most often referred to as multiculturalism and tolerance for difference expressed by means of representations consistent with changing configurations of societies and the challenges involved in shifting away from hegemonic whiteness on television. Yet racial hybridity, a growing social reality of mixed-race marriages and other mixed living arrangements around the world, and a thorny issue for many people in society as well as in the media community, was neither addressed nor given as an example of representations to be included in children's programming. Also missing were images of children who are not only interacting across race, but are also, themselves, a product of breaking racial barriers. For some, hybrid characters represent a true vision of a world of racial equality, one in which people create new life together based on who they are and the nature of their relationships, rather than on their biological and cultural heritages. For others, hybridity represents a form of "dissolving" or "erasing" race, instead of marking and celebrating it, and is therefore a true danger to the preservation of heritage and a threat to the most basic beliefs that constitute their identities.

Interestingly, as discussed in Chapter One, racial hybridity seems to be a growing feature of commercial children's television and related merchandizing, with popular images such as *Bratz*, *Lizzie McGuire*, and *The Cheetah Girls*. Hybridity and racial ambiguity can be interpreted as an acknowledgement of the lack of racial purity, yet at the same time it seems to work as a successful marketing strategy that attracts diverse audiences with limited characters that seem to speak to all of them. One ambiguous "brown" character can appeal to a wide range of ethnicities including Latin, Middle Eastern, Asian, and Native American, without alienating those of Caucasian descent.[5] With trends of colorism (see Chapter Three), the whitening of people of color, even some black populations can relate to the brown character as one of their own. This may explain the global success of *Dora*; the ease with which Japanese animation featuring racially ambiguous characters travels; and the popularity of *High School Musical*, whose lead female character is a Latina. An intriguing question might be whether the visibility and symbolic meaning of the present "hybrid" President of the US, Barack Obama (who referred to himself as "mix breed" when talking to journalists about the search for a family dog shortly after his inauguration in January 2009) will stimulate more hybrid characters on children's programming, as well.

In addition to the absence of reference to hybridity, there was also another central absence – that which relates to diversity of class. There was almost no discussion of the "sanitized" middle-class world that dominates children's television, clearly privileging modern urban life. This preference for a particular lifestyle is thus presented non-problematically, as a normalized, taken-for-granted way things are.[6] The fact that lower-class and rural children seem to be practically invisible on television screens around the world seemed to be a blind spot for my interviewees, many of whom were among the educated elite and members of the middle class in their respective societies. While the economic logic behind this absence may be explainable in that children of lower-income families and the poor – who make up a considerable portion of the world's children – do not make attractive audiences for advertisers, the absence of social awareness among interviewees suggests the need for further exploration of media professionals' social agenda and thinking.

As discussed in relation to gender equality, diversity is required everywhere, in all forms and types of characters in fiction and non-fiction formats, both front-stage and backstage. Different body and facial shapes and skin colors, costuming and apparel of all cultural styles and fashions, languages and accents, home interiors and foods, customs and religious traditions. It should reflect the urban and the rural ways of life, as well as the various classes that constitute and are representative of children's worlds. Good characters and exciting stories can appear in all colors, shapes, and forms.

These concerns build upon feminist reactions to the historical failures of a variety of media, including children's programming, to incorporate the diversity of voices of young people, non-heterosexual ones, disabled ones, and those of people of color and the lower classes of society. It is worth noting, however, that sensitivity to diversity issues has come to be understood not only as a moral and political issue, but also as a requirement for a central cognitive skill crucial for survival in the global world. The need to cultivate a "respectful mind" as Howard Gardner defines it[7] – responding systematically and constructively to differences among individuals and among groups, seeking to understand and work with those who are different – extends beyond mere tolerance and political correctness into the realm of flourishing and wellbeing.

Summary

The principle of diversity requires providing children with a wide range and variety of characters, both within as well as across each social category.
   The major strategies offered by interviewees for this principle were:

- Offer a diverse palette of human characters
- Present a variety of characters within and across each social category
- Legitimize and demonstrate inclusion and respect for difference
- Mainstream diverse characters and do not only present them as "sidekicks"
- Do not overcompensate by creating unrealistic "too good to be true" diverse characters
- Avoid being too pedagogical and moralistic about diversity

Complexity

> The principle of complexity embraces, to some degree, the "different but equal" position and, in practice, seeks to broaden the possibilities and traits for both boys and girls by producing more complex, rounded, and non-stereotypical characters.

The need for character complexity was one of the central arguments raised by interviewees, given their widespread critique of the general presence of underdeveloped characters and, more specifically, gender stereotyping. Their arguments claimed that unidimensional characters, built upon one specific trait (e.g. the "bitch-blonde" or "goody book reader" girl; the "bully" or "geek" boy), lend themselves to simplicity, stereotyping, and underdeveloped plots. While this is quite an accepted rule in scriptwriting,[8] interviewees insisted that it is essential in efforts that seek to break gender stereotypes, since underdeveloped characters almost always fall into the trap of reducing characters to a specific gendered

trait along traditional binaries such as active/passive, rational/emotional, leader/
follower, ugly/sexy, intellectual/fun-loving, manipulative/victimized, etc.

While the principle of diversity discussed above focuses on the inclusion of a
variety of character types, the principle of complexity requires that each character will be a "well-rounded," non-stereotypical, complete human being. So
while diversity focuses on the "between character" principle, complexity centers
on the "within" character principle. Stated in a different manner, a program may
have many diverse characters, yet some or all may be very stereotypical and lack
complexity. Many examples were provided by interviewees, beginning with very
familiar, well-discussed programs such as *The Smurfs*, a program that depicts a
world inhabited by blue figures, all male, whose names reflect their main personality trait (Lazy Smurf, Grouchy Smurf, Brainy Smurf, etc.) and only one
female character, whose name reflects her being female as her only trait:
Smurfette. This female character is not even one of the original Smurfs according to the storyline, because she was created by Gargamel, the evil wizard.
Interviewees also referred to the construction of television and film images
around celebrities such as the pop group The Spice Girls, adored in the 1990s by
tweens around the world, who came in the characteristic "spice" flavors of
"Baby" (Emma), "Sexy" (Geri), "Scary" (Melanie B.), "Sporty" (Melanie C.),
and "Posh" (Victoria).[9] In Mike's (US) view: *Stereotypes are due to a lack in
creativity. When someone is very creative, they are not going to create stereotypes, since stereotypes are a product of bad writing. If you create well-rounded,
complicated characters, they won't be stereotyped. Having interesting characters
means oftentimes going against types to keep them fresh and interesting. So I go
often against gender conventions.*

Beyond often-repeated, general statements – "I'd like to see complex characters," "characters are too stereotypical and not complex enough," "children
need to see that people do not have just one characteristic" – interviewees
rarely provided detailed explanations, as their claim was often embedded
within a discussion of other themes. Thus the statement by Julie (UK) is
exceptional in that she provided a more detailed explanation advocating complexity: *You know, as far as gender-presentation issues are concerned, it's very
important for us to have as balanced a view as possible. And I think the
answer to what we want or what we think will work or should happen is
complexity. I think the more complex we can make our characters, the more
sides of them that we can show, whether they are boys or girls, the richer the
characters are, and the more we address that issue. I think it's important not
to oversimplify any characters, regardless of the gender. You're in as much
trouble if you say: "Oh we need to have only tough, fidgety, take-charge kind
of girls and emotional, sensitive, intelligent boys. If you play that note exclusively, you're in trouble. So complexity is maybe the most important thing in
all the characters. So we try to show complex heroines, heroines that have
tough sides, sensitive sides, who deal with things with intelligence. If they're
emerging into a sense of their own femininity, how does that fit with the*

children they were before, as an emerging adolescent or their sexuality, you know, how does that all fit in? This is what I mean by complexity [...] Complexity of characters is what everybody should strive for. Yes you can ask if you have the right gender portrayals but what's really important is: Do we believe these characters? Do we understand them in that context? Do we believe them? Do we think they feel what they feel and behave how they behave?

A special document entitled *Girls and Boys and Television: A Few Reminders for More Gender Sensitivity in Children's TV*,[10] designed for producers and distributed during Prix Jeunesse 2008, provides specific guidelines that translate the request for complexity into specific suggestions in the development of boy and girl characters. The document states that "gender equality means to overcome one-dimensional, traditional constructs of masculinity and femininity, which over-simplify and fall short of reality and in contemporary society are neither beneficial to girls nor boys. Gender sensitivity means to reflect and be aware of one's own prejudices and question assumptions about gender that have become normalized through repetition." In specific reference to the presentation of girls on television, the guidelines suggest the following: "Gender sensitivity means to take girls and their preferences seriously. Create more interesting girl characters and avoid stereotypes. Quality in children's television means taking girls seriously and presenting them with perspectives which offer them spaces beyond the obvious interests and typical stereotypes." And what about the boys? The guidelines suggest that "gender sensitivity means to take boys and their preferences seriously [...] without using only violence. Create more attractive boy characters without stepping into the trap of clichés. Attaining excellence in children's TV means taking boys and their preferences seriously and moving beyond apparent stereotypes."

Each of the guidelines begins with a shift from the current state of affairs to prescriptive recommendations. The practical guidelines are integrated in the summary below.

Summary

The principle of complexity embraces, to some degree, the understanding of "different but equal" discussed above, but works towards broadening possibilities and traits for both boys and girls by producing more complex, round, and non-stereotypical characters.

The major strategies offered by interviewees and the Prix Jeunesse 2008 document for this principle were:

For the development of complex girl characters:

- Move from an emphasis on appearance to skills and values
- Expand girls' interest in romance and relationships to include interests in other things such as performance, adventure, career, hobbies, fantasy

- Allow girls to be caregivers responsible for others as well as oriented to themselves, in the sense of caring for their own needs and desires and acting to fulfill them
- Present girls who go beyond self-reflection and analysis and who act with self-confidence and without constant guilt
- Present girls who act to create harmony in relationships, but who are also able to stand up for their opinions, to handle conflict – if on occasion they are involved in confrontation, while learning to control their aggressive impulses even at the risk that others will be angry with them

For the development of complex boy characters:

- Present boys who are engaged in high-pressure performance activities that also involve reflection, as well as relaxation capacity – leisure activities that enable them to let go – physically and mentally
- Replace aggressive conflicts where rules are violated and borders of integrity are overstepped with the constructive quality of protecting and caring for others and oneself
- Permit boys to experience and to express a range of emotions
- Present boys who enjoy intellectual challenges and collaborations with others

Similarity

> According to the principle of similarity, the script shall emphasize the shared aspects of girls' and boys' lives, rather than dwell on differences that can evolve into conflict, stereotyping, status marking, and animosity.

The principle of similarity celebrates girls and boys as children who share the same challenges, aspirations, morality, dreams, and hopes; children who need love and friendships, have adventures and overcome difficulties; children who are curious and eager to explore their surroundings, and who struggle with their multiple identities; children who try to carve their place in the world. The principle advocates presenting children, both boys and girls, who are self-willed, positive, and share their problems and accomplishments. In such cases, the issues are presented not as girls' issues or boys' issues, but as issues of children's lives.

Good programming, so the interviewees told me, brings children closer to each other and at the same time closer to themselves. This desire to see a shared world on television, where similarities between boys and girls override the differences between them, stands in striking contrast to the popularity of the "Mars and Venus" framing discussed in Chapter Five. This perspective, as we recall, highlights gender differences and places the burden of bridging them onto styles of communication, and in doing so shifts "fixing" gender-related problems from women to the shared responsibility of both genders.[11]

Much of children's television and the toy industry, as argued above, celebrates the Mars and Venus model in children's culture in quite deterministic ways. It is thus remarkable to note the intense critique aimed at this dominant approach in many interviews and the interviewees' desire to emphasize similarities rather than differences between boys and girls. As Matt (US) put it to me very simply: *Appealing to every child is not a problem, because every child really wants the same things, you know. They want to be loved, they want to laugh, they want to cry, they want to learn, they want to celebrate their life, they want to feel like they can contribute in their local environment, they want all these things.*

With so much in common, sticking to gender stereotypes "is just plain lazy," as the interviewees often said, while developing fun and smart characters who are true to themselves but also do unexpected things is difficult. As many of the conversations unfolded, it became clear that breaking stereotypes and opening up the screen to blurring gender differences and to offering children real choice that cuts across the gender divide is seen by interviewees as a way to foster a safer and more healthy environment for children's growth and development.

Character

Several shared personality characteristics were central in the view of the producers in the presentation of both boys and girls on television. The most common theme expressed was the term "strong" character, as suggested by Maggie (Ireland): *A strong character is someone that takes the lead in action, who suggests solutions to problems.* When probed for more details, interviewees suggested that a strong character is, for example, energetic, intelligent, active, trustworthy, cooperative, someone who works towards a goal, overcomes difficulties and deals wisely with conflict. They are supported by good friends and caring adults. Abby (US) continued the monologue quoted above as follows: *[...] and I look at friends that have very tiny children and I think that we as program makers have a responsibility to those children, and we have to show them the good things in life. And the good things in life are not merchandizing and they're not television to sell things, they're embracing interesting characters, they're showing love, they're showing strength in individuals, morality, and when I say morality I mean individual morality, doing the right thing. And not all television does that.*

Indeed, character morality was seen as a central shared value of both boys and girls for several of the interviewees. Here, they seemed to be referring to an ethical dimension of personality that is respectful and caring of others, and is concerned about values that go beyond one's own self-centered and personal gains and satisfactions. Brad (US): *I think you would like to show that good character matters, that morality can be a successful formula for your life, that it's not only the nasty, thin, rich, obnoxious people who are successful. So for both boys and girls I think they need to see a way through to being good human beings as well as successful people. That good people can do well. Showing them a path through storytelling of being good, of good citizenship.*

The notion of "citizenship," as quoted above, is used here in the most basic sense – of conducting oneself as a member of a social grouping, a community of people, that extends one's view beyond oneself and, as such, in which one assumes shared responsibility. Acknowledging this status on television, even for pre-schoolers, was discussed by Cindy (US) in relation to instilling in young viewers the idea of civility in human relationships: *Being polite, you know. People being rude on the street and cutting you off in traffic. And, you don't hear please and thank you. I think if there was more civility within the world we would get along better. And that's one of the things I try to do with this program. I make sure that there is please and thank you in every show. Because I know that to our audience this is the time to learn those positive pro-social skills. And so, certainly, ... for me working on pre-school proper-ties, this is one of my big things ... showing decent people, polite people, responsible people, people who take responsibility for their actions, who see things through, that you can count on them, they are dependable, they are reliable. To me those are gender-neutral aspirations for every day.*

A related view was shared by Karoline (Sweden) in regard to her concern at the rise of violence among both boys and girls and the need to cultivate qualities that can help resist this trend: *[...] violence is a big issue in all societies right now, and what we see is not only physical violence among boys, but also violence among girls. So, we have to work a lot on empathy in boys and girls.* Boys' common physical violence and girls' more typical verbal bullying were perceived to be symptoms derived from similar causes and both required tele-vision's immediate attention.

Overcoming Difficulties

A theme repeated by several interviewees was the need for both boys and girls to see children overcoming difficulties and becoming stronger and better as a result of the challenge, along with stories of girls and boys who are survivors, and not victims. Beatriz (Ecuador) wanted to present a character who *knows very well where she wants to go, what she decides, but also able to show weaknesses, and how to deal with them ... to show the process how one can deal with weakness and convert disabilities into abilities.* Eric (Canada) shifted this thrust when he suggested that boys and girls need programs about finding one's mission in life: *It's not about role models, it's about becoming who you are. We have a wide variety of characters in our society and we need all these people with different skills. So, it is not about trying to convince them to become something else. Of course there are some role models, like I use athletes a lot [...] but the kids will have to discover who he or she is, so I don't want to portray a certain type of person they should be like, this is not my vision.*

Kate (US), too, believed that engaging characters are what make the difference in children's television: *I think that it's nice when you have characters that are heroic, you know, whether they are boys or girls. Where there are opportunities for the kids to see courage and be in a difficult situation and use an ability to reason to get out of it [...].* Mister Rogers *has great characters, and great stories and it's not for boys, and it's not for girls. And, if there was a wish that I had it was that there were more shows that were like that, that were not, "oh this is a girls show, this is a boys show." That doesn't matter with a lot of these action shows, the action is more important [...] That's probably not where the rest of the business is going, because a lot of movies are about a lot of special effects and they don't care much about characters. But to stand the test of time I think you have to have characters that kids relate to and connect with.*

But overcoming difficulties and struggling need not, in the opinion of interviewees, be presented only as serious matters. On the contrary, humor was integrated into the discussions, often as a crucial ingredient of programming for children and building up characters. For example, in endorsing his own network's production of the hit show *SpongeBob SquarePants*, which takes place in an ocean setting, Chris (US) stated: SpongeBob *is just a brilliant show ... they are mostly male, yeah. Um ... but, you know, he didn't have in mind that he was gonna create a show that was gonna be for boys or for girls, it was for kids, kids and adults, just because the way it was written. It's just funny and humor can transcend all age groups in all ethnicities and all sexes [...]* SpongeBob *is just a very naïve, wonderful character who gets himself into situations by trying to do the best he can possibly do in the most honest, forthright manner [...]. In the end it's his honesty and naïveté that solves whatever the problem is or what the issue is. And that's why it appeals to everyone [...] He's not a boy character and he's not a girl, he's just a really nice great character.* Humor and plain human honesty and naïveté, argued Chris, are appealing above and beyond gender and age barriers.

Similarly, Todd (US) described a program he was producing: *We have segments produced in Israel, Egypt, Palestine, Jordan, South Africa, Russia, Holland. And all of these are segments about a child in another culture mastering something difficult in their culture. They may have nothing to do with our culture, but it's the common sense of mastering and of struggle, of what is similar and different to the child in the audience ... so a child in Mongolia, a little girl who learns to balance balls on her head, is appealing to a young boy or a young girl here who is saying "I don't do that but I respect and understand the challenge of her learning how to do it, just as I respect the little girl in Holland who has to learn how to ride a bicycle because everybody rides a bicycle there to get from one place to another." It's the idea of struggle and it's a universal concept but it has its own particular attitude and angle, so I think one of the things we say we have to teach children not only to respect the differences but, after 9/11, how to stand up to intolerance, and so that's part of what we are trying to do in our shows.* As Todd explained, highlighting commonalities, despite their cultural manifestations, is perceived as a means of advancing tolerance and cultural understanding, beyond gender equality and respect.

Cultural Awareness

Indeed, the need for children's television to broaden children's horizons and introduce them to other cultures and societies was an associated, central theme. However, in non-Western countries it followed a concern, first and foremost, to love and take pride in one's own culture. As Sumita (Bangladesh) put it: *Good television for children means that you teach them that they should love their country, they should love their culture, and also they should gain knowledge of other cultures.*

Yet, in other societies, cultural differences were addressed in a different manner, as in Abby's (US) reflections about the particular global circumstances in which American children are raised today and on what she would like to see television provide children with, boys and girls alike: *I'd like children to feel comfortable in their world [...]. There are so many fears in children's lives now, all over the world, that television has a responsibility to children to try and make them feel safe and to feel good about themselves, and good about their world. Now their world might be their backyard, but also to understand different cultures and to embrace other cultures [...]. You know, the key for me in children's television is to make children feel safe and protected and excited about the world and I think that children are terrified of the world, terrified of traveling, and I know younger children who don't want to go anywhere, they want to stay at home. And I think that that makes very insular adults and I think that television has to expand the mind but it also has to give children courage.*

Children, so the argument goes, are facing similar global issues of personal safety, anxiety over the future of the global world and their place in it. And, in the face of this situation, interviewees claim that television has a responsibility to assist all children, boys and girls, to become courageous citizens of the world.

Gender Blurring

Raising the possibility of genderless texts evoked a different level of discussion of the shared world of boys and girls. In this approach, gender differences are so blurred that characters can be described as androgynous in many ways. Benny (Israel), for example, entertained the thought of experimenting with a program that would *inspire children to imagine different ways of being, different ways of thinking, different ways of doing, different ways for the future. To have at least one show that really presented a genderless world, maybe it could free the imagination up to think about things beyond gender constructs for half an hour.*

Few interviewees provided illustrations of such programs. Yamagishi (Japan), for example, described a program focusing on high technology that experimented with characters without gender traits. Kate (US) discussed *Mazie* – a girl character who is purposefully unmarked as a girl and combines a more "boyish" personality and occasional "girly" dressing up to create a non-stereotypical character. Mike (US) described the three androgynous animal characters in the unique photo-animation style of *The Wonder Pets*: A guinea pig, turtle, and duckling. *Linee, the guinea pig, is the leader of the group. Very curious, eager. I didn't think of her as a boy or a girl, but a guinea pig. Linee is not a common name, we purposefully wanted it to be vague so boys and girls will identify with her because of her personality, not because of her gender. There is no reference to her gender. We mix and match the clothes.* When attempting to explain the origin of these choices he related his personal background: *I come from New York City where everything goes. There is no rigid lifestyle. I grew up with some women who look masculine and men who look feminine, and for me it looks OK ... it is all there ... People's gender identity and sexuality is up in the air, it was never an issue. The preconceptions are that everybody is different in those ways, rather than that men are this way and women this way [...] It's part of the fabric of my life ... and when you look at the programs that we created, you would see that there are a variety of ways to be a boy or a girl, but it was never deliberate, just the way I was raised.* Mike's discussion of the influence of his personal background on his creative work echoes the discussion we had in Chapter Five about the content of children's television reflecting the creators' personal make-up.

Attitudes about the possibility of parting from gendered styles and formats (colors, music, camera work, clothing, accessories, etc.) in addition to personality traits and behavioral scripts were, thus, strongly rooted in interviewees' personal backgrounds and life circumstances. However, as the few illustrations in this study suggest, there are rare cases of applying this approach in contemporary children's programming. What exists is limited to genres that lend themselves to experimentation, such as animation or science fiction, and to the very young audiences that are still willing to share similar programs. No initiatives of this sort were reported in relation to older audiences and realistic genres

Summary

The principle of similarity refers to the need to foreground the shared aspects of the lives of girls and boys, rather than dwelling on the differences that tear them apart.

> The major strategies offered by interviewees for applying this principle were:
>
> - Present boys and girls as sharing similar qualities and aspiring to a similar vision of humanity
> - Present girls and boys as strong characters who can overcome difficulties and are survivors of life's ills
> - Engage boys and girls in cultural awareness and a sense of global citizenship
> - Employ images that blur and problematize gender differences

Unity

> Unity requires that friendships and relationships between girls and boys be constructed on equal terms.

The principle of unity refers to the possibility of presenting boys and girls as sharing life experiences together, collaborating with one another, united in their joint quest for happy growth and development. Following from previous discussions of similarities between boys and girls, applying the principle of unity will bridge existing gaps between the gender relationships and assist in overcoming barriers by presenting narratives in which children manage cross-gender friendships. Contrary to "the battle of the sexes" models – constructed through differences, competition, romantic pursuit, and sexual attraction – scripts seeking to achieve greater unity emphasize the basic qualities and aspirations that mark all children as human beings. In advancing unity, interviewees argued that demonstrating alternative relationships and encouraging cooperation would serve as an intervention in attempts to reform contemporary childhood segregation on television.[12]

Several illustrations were offered by producers in the interviews as role models for portrayals of positive relationships. *Kim Possible*, for example, is an animated series revolving around Kim's fight against her enemies, while she also has to deal with the ordinary life experiences of a young teen at school and home. One of the unique features of the program is her friendship with a boy, Ron. Despite the many mistakes that Ron makes, she does not devalue him or put him down. Their friendship epitomizes cross-gender, equality-based friendships devoid of sexual tension that are non-exploitive and non-manipulative. *Dora the Explorer* as well as *Maya & Miguel* were also suggested as programs that present healthy girl–boy friendships, as described by Abby (US): *In* Dora, [the lead character] *has an imagination. She doesn't always get everything right, she is willing to make mistakes and she admits her mistakes. She's not frightened of being a girl. She has good relationships with the other characters. The same with* Maya & Miguel. *Maya and Miguel are brother and sister, and they have a healthy, competitive brother–sister relationship. Maya is the stronger of the two characters, but not at the expense of Miguel. You know she is the decision maker. But it's done in a way which is not offensive to boys.*

The pre-school program *Wonder Pets* (discussed previously) is another example mentioned several times by interviewees. Here a trio of heroes rescue baby animals and demonstrate the benefits of teamwork, collaboration, and non-hierarchal cooperation that is gender blind. Thus, whoever among the group – which consists of two females and a male – comes up with the better idea or solution is supported and followed by the others. As Mike (US) explained, teamwork travels easily around the world as it is not controversial, particularly when it employs animals rather than humans and thus allows for more flexibility. It is much more difficult to create unity in programs that are aimed at older audiences and employ human characters.

Collaboration between boys and girls does not require them to relinquish central aspects of their lives. Kirstine (US), for example, would like to portray boys and girls who draw one another into their world of interests: *I want to see boys who are not interfering with and sabotaging girls' efforts or girls' friendships. I want to see boys who can deal with female authority and a girl calling a play* [in sports] *and having expertise that he may not have, and getting excited about it. I want to see boys who will follow a lead for imaginative play that they may have not thought about and enlarge it and add that sort of action and adventure and courage too. I love seeing boys out and about. I love boys, love it that boys are interested in mechanics. I love that the boys are interested in transportation and vehicles. I love it that boys are ... away from authority and I want to see them comfortable bringing the girls along. And I want to see them expecting that the girls will enjoy it all too.*

Interviewees also claimed that there is room for a more collaborative perspective even when dealing with the traditional romantic storylines to which girls are attracted, as Leona (Philippines) suggested: *[...] we paid attention to gender issues [...] for example of problem solving between genders and friendships between boys and girls. I have done workshops with practitioners of teenage productions quite often, to help them figure out storylines that are also beyond the boy-girl romance thing ... and girls always aiming to please boys ... and boys always trying to win them over and then being very demanding. I wanted to help them deal with more difficult storylines about sexuality and relationships. To help them understand issues like teenage pregnancy and how the dilemma must be a boy–girl responsibility and not just the girl's alone.*

Most central to interviewees' claims was the desire to see boys and girls collaborating on terms that are not reduced to sexual tension and romance. Samora (South Africa) expressed it directly: *I want to see boys and girls interact together, friendship without being sexual ... we lost that ...*

Figure 6.3 Little Peace of Mine © Filmmaker: Eyal Avneri; Producers: Edna & Elinor
   Kowarsky – Eden Productions, Israel

*everything on TV that shows interaction patterns is sexualized. I want to see
that they can go out and have fun together, share the same dance, share the
same hobbies, and it will change the dynamics of life together.*

A program from Venezuela that presented boys cheering from the sidelines
for an all-girl sports team is an example of a relatively direct portrayal. Kasper
(Denmark) shared an experience of producing a more complex program, with
a more complex message for viewers: *We tried to do something that shows
relationships between the two genders ... we have a game show right now
called* Amigo *and there we tried to make boy and girl friends that help each
other. They realize that they both have different skills that they can use, and
sometimes it is the girls that are based on the physical things and sometimes
the boys on the academic things, or vice versa. We are trying.*

A very different example was demonstrated in *Little Peace of Mine* (see
Figure 6.3), a documentary about a tense and complicated relationship between
two teens – a Jewish-Israeli boy and a Palestinian girl – who try to collaborate
in initiating a peace movement, and who challenge one another as they seek to
understand their deeply engrained political differences.

Other interviewees mentioned gender collaborations on equal terms, where
the girls do not assume the role of the disciplinarian adult type who controls
the "naughty" boys, as described by Kristine (US): *What I see over and over
again is the one little girl who is saying to the boys: "Ha, you guys have done
it again;" "You pick up this mess;" "Oh, now be careful, it's almost time to
go, we need to pick up our toys."* Unity, so the principle suggests, requires that
boys and girls be portrayed on equal terms, sharing friendships and adventures
in non-controlling and non-gender-manipulative ways.

Furthermore, such an approach argues for breaking the linkage between an attractive appearance and satisfying relationships, as well as exciting adventures. Eliminating such stereotypes suggests that boys and girls of all shapes, colors, and forms can be friends and enjoy good times together. More specifically, when sex and sexuality become part of friendship narratives designed for teens, the principle of unity requires presenting sexual relationships as part of intimate and close relationships of mutual respect and fondness. However, as the discussion in Chapter Four noted, few interviewees raised issues to do with the presentation of sex to teens.

Summary

The principle of unity features friendships between girls and boys constructed on equal terms.
  The major strategies offered for following this principle were:

- Present girls and boys who share friendships that are not based on romance and sexual tension but on common interests, values, personality traits, and mutual respect
- Avoid manipulative relationships where girls and boys play traditional gender roles
- Construct friendship relationships around equal terms, equal responsibilities, and equal contributions
- Present fulfilling friendships between boys and girls who do not adhere to stereotypical "beauty myths" for girls and "tough myths" for boys

Family

Family is the main social context of children's lives and, therefore, grounding children's experiences within a context of supportive, caring family life offers positive role models for human relationships, for parent–child as well as adult–child relations.

The centrality of family in children's programming was a major theme in interviewees' practice. Regardless of the kind of family structure accepted as desirable (or even moral), there was agreement that children need to be seen growing up in nurturing and healthy family environments. Harsh criticism was expressed against the trend in many American situation comedies and films to present dysfunctional families, generally represented by incompetent parents, or to just ignore families altogether, as part of the "home alone" trend.

These claims are consistent with previous research, as much family programming and many general-viewership films do feature children left alone to care for themselves in a world populated by ineffective adults and uninspiring role models.[13] While such images represent social transformations taking place in the Western world,[14] they also play an active role in constructing childhood in a novel way. Children are perceived, increasingly, as independent consumers and as leaders of the technological revolution (and less so as future citizens). The new technologies in particular have drastically changed the public–private division on which the family is based and have contributed to the erosion of parental authority, according to some critics. Indeed, in much of the media oriented to young audiences, parents are portrayed as superfluous: Children manipulate them, and the entire adult world more generally; overcome difficulties on their own; sustain themselves economically and socially; and, are generally at home alone in the world. The interviewees in this study resisted this trend wholeheartedly. In their family-centered view, childhood is a period requiring special care, in general, and adult characters who embody a vision and model of what children can, indeed should, grow into. Such attitudes were particularly strong with interviewees from societies marked by growing inequalities and child neglect.

The centrality of parents to children's healthy development and as models of parenthood, albeit ones that are changing, is expressed by Hanne (Norway): *But I must say that parents are very important; parents are always behind the relationships and stories … I think that we need also to be very careful in showing very traditional stereotypes of parents, especially because the people making the shows are basically my generation* [in their 40s–50s], *a little younger, and we are thinking about our parents. But parents today are really different from our generation […] there are also grandparents and I like to put them in roles of passing on traditions but highlighting more the ones that are more gender fair in their roles. And there is something to be said about our commitment to promote our own local culture and to highlight certain aspects of it.* Locating stories within an intergenerational context is thus a way to encourage connectivity to a collective culture and heritage as well as to specific family arrangements that foster healthier childhoods.

Many interviewees spoke specifically also about offering children parental role models who open up their visions about motherhood and fatherhood. Such, for example, was the following quote by Meghan (Canada): *I would like to present moms that work outside the home and are great moms, and I would like to present women who are great business people and have chosen not to have kids. I think, what I love to present is the fact that girls should realize that, as they get older … they can make any one of those choices. And that they should make it wholeheartedly and try to be all that they can be whatever path they decide to take. And with men I would like to do the same things. I would like to show strong fathers, especially fathers that stay with children.* Similarly, Kristine (US) said: *I want to see grown-up models. I want to see mothers whose authority is respected. I want to see mothers and fathers working together. I want to see men who cook. I want to really see men in kitchens. I want to see the focus on the jobs at home that need to get done and the work picked up by whoever is there to get it done.*

In many ways, the private sphere, which has been the most resistant to gender-equality change, was the focus of much of the discussion over the role television can play in offering children the possibility of different ways of life than those familiar to them.

The Role of Dads

The discussion of families was often translated more specifically into a discussion of fathers and new forms of masculinity. The desire to see positive role models of men who are neither dictators in their families nor stupid buffoons came up in many of the interviews, with professionals from all parts of the world, although it was particularly prevalent in interviews with northern-hemisphere interviewees.

The impact on families of paying attention to changing male characters was expressed by Caroline (US) in her discussion of a *Sesame Street* coproduction in the Arab world: [...] *the other thing that comes into play is to have very strong adult characters, both males and females; males that are integrated with females; males that are supporting women in their roles; males that are also very active with their kids. One of the things that came out with our Palestinian program was that men who were watching the show commented that they learned from the show about being more active with their own kids.[...] Many of them were saying, you know "I used to think of my role as somebody who was providing the financial structure to the family and in watching* Sesame Street, *where the men are so involved with the kids, I started to realize that I can get a lot of joy from being actively involved with my own kids."[...] there is a segment, for example from Egypt, where the father and his two kids are making a birthday cake for their mother, that's kind of sweet that way ...*

Discussion of representations of new masculinities ties strongly to the discourse about the "neglected boys" and "machismo" themes discussed in Chapter Three, as many interviewees see fathers as key players in enhancing the well-being of their children and in promoting more egalitarian societies. Grazille (Brazil), too, was concerned with having strong male role models for kids in her programs: *The idea is to balance two sexes and show them both, and to oppose stereotypes like kitchen-woman, science-man. So we are trying to change a little bit, to have a program where the presenter will be a young man, because kids in Brazil are raised by women and they don't have a masculine figure. I am trying to create a program with a male character who can talk to children.*

Many positive programming examples were presented in the events where this study was conducted and these productions were often referred to by interviewees when discussing their desire for more positive paternal images. Hope

(US), for example, praised such programs: [...] *if you have an opportunity to portray non-stereotypical behaviors ... like showing caring boys, taking care of their baby sisters or brothers or so on ... there is so much stuff that does that ... like the stuff I saw this afternoon* [during Prix Jeunesse 2004] *... wonderful, playful dads instead of the American stereotype that used to be that grumpy man in a suit that came home with a headache and yelled at the children. I just didn't see that at all today in programs from around the world. It is so wonderful. The one about the little girl who was a princess* [Konfje] *and her father built her a castle from blankets ... and the one called* [The Children's] *Supershow, a live-action variety show, and the dads were doing silly things and the kids were totally in charge, and the whole show was about why it is great to have a dad or if you don't have a dad it is still OK.*

Other programs that caught interviewees' attention were *Peppa Pig* (see Figure 6.4), an animation for pre-schoolers, where the mother is presented working at her computer while the father prepares dinner. *Hurray! Cool Daddy* (see Figure 6.5) was addressed by Nasing (Malasia): [...] *their program was very unique. A studio program with young children with their fathers* [attending] *and not the mothers. The whole program was designed to help fathers bond with their children ... that seemed like a very positive program, well received by the audience. Traditionally fathers don't have the time to spend with their children, the mothers are at home and even when they work they take responsibility for the children. But now the father sees his role being more important and wants to be part of this bonding and relationship; that it is his child too. So this program seemed to be very unique in its context and very effective in the way the program got that message across.*

The need to see male adults who relate to children, care for and nurture them, was echoed all around the world, albeit for different reasons. For some it was a reaction to traditional patriarchal families in which men exerted their authority in the private sphere but did not participate in raising or educating

Figure 6.4 Peppa Pig © Astley Baker Davies/E1 Entertainment 2003, created by Mark Baker and Neville Astley, UK

Figure 6.5 Hurray! Cool Daddy © EBS South Korea

their children. For some, it was a desire to counterbalance single-mother families and the absence of fathers altogether. And for some it was about correcting negative experiences with incompetent fathers in their real lives. However, common to all interviewees was a desire to see more caring males in children's lives on screen to somehow compensate for the reality of their absence, as Meghan (Canada) explained: *A major problem in black America is having dads stay with the moms. So there's a huge generation of kids being raised only by women and I think that's problematic. I think that you need to be raised by a man and a woman if it all possible, or at least by two strong characters, even if they're both women or both men. Having two adults in your life is better than having one. And so I would like to show men who are great dads.*

Kate (US) had a very specific role model in mind for this "great dad" ideal, a familiar children's television personality in the US: *This is a question I have been interested in for my whole career. I'd like to see more men figures in young boys' lives. I'm probably the most die-hard* Mister Rogers *fan in the universe ... there are so few Mister Rogers in the world, but I think that having role models, you know, male role models is so crucial ...* Fred Rogers personified the gentle, caring male figure who respected and understood young children, who talked to them at eye-level rather than talking down to them. In his programs he acknowledged the uniqueness of each child and affirmed his or her importance, at the same time fostering the development of imagination and the accumulation of knowledge of the world. He never raised his voice or resorted to verbal or physical aggression, and he instilled in his audience an optimistic, respectful view of their local environment and the people in it.[15] Men like Mister Rogers, argued Kate, are the kind of ideal male role models that she would have liked to offer children on television.

The presentation of children growing up while being supported and cared for by responsible and loving adults is claimed, by many, to be one of the major contributions that television can make to assist children: These may be street children in huge urban centers whose life circumstances have left them to fend for themselves or "latch-key" children of affluent families caught in the pressures of a competitive capitalist world, pampered with leisure technologies and accessories as a replacement for a real meaningful presence in their lives. Given this emphasis on change, we should also note that none of the interviewees spoke in favor of the restoration of a traditional family structure with a clear distinction between the private and public spheres, with a stay-home mom and a wage-winning dad. Neither did they specifically address children as the purpose and goal of family life, a central notion associated with capitalism.[16] Instead, they expressed a wish to recapture the view of families as responsible for the wellbeing of children, and particularly for adults as significant caregivers and upholders of culture and tradition.

Summary

The principle of family refers to the need to ground children's experiences within the context of a supportive, caring family life that offers positive role models for parenthood.

The major strategies offered for following this principle were:

- Break traditional gender-role division of labor within the private sphere
- Present fathers who enjoy caring and being involved in raising their children
- Present mothers who have their own professional lives outside of the home
- Present caregivers as upholders of tradition and culture

Authenticity

Authenticity leads television programs to be constructed with depictions of true-to-life characters, narratives, and social contexts.

The principle of authenticity reflects producers' calls for programs that present a social world that seems "true to life," with the potential to foster identification and attachment. Interviewees' use of the term "authenticity" seems to refer to the degree to which programs are true to their own culture and society as well as its spirit and character. This stance is particularly striking in the face of pressures exerted on producers by broadcasting authorities to conform to external, profit-driven market values that produce higher ratings scores; and to accede to political and ideological pressures to refrain from dealing with sensitive topics that might alienate audiences or undermine the *status quo* (e.g. homosexuality; opposition to ruling governments; fads and fashions that mean following winning formulas and successful clichés, and the like).

From psychological and individual perspectives, producers' discussions of authenticity speak to the need for presentation of characters who have the courage to live their lives according to their inner selves, rather than succumb to the demands and influences of society around them. The producers' testimonies echo philosophical concepts developed by existentialist philosophers and psychologists[17] who stressed the importance of living an authentic life, one in which creativity was considered to be essential. While the discussions of authenticity within the interviews were related to notions derived from existentialism and psychology, producers seem to be more sociologically oriented and critical of the social implications of commercial programming for children.[18] Despite the fact that the concept of authenticity, as an ideal social construction, is debated widely by social scientists, broad agreement was found to exist among this global collection of interviewees. They argued that most popular commercial television texts designed for children (as well as for adults) promoted behaviors and attitudes that are inauthentic, on some basic level, in relation to viewers' own inner selves and desires, while camouflaging the structural mechanisms driving them.[19] Non-fiction television programs, on the other hand, derive their power specifically from the fact that the images they provide seem to be believable, "real," and authentic. Those perceptions of "reality" are constructed through the use of documentary codes and conventions, including, for example, the incorporation of interviews, archival film footage, the use of hidden-cameras, "shaky" camera techniques that seem unedited, and the like.[20]

Character Credibility

The interviewees' focus, in regard to authenticity, was on the credibility of the characters themselves, as expressed by Lori (US), who said: *So, even if the program comes out looking like it is pure entertainment, there's a lot of thought that goes into a realistic portrayal of capturing what they really experience in their lives. Degrassi is a good example of such a show. They are working out issues with friends and friendships, and cliques in high school. They're working out issues of identity, like a gay character on Degrassi who is struggling with issues of identity. They're working through how they take risks, and how far to go, and does that make them feel like outsiders. And there are episodes that deal with experimentation with drugs, too. It is such a range. I think that they [viewers] need to see characters who are struggling with the things that they are struggling with. How they are relating to their families ... you know, what's happening at that age is that, you know that kind of gap between you and your parents starts to widen and you don't speak the same language anymore, and how difficult that is, and what's happening with your friendships [...] you don't know who you are, all the identity issues, I think, seeing characters struggling with those issues so that they are not feeling alone in what you're going through.*

The Canadian teen series *Degrassi* (see Figure 4.6) was mentioned by several interviewees as a positive example of authentic programming. Brad (US), for example, explained: *We talk a lot of being authentic. Degrassi tries very hard to be authentic. Every character in the show is acted by a person who's actually the age of the character. They don't have twenty-five-year-olds playing sixteen-year-olds. They're all sixteen with acne and the rest, and they take great pride in this, as they should.*

A female Hollywood producer on one of the LA conference panels explained that in her experience employing underage actors and actresses is more expensive due to labor laws protecting child employment in the industry in the US (e.g. restrictions on the number of hours of work per day, rest requirements, etc.). In order to cut expenses and to ease the process by working with experienced talent, US broadcasters tend to cast older actors to portray teenagers. The result is that they appear and behave in more mature and sexy ways than their characters' ages would suggest, and thus inhibit authenticity.

Tina (US), too, discussed characters' appearance: *They are real kids and so, you know, they've got pimples, their hair looks bad some days, and they are not perfect looking. And I actually think that this is just right, something as simple as that is very empowering to see. Just to see yourself reflected back on screen, particularly girls, because I think that it's been the standard and the ideal for young girls in the US – skinny, being pretty, being perfect, in all the magazines they read nobody is real. I think this is really groundbreaking to present really just genuine authentic looking kids.*

That this is, indeed, "groundbreaking" and rare in US-produced commercial programs was argued also by Natalie (France): *In my TV station we need to distinguish between the programs we buy and the programs we produce. In the programs we produce in France, girls are not like dolls. What I regret in American programs is that the girls look just like big girls with make-up; they are supposed to be thirteen to fourteen and there is make-up on their face like women of twenty to twenty-five years, and I don't like it ... When I am in production in France, we have normal girls that are not as nice looking as in American programs. We try to let them look natural, to be closer to reality, to what teenagers really are. Our audience was saying that they are not beautiful*

enough, because they are used to American programs, so we have to be rea-
listic, but not fully realistic …

In her interview Natalie raised the dilemma, mentioned by several interviewees, that the external beauty standards of American TV, spread globally,
impinge on their ability to be authentic, as their viewers have internalized the
US-based expectations. Brad (US) was even more critical of the manner in
which young audiences in the US have lost their sense of authenticity and have
fallen prey to external, profit-driven social pressures: *When we go to research*
and talk to our audience about what they want and what they don't want,
they say they want to see prettier people. It's like "But come on, don't you
want it to be real?" "No I don't want it to be real. I want it to be my version
of television. We don't want ugly people. We don't wanna look at ugly people.
We're not interested in ugly people." … it's really disturbing. And one of the
phrases we sort of made up for ourselves was that our audience is accusing us
of being a mirror and they would like us to be a window. "Tell me who I can
become. Don't tell me who I am. I know who I am. I spend all day with me,
I'm sick of me. I want to look older. I wanna imagine myself as a more fan-
tastic adult than I might turn out to be."

For our audience, TV is first and foremost escape and entertainment. And
there are so many times when we wish it to be something different, but they
bring it back to: "You're here to entertain. Do your job". It's not always
rewarding to hear that from them, but they say it with consistency. And it
doesn't mean we have to dumb it down or make it stupid or make it horrible,
but it does need to fulfill its social purpose. And if our job is to be a teen
brand, it needs to feel like somewhat the teenagers they want to be, not just
the teenagers they are. […] They want their TV people to feel more mature
and more polished.

At the same time that Brad and his colleagues are struggling with the tension between being true to reality and satisfying audience pressure to beautify
their world, they also take painstaking efforts to portray teen experiences in a
valid and credible way: *In the program we've got the girl figuring out her*
sexual identity, so we are getting advice from GLAAD [21] *… a group of young*
people who are gonna help us understand what it's like to come to terms with
discovering you are gay; getting the language right and knowing what it feels
like, and making sure the emotion is true. We are also making sure that there
is a group of black people who have been adopted by white families who are
advising us as we develop the story process, because unless you've gone
through it you can't really know.

Relevancy

The relevancy of TV characters to their audience's everyday experiences was a
central theme in relation to authenticity. Such, for example, was the discussion
offered by Omar (Syria): *When we adopt imported animation programs from*

China, Korea, Japan, we have to adjust them to fit Arab children. They need to make it familiar to the children, so it won't look strange to them; for example, in things like relationships between children and parents, or in schools, their treatment of authorities. Disrespect to adults is foreign to Muslim cultures and perceived as undermining their mores and values. Alternative forms introduce inauthentic experiences of what social life is or should be like into the homes of children, in this case in Syrian society. Similarly, Ralf (Germany) made the following argument in discussing pressures to adopt an American social scene in a German–US coproduction: *We don't want to have this kind of cultural diversity, because for one thing, the African-American experience is just that. It's African-American, it's not African-German, and the Africans that are in Germany are wearing different clothing, speaking a different dialect ... and so why would we want to try and imbue upon the children of Germany this experience which is not Germanic?* As Ralf's question demonstrates, the discrepancy between reality and its presentation in the program is perceived as disturbing the possibility of children feeling that they are inhibiting an authentic place through their viewing experiences.[22] It promotes an expectation from children's television to form a sense of community among viewers so they feel that it "reaches people like them, resonates with their personal beliefs, and helps them chart their position in the larger world."[23]

The need to transform the viewing experience into an authentic space requires that the reality is familiar rather than foreign, so it does not alienate children. Even minute but recognizable visible signs such as clothing, mannerisms, or dialect can create an affinity for the program, build loyalty,[24] and foster a sense of "locale patriotism." Such was the testimonial provided by Leonora (Mexico) for example: *[...] we had telephone calls from little girls from the public, they say – "Why is she wearing pants, she is a girl, she should be wearing a dress or a skirt." So now, even ten years later, sometimes they wear skirts and dresses, and sometimes they wear pants, but whenever we have a public performance I always say "please let all the girls and the women hosts wear skirts," otherwise. ...*

Social Change

The search for authenticity can also attract strong audience disapproval, as reported by Kasper (Denmark): *When we did the program ... we actually had this twelve-year-old smoke a cigarette on screen ... it is highly unusual in Denmark to show this, as everybody would say "Don't do that!" But, we showed it because this is actually how he is; we are trying to show that this is not something you should be proud of, that it is actually very bad. But, in other countries they would have never show that. We try to reflect our country and our culture. Our children sometimes swear on screen, although we try to make it so they won't swear more than the average kid, actually even less, but we wouldn't make a drama where there is no swearing because it wouldn't be credible to children, as there are no children who talk like that. So we try to reflect it in that way.*

Interviewees often addressed the possibility of change in relation to authenticity. Indeed, since authenticity was mainly perceived as lending "credibility" and truth to reality, those mentioning it also referenced situations in which reality was in dire need of social change. Thus, being authentic to some traditional aspects of society was not necessarily perceived as a positive characteristic of a program, but rather it was viewed as a debilitating factor in some situations, even one that prevented or blocked them from presenting a positive movement advancing a better social vision. The question thus became – how far from authentic reality can a program go before losing its audience? Or as Kirstine (US) put it: *I think it is complicated because children work hard to organize their worlds and if you violate many of their expectations, they either won't pay attention to you or they won't register what they are watching.*

The need to find a balance between introducing some change and maintaining authenticity was a theme that repeated itself among several interviewees. Samita (Bangaladesh) shared her experience of a situation in which the TV image conflicted with life circumstances and thus introduced unrest: *I often went outside Dakar for a UNICEF assignment and when I saw girls I asked them – "Do you like to be active like Meena"–and they say "Yes, but my mother sometimes tells me don't talk too much."* Meena (see Figure 6.6), a very popular cartoon featuring a South Asian girl, was created by UNICEF. Since its original appearance in Bangladesh in 1991, it has since spread to many Asian countries. It provides an example of television as a social intervention, as the series was created with the intention of fostering social change by specifically addressing issues of gender discrimination (e.g. in food, education, and domestic workloads). While many of these aspects are unique, the soap-opera dramatic style of *Meena* has been criticized by some as being inappropriate for children, and for including, most probably unintentionally, a variety of negative, alongside more gender-progressive, social messages.

Figure 6.6 Meena © UNICEF

Based on a lovable cartoon girl character who stimulates identification, it has been argued that *Meena* has succeeded in presenting a role model who challenges traditional value systems without threatening the audience.[25] However, the girls' reactions reported in the quotation above tell us that they are aware that the character of Meena offers a role model that diverges from their own everyday experiences, as demonstrated by the confrontation with the mother. As in other societies, mothers are often the most effective conveyers of patriarchal values as they realize that it is their responsibility to socialize their girls to fit into societal demands as they grow up (including being the ones in charge of facilitating what many Westerners and human-rights activists argue are repressive practices, such as: genital mutilation in some Islamic societies; forced early marriages and sex-trafficking around the world; the binding of feet in China's past; and the like).[26]

Most interviewees who referred to tensions between television images and life in the material world suggested that change needs to be introduced incrementally, in small steps, and very subtly, so the sense of authenticity is not hampered. As Paradise (South Africa) suggested: *I think that the messages should be salient ... I think it needs to be subtle but clear, as part of ordinary life, but not in your face. But the reality is that our children are growing up in different societies, and some cultures don't want you to tamper with that ... that is where the challenge lies, because there is the question of what are the traditional values, and how strong are they, and how do they hold true, and how do they resonate in our lives? ... I think people do that* [continue traditions] *because it is what they know, and what they are comfortable with, the cushioned life, don't change it too much because you might shock somebody. So, it is again the issue of subtlety. How do you, slowly, as you are making the program, begin to question and challenge things in a nice way; so your male characters have something feminine, something that is soft on a deeper level of the character rather than what has been accepted.*

Kim (The Netherlands) expressed the same idea: *You do it slowly, because when you make a whole program of a very successful mother and a stay-home father it doesn't work. But when you start with a father helping in the household, maybe they do the dishwashing together, little things, then you can do it step by step, and then they accept it. So, otherwise they don't broadcast it or it doesn't work.*

Overall, most interviewees were in favor of introducing change gradually, so that it is less threatening and more easily accepted. Rather than treating the current state of affairs as morally wrong, they also suggested, as did Taylor (Tanzania), that it should be approached playfully as something both practical and worthwhile. In illustrating his approach in regard to polygamy in his country, he argued that rather than critiquing this phenomenon and claiming that it is bad or immoral, it is better off to explain its historical and economic roots and why it makes no sense anymore in current life. The same logic, he argued, should be employed in television's efforts to discourage girls from dropping out of school: *Rather than making it a moral issue, make it a practical one. Girls should look at school as a stepping stone to go to Europe, to go to China, to go to America. Don't just stay home and get married, but go to school and the world opens up for you.*

Some, like Salma (Pakistan), suggested recruiting religion, since religion is part of the authentic sense of reality in everyday life in Pakistan and thus offers a common and respected basis for change: *Change has to be realistic. For example, you need to say in the program that girls need to be educated not so they can go to work, as this would be too big a change, but in order to be better mothers. When a boy says – "Girls can't do that" – the girl can respond – "Why not?" Introduce gradual change, not revolutionary, but gradually.*

Use religion to promote gender equality, because people are religious – like using Koran sentences that talk about women's rights. Use religious programs on TV to promote gender equality. The best way to counter these traditions in Pakistan, and elsewhere I think, is to bring religion into it because a lot of religious teaching is slightly biased and not very balanced and a lot of it is there, and the Koran says that women are equal to men, and those things are kind of interpreted the wrong way. So the way I have handled all of my programs and brought in extremely loud and clear revolutionary ideas about women, is to bring religion into it, and interpret it as it was meant to be.

The non-traditional reading of the Koran offered by Salma resonates with a growing trend in feminist thought that offers alternative interpretations to religious texts and practices, suggesting that a religion's patriarchal development is historically and culturally grounded and not inherent in the sacred intentions and writings of the original spiritual leaders or divine forces.[27] Such attempts at "depatriarchalizing" religious traditions by feminist scholars seem to have infiltrated the consciousness of several producers from religious societies who are struggling to make peace between their feminist orientations and their religious beliefs and traditions.

Thus, authenticity for the interviewees, in the sense of presenting a credible reality and being "true to life," offers not only criteria for evaluating the quality of programs and their potential to resonate with audiences, but perhaps more importantly, a criterion for introducing change in an effective and meaningful way. It is interesting to note that interviewees rarely alluded to the critical sense often associated with authenticity as a way of legitimizing the pursuit of American values of individualism (e.g. "be true to yourself"), and as a result, also promoting social unrest and radical anarchism (if "being true to yourself" means denouncing social norms and laws). Indeed, authenticity in the context of producing television for children was only invoked as a positive principle, one that could be summarized colloquially as not "selling out;" not surrendering to external pressures to abandon inherited local culture and values, but rather trying to create programs which are true to social reality.

Furthermore, another perspective rarely shared by interviewees in discussions of presenting an authentic reflection of reality relates to the question of "whose reality" is being reflected? Clearly, when one particular reality is chosen to be presented, other authentic realities are excluded. For example, when programs in Africa tackle the issue of safe sex and HIV/AIDS prevention, they exclude discussion of the reality of non-sexually-active teens; and when European programs center on middle-class children's lifestyles, they lack authenticity for the significant populations of working-class and immigrant children. Thus, this question relates to producers' social consciousness, values, vision, and understanding of their audience.

Summary

The principle of authenticity refers to the need for children's television to depict true-to-life characters, narratives, and social contexts, as this is critical to enabling children develop an authentic understanding of social reality.

The major strategies offered for following this principle were:

- Employ characters who are in real life actually close to the age and background of the fictional characters they will be playing

- Present characters who are not ideal beauty models

- Create plot lines that have relevancy to children's everyday lives, cultures, and values

- Introduce change in small and non-threatening steps

- Introduce change that is feasible and beneficial

- Recruit alternative interpretations of religion and traditions in order to introduce acceptable change

Voicing

Voicing is achieved when television programs are organized in such a manner as to present the perspectives of children themselves, as they view and express them.

The final principle offered by the interviewees was to "give voice" to children themselves. The notion of empowering underrepresented and misrepresented groups by giving them a voice in the media has been discussed extensively by scholars with diverse interests, from a variety of theoretical approaches.[28] Children, in particular, lack space, a voice and hence agency in both the theorizing of childhood as well as in its representation, in all cultural and media forms. The extremely limited presentation of children's voices in research has led some scholars to question our ability to make sense of "girls' voices" (and for that matter, boys' voices as well, although they have received less attention until more recently) and of what can be concluded about their inner worlds. The call has been to develop "a method for listening 'beyond and around' girls' words, interrogating especially troublesome talk rather than simply recording 'obvious' meanings."[29]

One form of "giving voice" is the development of child- and youth-made media (e.g. independent blogging, posting photos and artwork, and producing home videos and biographical documentaries, as well as guided school projects, aided productions in training workshops and special classes, and involvement in social movements and activism via the use of media and the production of messages). The value of these activities in the development of literacy skills, civic engagement, and personal growth has been widely discussed.[30] The primary consequences of such activities cited in this literature include enabling adults to obtain an "insider" view into the world of young people, to be more attuned to their needs and wellbeing, and thus to help bridge barriers between teen and adult worlds. In addition, the creative process of expression has been found to have therapeutic and empowering benefits to youngsters themselves, providing them with opportunities to engage in collaborative teamwork, to bridge differences, and to engage in productive negotiations. In addition, experience producing media messages is perceived to be a necessary means – as well as goal – of media literacy. While currently understood to be a complicated and multilayered term, media literacy, generally, is perceived to be a form of literacy necessary for participation in civic and cultural life that requires informed, critical, and creative citizenry. It is understood to refer to the ability to analyze and evaluate messages, as well as the ability to communicate in a variety of ways.[31]

However, in the context of our discussion, "giving voice" has quite a different (albeit related) meaning as it refers, essentially, to enabling children's perspectives to be expressed in adult-produced media. For the most part, this is rationalized by producers in terms of the importance of "authenticity," discussed above, as well as a principle for producing higher quality and programming of better "value" for the child-audiences viewing these programs. It is the value of "children talking to children" that is highlighted in these calls for "giving voice" rather than "children talking to adults" or children "working out" their inner world for their own benefits.

Several different views of this rationale were shared in the interviews. Some interviewees, like Julie (UK), felt that adults impose nostalgic aspirations on children rather than listening to their needs and desires: [...] *the trap for making children's programming, particularly children's drama, is that for adults it is the nostalgia factor. You can easily fall into: "Oh I loved that when I was a child, I want to show children what that was like." It's over, you know, you really actually have to understand what they want to see, and what's going on with them in their lives, and make programs for them.*

Others felt that creators of children's programs often talk about children rather than letting children talk for themselves. This was also expressed in the form of a distinction between programs that are *about* children and those *for* children. This distinction suggests a program featuring children does not necessarily have children's wellbeing and needs as its goal. Casting children as characters may be a necessary but not a sufficient condition for consideration as a quality program for children. Several examples illustrate this argument: Emma (Bolivia) said: *We made a series with the title* With Our Own Voices *where children talk about their lives, about their rights. They can speak, they can talk with their point of view; and I think it's very important that they do so in their language [...].* Margaret (Kenya) shared: *We were watching a program from Asia about a girl who wants to go to school and it is very interesting because it was a story from a girl's point of view [...] so the issues are still the same but from a different point of view.* And Mpule (Botswana) recommended: *I give them all voices so that they share how they feel, they share their success stories, their fears, their disappointments together. Let them have a face.* A unique example of giving voice was presented in *Children of Nomads*, a program from India in which the camera follows a six-year-old girl who interviews nomad children about their lives and gets acquainted with them from a child's perspective.

A specific example demonstrating the complexity of the issues involved in adults speaking for children rather than letting them speak for themselves developed in one of the discussion groups I attended during Prix Jeunesse 2008. A Muslim woman from South Africa, who had her head covered herself (a relevant detail, as will become clear shortly), shared the following in the heat of the argument: *It is difficult if you are going to break stereotypes. I had a program assignment with the French government about the Muslim head-scarf, a religious issue, and the way it was argued, it was completely not about the girl herself. And I say – let's look at what the girl says, what does it mean to her, does she want to have it on? Does she want to take it off? Where is her voice? And the counter-argument was that – "No, no, no, if girls take off the headscarf then the boys will call them names." But nobody is saying this is what it is indeed for girls. Is this what really happens to them? Give them a voice of their own.*

As the discussion unfolded, it became clear that not giving girls a voice, in this case as in many others, is not necessarily a result of a naïve lack of awareness of children's needs, but a calculated strategy to ignore children's positions and perspectives, and to impose upon them an adult one. What was radical about the proposal made by this participant was not so much the matter of "giving voice" to girls for the sake of creating an authentic and more appealing program, but rather the proposal that the program examine a complicated religious, social, and political issue that has attracted so much heated debate. Indeed, this speaker combined both elements: examine an issue and enable the girls to present the view of those required to take off their *hijabs* (or, alternatively, in other cultures, to put them on). In doing so, viewers would learn about the issue as well as what those most directly involved have to say about it.

It is interesting to note that the concern for "giving voice" was mostly expressed by non-Western participants, as part of a general normative discourse among media professionals that called for privileging the marginalized and disenfranchised. One possible explanation for this was offered indirectly by Chan-ho (Korea) who talked about the unique characteristics of her society: *I prefer to see somebody who is very natural, to be themselves, whoever they are, comfortable; because Asian, Korean, are very rigid in a way, very polite, very conservative [...] we need to learn how to express ourselves, not to constrain ourselves [...] girls are usually cold and shy on TV, but today young girls are asking questions [...] it is getting better.* What Chan-ho is alluding to is more typical of societies in which family structures are hierarchical, where respect for adults and authorities is highly valued, and where children have less space to express themselves within the adult world. Many illustrations of these cultural differences are spread within the pages of this book. In contrast, in many Western societies, more specifically within the norms of the middle-educated classes, children are treated more as equals to adults and families practice a more democratized everyday life (as we have discussed above in relationship to the principle of family), to the point that many would argue that children talk "too much" and that their "voices" have over-shadowed those of experienced and responsible adults.

A special case illustrating this point was a discussion of the Swedish program *Radical Cheerleaders* (see Figure 6.7) that developed among participants in the Japan Prize 2006 event where it was screened as a finalist in the youth category. The documentary followed the leader of a group of teenage girls in Sweden protesting gender inequality through a performance of a different kind of "cheerleading" routine that included "punk style" dress codes and "dirty-aggressive" language and gestures that break gender expectations regarding "good girl" codes of appearance, behavior, and speech. The program agitated and elicited much objection among the viewers, including those who considered themselves avid fighters for gender equality in their own organizations. The central concern was the "in-your-face" rebellious approach portrayed in the program: "Well, yes, we understand. We agree with the message, but does it have to be so harsh? Why do they have to use 'fucking' all the time and the 'cut their cocks' language?"

Indeed, as reported by Anneli (Sweden), who was involved with its production, the program ignited a public debate in Sweden when it was first aired: *We have never gotten so many hate letters mailed about a program before. It was so many, mostly from men around forty-five, fifty, who suddenly started to write angry letters and they tried to stop the program ... and wanted to*

Figure 6.7 Radical cheerleaders © UR, Sweden

take us to court, because of the "cutting off the men's cocks" language [...].
It is one episode in a series. The series is not about feminism [...] it's about
expressing yourself as a teenager. If you have something you really want to
say, you can express yourself in different ways. And this is one kind of
expression. Another episode was about an African princess living in Stockholm
with her father and she writes her own lyrics. And she went to audition to
some contest in Sweden and we decided to do a story about her. She was
trying to get into a restaurant together with her mother and her brother, and
she was molested by the guardians, and they hit both her and her mother. It
was a very famous restaurant in the middle of Stockholm [...] they thought
she was hustling and she was really not doing anything wrong. And then she
started a network for people with different backgrounds living in Sweden who
can't get into restaurants. So that was a side story about discrimination and
how she worked with it.

   When asked specifically about the harsh language chosen in *Radical*
Cheerleaders Anneli responded: *That's the way they express themselves. We*
would never censor them; that would go against the whole idea [...] and I
liked the fact that she sometimes was so childish, and sometimes so grown
up. You know, when they were laughing about someone farting in the
bookstore, very childish ... and then she had these really analytical
thoughts. Thus, since retaining the original and authentic voice of the characters was a main goal of the program, presenting teenage girls in the ways

they wish to present themselves included allowing them to express themselves in their own uncensored ways, which sometimes appeared childish to an adult eye, sometimes mature, sometimes aggressive, and sometimes sweet and shy.

As with references to the other principles of gender equality, here there was an assumption behind the interviewees' calls for "giving voice" that such a strategy would contribute to social change by allowing children to be agents of change themselves, and that it would also benefit children, both on and off screen. It was believed that it has the potential to empower children, girls in particular, who are still silenced to a great degree in many societies around the world.

Summary

The principle of voicing refers to constructing television programs in such a manner as to present the perspectives of children themselves as they view and express them.

The major strategies offered for following this principle were:

- Incorporate in storylines the points of view of real children experiencing similar situations
- Produce documentary programs that feature children's perspectives
- Do not impose adults' points of view on children as if they represent their world
- Give voice to children's diverse perspectives

Chapter 7

Beyond The Principles

Concluding Notes on Changing Gender Representations

How does one summarize the insights and propositions offered by so many well-intended professionals, from very diverse backgrounds, who share a love for children and a concern for their wellbeing? These concluding notes highlight some of the strands with which we can braid their thoughts together with my analysis, interpretations, and vision.

First, as a general term of reference and set of criteria, we remind ourselves of the communication rights of children, as delineated in the United Nations Convention on the Rights of the Child, which include the rights to be heard and to be taken seriously; to free speech and to information; to maintain privacy; to develop cultural identity; and to be proud of one's heritage and beliefs.[1] Yet, whether boys and girls live in deprived and resource-poor societies, or in overwhelmingly commercialized and profit-driven ones, their voices are mostly neither heard nor taken seriously; they have limited possibility for free speech or access to much-needed information; their privacy is often not respected and their cultural heritage is often ignored or erased. This situation has led some concerned adults to seek to limit children's access to media, to legislate the regulation and control of content, and even to advocate the use of direct censorship.

Two alternative courses of action have been advanced by those who, too, are concerned about children's wellbeing, but oppose direct government intervention and the use of censorship: First, according to some proponents, parents should be encouraged to regulate and to mediate their children's media use at home; second, children should be educated in their schools to become literate media users. However, the limited yet very specific research evidence gathered to date indicates that neither of these strategies has yet proved its efficiency in mediating the processes of meaning-making and in counteracting the type of values and worldviews promoted by much television fare.[2]

A complementary third approach, advocated here, argues that media professionals should develop a critical awareness of their work, engage in self-regulation of their industry, roll up their sleeves and become engaged in the development of a more socially engaged, just, and richly symbolic presentation of the world to children. Thus, responsible production together with engaged parenting and education may provide the fertile ground for social change towards more gender equity.

In addition, the study's findings can be strongly tied to the field of development communication, which systematically applies processes and strategies of communication to promote social development and change. Indeed, many of my interviewees' quotations regarding gender images on television integrated assumptions, overt statements, and prescriptions for change: Be it in schooling for girls and the struggle to end illiteracy, HIV/AIDS prevention education and the promotion of health and tolerance, or the reduction of domestic violence through promoting change in portrayals of masculinity. Most of this work has been associated with transforming resource-poor and underdeveloped societies, making them more socially and economically advanced and more liberated in terms of social equity.[3]

The type and quality of social change suggested here can be framed as part of the growing interest in and development of social marketing, and more specifically in the entertainment-education ("edutainment") interventions alluded to in previous chapters. Conceptualized as bridging the arbitrary dichotomy between entertainment and education, by combining the benefits and strengths of both, edutainment involves designing and implementing media productions with educational messages that are also entertaining. In this manner, the appeal and popularity of entertainment genres are capitalized on in order to promote social change oriented to wellbeing at individual as well as social levels. A variety of successful edutainment interventions have been documented and studied in areas such as health, the environment, and social issues.[4]

Toward Gender Equity in Children's Television

As discussed throughout this book, we live in an era in which new expressions of masculinities and femininities, as well as changes in gender relations, have emerged. As constructions of gender are pluralized, they become increasingly fragmented, and some would even argue – tenuous. As a result, a current debate questions if we are facing the "bending" or even the "ending" of gender.[5] Yet, in contrast to these views, we have seen that the vast majority of television programming for children continues to present a binary, segregated, stereotypical, and unequal gender world. This enduring discrimination has a long, complicated social history and it is intimately involved in the retention of the most central, obvious, and universal material forms of gender inequality. Interviewees' testimonies supported the assertion that men retain most of the decision-making positions and responsibilities in the industry. This conclusion is particularly dramatic given the extensive feminization of media professions, particularly within the area of children's television, and the fact that many women now occupy key positions of power and influence within this professional world.

The industry continues to rely to a significant degree on familiar genres and proven formulas, to employ stereotypes and clichés, and to follow "axioms" about what boys and girls like and what they will or will not watch. While significant and impressive changes have been introduced via innovative, gender-sensitive, high-quality programming for children (some of which has been noted in the previous pages), many global and local broadcasters continue to rely on recycling old-fashioned programs stored in their archives, and will probably continue to do so for economic reasons for decades to come. The result is that the introduction of overall, significant change in children's television is very slow, with only isolated islands of innovation.

Introducing gender sensitivity into television for children – both explicitly and implicitly – can be perceived as promoting a universal humanistic value incorporated within entertainment. The eight working principles delineated in Chapter Six – equality, diversity, complexity, similarity, unity, family, authenticity, and voicing – may be seen as guidelines for advancing such change, along with the many specific production strategies shared by inter-viewees. These principles may seem obvious to some readers. Yet, the produ-cers with whom these findings have been shared in several recent conferences and meetings did not think so. For example, it is one matter to argue on the basis of Cultural Studies' scholarship that commercial texts "colonize" local cultures by perpetuating a Western beauty myth and way of life. It is quite a different matter to investigate what no-less-educated producers working in these countries actually think about these texts and their influence on their own child audiences, as they confront these issues in their everyday work practices. The fact that both scholars and professionals may agree overall with the above observation, while gratifying, does not make it superfluous – as the two groups arrive at their understanding through entirely different experiences, sources of data, and analyses.

This critical reading of the obstinate status of children's programming was shared by many interviewees, and even by top executives of major US media corporations. And, interestingly, there seems to be widespread agreement that since "it is all about money," the most effective arguments for advancing change should not be moralistic ones about social responsibility, but rather those that are framed as profit-driven: Demonstrate how money can be made by changing images and catering to growing demands from the child audience. As one top executive who spoke to me on the promise of anonymity observed: *The best way to promote change is to show there is profit in it.* In reflecting on this proposal, a Latin-American executive sighed: *No wonder what it is called, in the US, television is industry.* She explained in response to my request for clarification that the choice of the term "industry" (over, for example, "arts," or "world") reflects the ideological value system behind it: This is a corporate world driven by profit considerations, producing products on an assembly line to be sold to mass consumers. Thus, "better" programming, for the industry, does not mean "socially better," rather – "more profitable."

In striking contrast, many interviewees – particularly those more gender-sensitive, socially engaged, and involved in advancing change – reflected on the need to continually develop their own awareness and social consciousness, because they admitted to regularly falling into gender-bias traps, given that most of us have been so strongly acculturated to gender blindness. Interestingly, they employed a model of social epistemology that assigned researchers a very important role: Scholars can assist them by conducting action research that will provide them with data and observations about attempts to advance programming and organizational changes related to key social issues. Furthermore, their critical perspective challenges axioms discussed in this study and poses a rich agenda for socially engaged research that is involved in policy and programming changes: Is it true that boys will not watch girls' programs? Will introducing more diversity expand or lead to a decline in audience numbers? Do new images of boys and girls as well as new relationships and collaborations between them appeal to various young audiences? How do children react to seeing people who do not fit the "ideal appearances" of the people on their screens? Do boys relate to boys who talk about their inner worlds, and to girls who are leaders and who are more concerned about their character than their looks? How are decisions made in organizations producing and broadcasting for children?

Overall, I concluded that most of these interviewees want to be listened to and to learn from relevant research that will help them in their decision-making processes. This finding stands in sharp contrast to another accepted "axiom" employed in both academic as well as industry circles, one that argues that these two professional worlds are mutually suspicious, disrespectful, and dismissive. Accordingly, so the axiom goes, professionals believe that academic research functions in an unapproachable and generally out of touch "ivory tower," and that the pronouncements of academics are irrelevant because they are unaware of or do not account for the constraints of "the real world." In turn, academics believe that many professionals are too arrogant and uninformed to listen to solid, substantiated, and evidence-based advice. The findings of this study support a view that is diametrically opposed to both claims: the media professionals who participated in this study called for serious, in-depth, and productive collaboration between these two worlds of expertise.

The professionals' desire for collaboration with academics is encouraging given the rise in current debates in academic associations and published scholarship about the role of communication scholars as public intellectuals.[6] Indeed, this study can be seen as an example of how engaged scholars of gender and media professionals can move beyond conventional studies of media representations toward developing our understanding of the ideologically driven mechanisms, political-economy constraints, as well as means of production that drive the images that both academics and media professionals have been criticizing for so long.

Furthermore, in keeping with these producers' engagement, I hope this book moves beyond description and analysis of the professional world involved in producing these images. It has attempted to do so by presenting a collective set of recommendations for desirable portrayals and guidelines for advancing change. The analysis of the views shared in the interviews contributes to an evolving conceptualization of how gender-bending can be advanced by media professionals involved in the production of children's television programs. Indeed, much of what they said, indeed the spirit of what they shared with me, extends well beyond what they had to say about gender *per se* to a vision for social equality in more general terms. As such, I hope this book can be of value to media professionals, scholars, and students engaged in creating and studying the social construction of reality portrayed on the screen – for children and adults alike who aspire to advance the use of television to promote a more humane and just world.

The Power of Imagination

This long five-year journey around the world taught me that gender "bending" is possible – and perceived to be desirable – through practices and performances that resist gender norms and take social risks in behaviors, appearances, characters, roles, relationships, language, mannerism, sexualities, dreams, and so forth shared in children's television programming. This reminds us of the famous feminist slogan that has inspired the imagination and supported women (and some men) involved in advancing gender change over the last thirty years: "Well-behaved women seldom make history."[7] While interpreted in a multiplicity of ways, it has come to suggest that conformity and adhering to traditional gender norms that expect compliance and the subordination of women does not bring about significant changes for women (or other oppressed groups, for that matter). Offering girls and boys images of girls and boys who are not afraid to deviate from traditional gender norms, who break away from them in making the world a better place for themselves and for others, may be just what this television "safe space" can symbolically do. As Mike (US) expressed passionately: *Television can be forward-thinking. It can show people different ways of living and accepting. I don't want to reflect reality the way it is, but reflect reality the way I think it should be [...]. As we grow up we forget about love. We get busy, we get smart, we become greedy. All these things happen to us [...] I don't mind modeling a utopian world, I would rather have people who say I have learned something from that show, that's what I want to do. I want to make a positive change, even small, rather than validate the problems.*

One of the unique advantages of studying gender with media professionals from so many different societies around the world is that it enables us to gain an insight into alternative ways of being a girl or a boy while addressing the limits of Western theories and ideologies about gender which dominate our scholarly work in the field of feminist media studies. Many questions remain and none of the interviewees was so naïve as to believe in dramatic, overnight changes in the content viewed by children on screens around the world. As Nasing (Malaysia) said to me with a sigh: *I think these things take a lot of time. Even if it is going to happen, it is going to happen slowly. We are talking about many thousands of years of ingrained, inherited traits and values, and characteristics; it's not going to happen overnight, but it is changing and I am happy that it is for the good!*

By way of putting change strategies in perspective, I recall that on more than one occasion I incited a discussion regarding embedding religious symbols in programs for children when sharing with a group of producers a story related to me by Dikla (Israel). According to Dikla, she very reluctantly relinquished a programming idea to present a Jewish boy wearing a Star of David playing with a Palestinian girl wearing a religious scarf (the *hijab*) in a pre-school program in Israel. Her pilot test of the idea revealed that parents on both sides of the seemingly intractable divide were resistant, because they viewed the religious symbol of their opponents to be so foreign, inducing so much immediate fear and hate, that they were not willing to tolerate the idea of their children being exposed to it. Reactions to this episode reinforced the notion that ruptures in the presentation of familiar reality caused by introducing "shocking" challenges are mostly unwise and ineffective, and that change needs to be achieved by stretching authenticity gently and gradually, in such ways as were suggested by many interviewees in Chapter Six.

Yet Paradise (South Africa) offered a striking alternative view of how change should be advanced when she responded to my account of Dikla's initiative: *Yes, you show them the* hijab, *because if they don't see it they can't imagine it. Children need to have a vision, a dream. If you can't imagine something you can't work towards achieving it.* At a different event, Senait (Ethiopia) surprised me when she shared the bold efforts of *Tsehai Loves Learning* (see Figure 3.1) to face gender stereotypes head-on in a very traditional environment. Similarly, Lindsey (US) suggested: *Put the character in a situation to see something you haven't seen before. If you can't think it, you can't talk it, and you can't do it.*

Thus, some producers believe that there is value in "shocking" the audience, as suggested by another educator who coordinates production workshops for UNICEF in resource-poor societies. She shared what she calls the "stare factor:" By allowing children to stare at the unimaginable (e.g. a severely disabled person; a person of an unfamiliar race), they become comfortable with it. Examples of such a strategy were presented in the documentary *Stark! Kevin Hear Me Out* (see Figure 7.1) that followed the struggle of a stuttering boy as he faced his disability; or following the friendship created between a blind Caucasian girl and an Asian girl in the fiction *Genji* (see Figure 7.2). Both force the viewers to boldly stare at the disabled children in their moments of vulnerability and pain. Another interviewee was moved to cite Martin

Figure 7.1 Stark! Kevin Hear Me Out © ZDF, Germany

Figure 7.2 Genji © KRO Youth / Eyworks Film & TV Drama, The Netherlands

Luther King's famous "I have a dream" speech[8] as evidence of the promise in offering children a dream that may seem unattainable, in order to hold it up as a light for the future.

Being challenged to imagine the impossible can be illustrated by another interview conducted by Larry King,[9] the prominent television-show host, this time with Thomas Beatie and his wife Nancy. Thomas is a transsexual who became known as the first man to become pregnant and to give birth to a child (and at the time of writing, was pregnant for the second time).[10] At a certain point in reconstructing the early stages of their relationship (before Thomas started his hormonal treatments), Larry King turned to Nancy and asked her with noticeable unease: "So when you fell in love with Thomas, he was still a woman, right?" Nancy looked at him with a very content, gentle smile, and responded: "I did not fall in love with a woman or a man. I fell in love with a person."

Thomas and Nancy's discussion, and indeed their appearance on this popular television program, reminds us of the power of imagination. For me, it was not about preaching this or that gender identity or glorifying the science of gender-reassignment. It was not about providing a role model or a normative prescription for this or any other personal choice. Rather, it was about the possibility of breaking expectations, thinking outside the gender box; imagining something that I, as a viewer, had never imagined before.

Television images have the power to do just that, and so much more, toward advancing gender equity, if we act to do so.

Glossary of Programs

Alam Simsim A coproduction of Sesame Workshop and Al Karma Edutainment launched in 1997 and broadcasted since 2000 on Egyptian Television (ETV). See also: *Sesame Street*.

Amigo A humorous children's game show with a studio audience produced by Denmark Radio TV (DR TV).

Angelina Ballerina An animated series about a fictional mouse based on a book series by author Katharine Holabird and illustrator Helen Craig, produced by HIT Entertainment, UK. A new series *Angelina Ballerina: The Next Steps* has been produced since the fall of 2009 by CGI for PBS Kids in the US and Nick Jr. in the UK.

As Told By Ginger An animated series premiered on Nickelodeon in 2000, focusing on Ginger Foutley and her adventures in Jr. High, as she records them in her diary.

Atomic Betty An animated series coproduced by Atomic Cartoons, Breakthrough Films & Television, and Tele Images Kids, Canada. It tells the story of an adolescent named Betty who is secretly also a Galactic Guardian, dedicated to peacekeeping and law enforcement.

Barney & Friends A pre-school program featuring a purple dinosaur and his human friends, promoting learning through songs and dance with a friendly and optimistic attitude. Originally created by Sheryl Leach, US and picked up by PBS in 1992. Production and ownership has changed hands many times since, and it is currently distributed by Twentieth Century Fox Home Entertainment.

Batman A film series featuring a superhero based on a comic character created by Bob Kane, financed and distributed by Warner Bros. Pictures. The first series was directed by Tim Burton and Joel Schumacher and released between 1989 and 1997. A second series was launched in 2005 and directed by Christopher Nolan. The role of Batman was portrayed by various actors: Michael Keaton, Val Kilmer, George Clooney, and Christian Bale.

Bob the Builder A claymation series created by Keith Chapman in the UK and aimed at young pre-schoolers. Bob is a building contractor who works with friends and equipment and emphasizes conflict resolution, cooperation, and various skills. In the US it originally aired on Nick Jr., then moved to Noggin, and since 2005 it has been broadcast by PBS Kids.

Boxing Beauty (Figure 6.1) Produced and broadcast on Israeli Broadcasting Authority (IBA). A documentary about a multi-talented teenage girl who is a boxer, singer, and a model, as she is practicing for the Israel National Boxing championship.

Bratz A computer-animated series based on a line of toy dolls following the adventures of four girl characters with "a passion for fashion." Produced by Mike Young Productions and MGA Entertainment and airing in the US on FOX Kids TV.

Buffy the Vampire Slayer A supernatural drama series created by Joss Whedon which went on the air on WB Television Network, US in 1997. It follows the adventures of Buffy Summers, played by Sarah Michelle Gellar, who battles against forces of darkness such as vampires and demons.

Bugs Bunny An animated grey rabbit character, created originally in 1940 by Tex Avery and Robert McKimson in NY and featured in series of animated films and television animations, becoming the mascot for Warner Bros.

Caillou A pre-school animated series based on the books by author Christine L'Heureux and illustrator Hélène Desputeaux featuring a curious four-year-old boy and his friends and family. Produced by Cookie Jar Entertainment, it was originally aired on Teletoon channel, Canada in 1998, and from 2000 on PBS, US.

Cheetah Girls A series of original Disney Channel movies first released in 2003 and based on a series of books by Deborah Gregory that tell the story of a four-member teen girl group of pop-singers.

Children of Nomads Produced by Leorats Communication and broadcasted by Gyan Darshan/EMPC Ignou, New Delhi, India. The program features the meeting of a privileged six-year-old Indian girl with marginalized nomad children.

The Children's Supershow Produced and broadcast by the Norwegian Broadcasting Corporation (NRK). A variety program featuring children and dads and other adult males who are fun and kind.

Cinderella An animated feature film produced in 1950 by Walt Disney based on a fairy tale about romantic love. The film won awards for its music score and the "Bibbidi-Bobbidi-Boo" song.

Clarissa Explains It All A teen situation comedy series created by Mitchell Kriegman, originally aired on Nickelodeon from 1991–94. It featured the everyday life of a pre-adolescent girl, Clarissa, played by Melissa Joan Hart.

The Cosby Show A situation comedy starring Bill Cosby, first airing on NBC in 1984. The show focuses on the life of an upper-middle-class African-American family living in Brooklyn, New York and raising their five children.

Dancing Produced by VPRO Broadcasting Organization and broadcast on the Netherlands Public Broadcasting (NPO). A non-fiction program for pre-schoolers featuring diverse people dancing.

Danny's Parade (**Figure 4.3**) Produced by NPS and broadcast on the Netherlands Public Broadcasting (NPO). A non-fiction program documenting the activism of a fourteen-year-old gay boy organizing a gay and lesbian youngsters' float in Amsterdam's annual Gay Canal Parade.

Daria An animated series and two TV movies created by Glenn Eichler and Susie Lewis Lynn that ran originally on Cable Network MTV. Daria, a spin-off character from MTV's *Beavis and Butt-head,* is a high-school girl who presents a satirical view of school life and many allusions to popular culture.

The Day I Decided to be Nina (**Figure 4.2**) Produced by VRPO and broadcasted by the Netherlands Public Broadcasting (NPO). The documentary follows an eleven-year-old boy who wants to live as a girl.

Degrassi (**Figure 4.6**) A drama series composed of *The Kids of Degrassi Street; Degrassi Junior High;* and *Degrassi High* (produced by Playing With Time Inc.), and *Degrassi: The Next Generation* (produced 2001–present by Epitome Pictures Inc.) Canada. The series follows the lives of a group of teenagers and the challenges they face.

Dora the Explorer An animated pre-school series that has aired on Nickelodeon since 2000 as well as other networks. It features Dora, a Latina girl, and her friends, who go on exploring trips to find something or help somebody while involving the audience. In the American version she also teaches children Spanish (in other countries where the program is dubbed into the native language, e.g., Israel and Germany, she teaches English).

Daffy Duck An animated cartoon character in the Warner Brothers *Looney Tunes* and *Merrie Melodies* series. Since his 1938 debut, the character has evolved and changed.

Fatma (**Figure 3.2**) Broadcast by Nile Thematic Channels on Egyptian Radio & Television Union. A documentary telling the story of a village girl who insists on going to school despite all difficulties.

Friends A situation comedy created by David Crane and Marta Kauffman and premiered on NBC, US in 1994. The series revolves around a group of six young people who are friends and live in Manhattan, New York City.

Genji (**Figure 7.2**) Produced and broadcast by KRO Youth, The Netherlands. The drama tells the story of the friendship between a Chinese girl and a Caucasian blind girl, and overcoming fears.

Girls (**Figure 4.4**) Broadcast on the Netherlands Public Broadcasting (NPB/IKON). The documentary features three teenage boys who talk about their inner world, and particularly their thoughts about, and relationships with, girls.

Hey Arnold An animated series created by Craig Bartlett and aired originally on Nickelodeon from 1996–2004. The series features Arnold, a fourth-grader who lives with his grandparents in a boarding house in a fictional American city and helps his school mates solve problems.

High School Musical A series of three hit Disney Channel movies, airing since 2006, featuring a love story between two high-school teens belonging to rival social groups – Troy Bolton (Zac Efron) and Gabriella Montez (Vanessa Anne Hudgens) – which broke viewing records worldwide.

Hurray! Cool Daddy (**Figure 6.5**) Produced and broadcast by Educational Broadcasting System (EBS), Korea. The studio-based series features fun and games for children 5–7 years old and their fathers.

Invisible Wounds (**Figure 4.1**) Produced and broadcast by Swedish Educational Broadcasting Company (UR). A six-part non-fiction series dealing with children who have suffered sexual and physical abuse by allowing them to open up and talk about it.

Konfje Produced by BOS Bros Film & TV Productions and broadcast on the Netherlands Public Broadcasting (NPB/KRO). The fiction series tells the story of a four-year-old and her adventures at home, including an episode where her father pretends she is a princess and builds her a pretend castle.

Kim Possible An animated series created by Mark McCorkle and Bob Schooley and originally aired on the Disney Channel from 2002–7. The action-oriented series features Kim Possible, a teenage crime fighter living a double life who deals with supervillains as well as her own school life.

Larry King Live An American nightly talk show hosted by Larry King on CNN since 1985 and broadcast worldwide on CNN International. In the program King interviews individuals such as celebrities and politicians.

The Little Mermaid An animated film produced by Walt Disney Feature Animation and released in 1989. The film is based on the Hans Christian

Andersen fairy tale and tells the story of the mermaid Ariel who falls in love with a human prince.

Little Peace of Mine (**Figure 6.3**) Produced by Eden Productions and broadcast by Telad, Israel. The program follows a twelve-year-old Israeli boy who forms a new children's movement for peace and the harsh reality they uncover of Palestinians and Israelis living in conflict.

Lizzie McGuire A pre-teen and teen series created by Terri Minskly and produced by Stan Rogow aired originally on the Disney Channel from 2001–4. The series features a well-behaved Lizzie, and her animated *alter ego* who occasionally expresses her true feelings.

Maya & Miguel An animated series produced by Scholastic Studios airing on PBS Kids Go! since 2004. The series features the pre-teen Hispanic twins Maya and Miguel and their friends and is aimed at promoting multiculturalism.

Meena (**Figure 6.6**) A television series created by UNICEF for the promotion of gender equality in South East Asia by encouraging girls' education and preventing child-marriage.

Mickey Mouse A comical mouse cartoon character was created in 1928 by Walt Disney who has become an icon for the Walt Disney Company.

Mortified (**Figure 4.5**) Produced by the Australian Children's Television Foundation and broadcast on Nine Network. The drama series features the challenges facing a twelve-year-old girl as she shifts from childhood to adolescence.

Mr. Rogers' Neighborhood A pre-school television series, created and hosted by Fred Rogers in Pittsburg, Pennsylvania, and was longest running series on most PBS stations until September 2008. The series used a mixed format of drama and puppetry and was characterized by its gentleness and respect for children.

Mulan An animated feature film produced by Walt Disney Feature Animation and released in 1998. The film is based on the Chinese legend of the brave female character of Hua Mulan during the time of the invasion of China by the Huns.

Odd One Out Produced by VRPO Broadcasting Organization and broadcast on Netherlands Public Broadcasting (NPB). A non-fiction series that looks at the lives of unique children.

Pelswick An animated series produced by Nevlana for CBC Television in Canada and Nickelodeon in the US and aired originally in 2002. The series relates the normal life of a teenage boy who uses a wheelchair and is based on books created by John Callahan.

Peppa Pig (**Figure 6.4**) An animated series created and produced by Astley Baker Davies and El Entertainment and broadcast originally on Five, UK in 2004. It revolves around the life of Peppa, a young pig and her family and friends.

The Peace Initiatives Institute's (Pii) Media Initiative For Children (**Figure 6.2**) A series of 60-second animated episodes directed by Paul W. Harris, produced and regularly broadcast on television in 2003–9 by the Peace Initiatives Institute and integrated with a curriculum developed and taught in Northern Irish pre-schools by Pii's in-country partner, "The Early Years" organization. The episodes convey simple messages about the inclusion of others in the everyday life of young children.

Pimp My Ride A show produced by MTV which revolves around restoring cars in poor condition and customizing them.

Pocahontas An animated feature film in the Walt Disney Animated Classics series released in 1995. The film is based on the story of a real Native American woman and her fictionalized romance with the Englishman John Smith.

Pokémon A media franchise originating with the Nintendo video game created by Satoshi Tajiri and later including among other products a Japanese animated television series which tells the adventures of Ash, a Pokémon trainer, his friends and the many creatures inhabiting their world.

Powerpuff Girls An animated series created by Craig McCracken and produced by Hanna-Barbera until 2001 when Cartoon Network took over. The series revolves around the adventures of three superhero girls who use their powers to defend their town from villains and monsters, as well as with normal everyday issues.

Power Rangers An animated series produced by Saban Entertainment (later BVS Entertainment under Disney) and premiered on Fox Kids in 1993. The series revolves around the adventures of five people who morph into superheroes in colorful costumes and fight evil forces.

Radical Cheerleaders (**Figure 6.7**) Produced and broadcast by the Swedish Educational Broadcasting Company (UR). This non-fiction program follows a Swedish teen who organizes a group of alternative cheerleaders, independent and articulate teen girls who are critical of gender relationships and seek their independence.

Ready Steady Grow Produced and broadcast by the Swedish Educational Broadcasting Company (UR). This non-fiction series discusses puberty in both boys and girls and the changes they go through physically and emotionally.

Rugrats An animated series created by Arlene Klasky, Gábor Csupó, and Paul Germain for Nickelodeon and aired originally from 1991–2004. The series centers on the adventures of four babies.

Scooby Doo Animated series produced by Hanna-Barbera Productions and later Warner Bros. Animation for American Saturday morning television in different versions from 1969 to the present. The series features a talking dog and four teenagers.

Sesame Street An acclaimed educational multi-genre magazine-format series for pre-school children produced by Sesame Workshop (formerly Children's Television Workshop) that premiered in the US in 1969. The program has since been broadcast in over 100 countries around the world as well as in the form of many local coproductions.

Sex and the City A drama/comedy series broadcast originally on HBO from 1998–2004. The show focuses on the friendship of four professional women who live in New York City and their intimate relationships with men.

Sexteens A five-minute animation program which is part of the project "Cortos que animan" developed by Fundacion Huesped for Artear S.A., Buenos Aires, Argentina. The series consists of five animated stories dealing with different aspects of HIV as they relate to the lives of three teenage girls at the start of their sexually active life.

The Simpsons An animated adult-oriented sitcom series created by Matt Groening for Fox Broadcasting Company since 1989. The series is a satirical parody of the blue-collar American family. A feature-length film based on the series was also released in 2007.

The Smurfs An animated series based on comic strips by the cartoonist Peyo in Belgium that was developed in the 1980s by Hanna-Barbera Productions. The series describes a fictional community of blue creatures who live in a village in the woods.

Snow White and the Seven Dwarfs A 1937 Walt Disney animated feature based on the Brothers Grimm fairy tale. It relates the adventures of a beautiful princess running away from her wicked and jealous stepmother and finding a home caring for seven dwarfs. When she is tempted to eat a poisoned apple she falls unconscious but is rescued from this fate by a kiss from a handsome prince and "lives happily after." The tale of Snow White has become part of the canon of classic animation, and has been subject to a wide range of scholarly analysis relating to the messages it conveys about gender roles.

SpongeBob SquarePants An American animated television series created by United Plankton Pictures, Inc. and aired on Nickelodeon.

Stark! Kevin Hear Me Out (**Figure 7.1**) Produced by e+u-tv and broadcast by ZDF, Germany. This documentary program follows Kevin, who goes through a challenging training course to overcome his stuttering problem.

The Spice Girls An English pop girl group popular in the 90s consisting of five women. Following the success of their albums they were also featured in the movie *Spice World*. The group known for introducing the iconic term "Girl Power."

Spiderman A series of comic-based superhero films by Columbia Pictures first released in 2002. The films feature the character of Peter Parker, who turns into Spiderman, and his adventures as he protects his friends.

Superman A comic-based superhero film of 1978 staring Christopher Reeve, which established the superhero film genre. The film features the character of Clark Kent who turns into Superman and fights for justice.

Takalani Sesame (**Figure 3.3**) Coproduction of Sesame Workshop and broadcast since 2000 by the South African Broadcasting Corporation, in both English and Sotho. See also: *Sesame Street*.

Teletubbies A series aimed at toddlers produced from 1997–2001 by Ragdoll Productions and broadcast on the BBC, UK. The program features four colorful child-like figures who interact with nature and technology.

Thomas the Tank Engine An animated series created by Britt Allcroft and broadcast first on ITV, UK in 1984. The series is based on *The Railway Series* of books by Reverend W.V. Awdry that deals with the adventures of a group of trains and road vehicles.

Tsehai Loves Learning (**Figure 3.1**) Produced by Whiz Kids Workshop and broadcast by Ethiopian Television. This is the first pre-school educational television series in the Amharic Ethiopian language.

The Three Amigos A series of twenty Public Service Announcements (PSAs) in the form of short comedic sketches, featuring three animated, talking condoms to stop the spread of HIV/AIDS. The PSAs were created by Firdaus Kharas in Canada and have been adopted in 41 languages.

Totally Spies An animated series produced by the Marathon Production, France, originally aired between 2001–9. The program stars three teenaged superspies from Beverly Hills, California who secretly fight international crime.

Winnie the Pooh A Walt Disney Company franchise based on animated characters from the books by A.A. Milne. The adventures of the bear, his friends, and his owner Christopher Robin appear, among others, in a film from 1977 as well as an animated television series introduced originally on ABC, US in 1988 and later on the Disney Channel and Toon Disney.

Wonder Pets An animated pre-school series produced by Little Airplane Production that premiered on Nick Jr. of Nickelodeon in 2006. The series feature the adventures of three pets who collaborate in helping animals in distress around the world.

Xena: Warrior Princess A drama series produced by Pacific Renaissance Pictures Ltd in association with Universal Studios and aired originally from 1995–2001. The series feature Xena's (Lucy Lawless) quest for redemption by using her fighting skills to help people, with the help of her companion Gabrielle (Reneé O'Connor).

Notes

Preface

1 Buckingham, D. (2008). Children and media: A cultural studies approach. In K. Drotner & S. Livingstone (eds), *The International Handbook of Children, Media and Culture* (pp. 219–36). Los Angeles: Sage.
2 Valdivia, A. (1999). A guided tour through one adolescent girl's culture. In S.R. Mazzarella & N.O. Pecora (eds), *Growing up Girls: Popular Culture and the Construction of Identity* (pp. 159–71). New York: Peter Lang, p. 159.
3 Hooks, B. (2000). *Feminism is for Everybody: Passionate Politics*. UK: Pluto Press.
4 Lemish, D. (2002). Gender at the forefront: Feminist perspectives on action theoretical approaches in communication research. *Communications* 27(1), 63–78.

1 Gender Representations and Their Socializing Role

1 This chapter is based on earlier writings, including Lemish, D. (2008). Gender representation in media. In W. Donsbach (ed.), *International Encyclopedia of Communication* (pp. 1945–51). Oxford: Blackwell Publishing; Lemish, D. (2007). Gender roles in music. In J.J. Arnett (ed.), *Encyclopedia of Children, Adolescents, and the Media* (pp. 365–67). London: Sage; Lemish, D. (2007). *Children and Television: A Global Perspective*. Oxford UK: Blackwell Publishing.
2 See for example: Barner, M.R. (1999). Sex-role stereotyping in FCC-mandated children's educational television. *Journal of Broadcasting & Electronic Media, 43,* 551–64; Browne, B.A. (1998). Gender stereotypes in advertising on children's television in the 1990s: A cross-national analysis. *Journal of Advertising, 27,* 83–96; Signorielli, N. (1989). Television and conceptions about sex roles: Maintaining conventionality and the *status quo. Sex Roles, 21,* 341–60; Smith, S.L. & Moyer-Gusé, E. (2005). Voluptuous vixens and macho males: A look at the portrayal of gender and sexuality in video games. In T. Reichert & J. Lambiase (eds), *Sex in Consumer Culture: The Erotic Content of Media and Marketing* (pp. 51–65). NY: Routledge.
3 Brown, L.M., Lamb, S., & Tappen, M. (2009). *Packaging Boyhood: Saving Our Sons from Superheroes, Slackers, and Other Media Stereotypes*. NY: St. Martin's Press; Lamb, S, & Brown, L.M. (2007). *Packaging Girlhood: Rescuing Our Daughters' from Marketers' Schemes*. NY: Macmillan; Seiter, E. (1995). *Sold Separately: Parents & Children in Consumer Culture*. New Brunswick, NJ: Rutgers University Press.
4 Smith, S.L. & Cook, C.A. (2008). Children and gender in film and television. Presented at the conference of the Geena Davis Institute on Gender in Media. Los Angles, CA.
5 Götz, M., Hofmann, O., Brosius, H.B., Carter, C., Chan, K., Donald, S.H., Fisherkeller, J., Frenette, M., Kolbjørnsen, T., Lemish, D., Lustyik, K., McMillin, D.C.,

Walma vn der Molen, J.H., Pecora, N., Prinsloo, J., Pestaj, M., Ramos Rivero P., Mereilles Reis, A.H., Sweys, F., Scherr, S., & Zhang, H. (2008). Gender in children's television worldwide. *TelevIZIon, 21*, 4–10.

6 Herche, M. & Götz, M., (2008). The global girl's body. *TelevIZIon, 21*, 18–19.

7 Urla, J. & Swedlund, A.C. (1995). The anthropometry of Barbie: Unsettling ideals of the feminine body in popular culture. In L. Schiebinger (ed.), *Feminism and the Body* (pp. 397–428). Oxford, UK: Oxford University Press.

8 Smith, S.L. & Cook, C.A. (2008). Children and gender in film and television. Presented at the conference of the Geena Davis Institute on Gender in Media. Los Angles, CA.

9 Report of the APA on the sexualization of girls (2007). American Psychological Association www.apa.org/pi/wpo/sexualization.html

10 Durham, G. (2008). *The Lolita effect: The Media Sexualization of Young Girls and What We Can Do About It*. Woodstock & New York: The Overlook Press.

11 Ibid.

12 Thomson, T.L. & Zerbinos, E. (1995). Gender roles in animated cartoons: Has the picture changed in 20 years? *Sex Roles, 32*, 651–73.

13 Please refer to the Program Index for an annotated listing of all programs and films cited. For a discussion of *Dora the Explorer*, see Diaz-Wionczek, M., Lovelace, V., & Cortés, C.E. (2009). *Dora the Explorer*: Behind the scenes of a social phenomenon. *Journal of Children and Media, 3*(2), 204–9.

14 Banet-Weiser, S. (2004). Girls rule!: Gender, feminism and Nickelodeon. *Critical Studies in Media Communication, 21*(2), pp. 119–39; Banet-Weiser, S. (2007). *Kids Rule!: Nickelodeon and Consumer Citizenship*. Durham, NC: Duke University Press.

15 Portman, T.A. & Herring, R. (2001). Debunking the Pocahontas paradox: The need for a humanistic perspective. *Journal of Humanistic Counseling, Education and Development, 40*(2), 185–200.

16 See for example: Kearney, M.C. (2006). *Girls Make Media*. London: Routledge; Mazzarella, S. (ed.) (2005). *Girls Wide Web: Girls, the Internet, and the Negotiation of Identity*. New York: Peter Lang; Sweeney, K. (2003). *Maiden USA: Girl Icons Come of Age*. New York: Peter Lang.

17 Lemish, D. (1998). Spice Girls' talk: A case study in the development of gendered identity. In S.A. Inness (ed.), *Millennium Girls: Today's Girls Around the World* (pp. 145–67). New York: Rowman and Littlefield; Lemish, D. (2003). Spice World: Constructing femininity the popular way. *Popular Music and Society 26* (1), 17–29.

18 Hains, R.C. (2008). Power(Puff) feminism: The Powerpuff girls as a site of strength and collective action in the third wave. In M. Meyers (ed.), *Women in popular culture: Representation and meaning* (pp. 211–35). Cresskill, NJ: Hampton Press.

19 Inness, S.A. (1999). *Tough girls: Women Warriors and Wonder Women in Popular Culture*. Philadelphia: University of Pennsylvania Press; Inness, S.A. (ed.) (2004). *Action chicks: New images of Tough Women in Popular Culture*. New York, NY: Palgrave Macmillan.

20 See for example: Early, F.H. (2001). Staking her claim: Buffy the Vampire Slayer as transgressive woman warrior. *Journal of Popular Culture, 35*(3), 11–27; Owen, A. (1999). Vampires, postmodernity, and postfeminism: Buffy the Vampire Slayer. *Journal of Popular Film and Television, 27*(2), 24–31.

21 Ross, S. (2004). "Tough enough": Female friendship and heroism in *Xena* and *Buffy*. In S.A. Inness (ed.), *Action chicks: New Images of Tough Women in Popular Culture* (pp. 237–55). New York, NY: Palgrave Macmillan.

22 Inness, S.A. (ed.) (2007). *Geek Chic: Smart Women in Popular Culture*. New York: Palgrave Macmillan.

23 Hains, R. C. (2007). "Pretty smart": Subversive intelligence in girl power cartoons. In S.A. Inness (ed.), *Geek Chic: Smart women in Popular Culture* (pp. 65–84). New York: Palgrave Macmillan.

24 Valdivia, A.N. (2009). Living in a hybrid material world: Girls, ethnicity and doll products. *Girlhood Studies*, 2(1), 73–93; Valdivia, A.N. (2008). Mixed race on Disney Channel: From *Johnnie Tsunami* through *Lizzie McGuire* and ending with the *Cheetah Girls*. In M. Beltrán & C. Fojas (eds), *Mixed Race Hollywood: Multiraciality in Film and Media Culture* (pp. 269–89). New York: NYU Press.

25 Media Education Foundation (MEF) (2002). *Tough Guise: Violence, Media and the Crisis in Masculinity with Jackson Katz* (DVD) www.mediaed.org.

26 London, R. (2007). Producing children's television. In J.A. Bryant (ed.), *The Children's Television Community* (pp. 77–93). Mahwah, NJ: Lawrence Erlbaum Associates.

27 Stipp, H. (2007). The role of academic advisors in creating children's television programs: The NBC experience. In J.A. Bryant (ed.), *The Children's Television Community* (pp.111–28). Mahwah, NJ: Lawrence Erlbaum Associates.

28 de Beauvior, S. (1989[1949]). *The Second Sex*. New York: Vintage Books.

29 de Lauretis, T. (1987). *Technologies of Gender: Essays on Theory, Film, and Fiction* (pp. 1–30). Bloomington, Indiana: Indiana University Press.

30 Douglas, S. J. & Michaels, M.W. (2004). *The Mommy Myth: The Idealization of Motherhood and How it has Undermined Women*. New York: Free Press.

31 For a discussion of these challenging theories, which are beyond the scope of this book, consult Butler, J. (1990). *Gender trouble: Feminism and the subversion of identity*. New York: Routledge; Sedgwick E.K. (1990). *Epistemology of the Closet*. Berkeley: University of California Press; Wittig, M. (1992). One is not born a woman. In *The Straight Mind and Other Essays* (pp. 9–20). Boston: beacon Press.

32 Butler, Ibid.

33 Rakow, L., & Wackwitz, L.A. (2004). Representation in feminist communication theory. In L. Rakow & L.A. Wackwitz (eds), *Feminist communication theory: Selections in context* (pp. 171–86). Thousand Oaks, CA: Sage Publications,

34 Ganguly, K. (1992). Accounting for others: Feminism and representation. In L.F. Rakow (ed.), *Women making meaning: New feminist directions in communication* (pp. 60–79). New York: Routledge.

35 Russo, A. (1992). Pornography's active subordination of women: Radical feminists re-claim speech rights. In L.F. Rakow (ed.), *Women making meaning: New feminist directions in communication* (pp. 144–66). New York: Routledge.

36 Cirksena, K. & Cuklanz, L. (1992). Male is to female as _ is to _: A guided tour of five feminist frameworks for communication studies. In L.F. Rakow (ed.), *Women making meaning: New feminist directions in communication* (pp. 18–44). New York: Routledge.

37 Craig, S. (ed.). (1992). *Men, Masculinity, and the Media*. Newbury Park, CA: Sage; Hanke, R. (1998). Theorizing masculinity with/in the media. *Communication Theory*, 8, 193–203.

38 Barthes, R. (1957). *Mythologies*. Paris: Seuil.

39 Wolf, N. (1991). *The Beauty Myth: How Images of Beauty are Used Against Women*. New York: Doubleday.

40 Said, E. (1978). *Orientalism*. London: Routledge & Kegan Paul.

41 Hall, S. (2003). The spectacle of the other. In M. Wetherell, S. Taylor, & S. Yates (eds), *Discourse Theory and Practice: A Reader* (pp. 72–81). London: Sage.

42 Valdivia, A.N. (ed.) (1995). *Feminism, Multiculturalism, and the Media: Global Diversities*. Thousand Oaks, CA: Sage Publications.

43 Hegde, R.S. (1998). A view from elsewhere: Locating difference and the politics of representation from a transnational feminist perspective. *Communication Theory, 8* (3), 271–97.

44 Gill, R. (2007). *Gender and the Media.* Cambridge, UK; Macdonald, M. (1995). *Representing Women: Myths of Femininity in Popular Media.* New York, NY: Arnold. Meyers, M. (ed.) (1999). *Mediated Women: Representations in Popular Culture.* Cresskill, NJ: Hampton Press.

45 Lotz, A.D. (2001). Postfeminist television criticism: Rehabilitating critical terms and identifying postfeminist attributes. *Feminist Media Studies, 1*(1), 105–21.

46 Lemish, D. (2007). *Children and Television: A Global Perspective.* Oxford UK: Blackwell Publishing.

47 See for example: Clark, L. & Tiggemann, M. (2007). Sociocultural influences and body image in 9- to 12-year-old girls: the role of appearance schemas. *Journal of Clinical Child and Adolescent Psychology, 3*(1), 76–86; Hargreaves, D. A. & Tiggemann, M. (2004). Idealized media images and adolescent body image: "comparing" boys and girls. *Body Image. 1*(4), 351–61; Harrison, K. (2003). Television viewers' ideal body proportions: The case of the curvaceously thin female. *Sex Roles, 48*(5), 255–64; Harrison, K. (2000). NWL – The body electric: Thin-ideal media and eating disorders in adolescents. *Journal of Communication, 50*(3), 119–43; Harrison, K. & Cantor, J. (1997). The relationship between media consumption and eating disorders. *Journal of Communication, 47*(1), 40–67.

48 Report of the APA on the sexualization of girls (2007). American Psychological Association   www.apa.org/pi/wpo/sexualization.html; Brown, J. (ed.) (2008). *Managing the Media Monster: The Influence of Media (From Television to Text Messages) on Teen Sexual Behavior and Attitudes.* Washington, DC: National Campaign to Prevent Teen and Unplanned Pregnancy.

49 Götz, M., Lemish, D., Aidman, A., & Moon, H. (2005) *Media and the Make Believe Worlds of Children: When Harry Potter met Pokémon in Disneyland.* Mahwah, NJ: Lawrence Erlbaum.

50 Media Education Foundation (MEF) (2002).*Tough Guise: Violence, Media and the Crisis in Masculinity with Jackson Katz* (DVD) www.mediaed.org

51 Ibid.

52 Buckingham, D. (2008). Children and media: A cultural studies approach. In K. Drotner & S. Livingstone (eds), *The International Handbook of Children, Media and Culture* (pp. 219–36). Los Angeles: Sage.

53 See for example: Currie, D.H. (1997) Decoding femininity: Advertisements and their teenage readers. *Gender and Society, 11*(4), 453–77; Douglas, S. (1994) *Where the Girls Are: Growing Up Female with the Mass Media.* New York: Penguin Books; Lemish, D. (1998b) Spice Girls' talk: A case study in the development of gendered identity. In S.A. Inness (ed.), *Millennium Girls: Today's Girls Around the World* (pp. 145–67). New York: Rowman and Littlefield; Mazzarella, S. and Pecora, N. (eds) (1999). *Growing Up Girls: Popular Culture and the Construction of Identity.* New York: Peter Lang.

54 See for example Singhal, A. & Rogers, E.M. (1999). *Entertainment-Education: A Communication Strategy for Social Change.* Mahwah, NJ: Lawrence Erlbaum.

55 See for example: Lemish, D. (2007). *Children and Television: A Global Perspective.* Oxford UK: Blackwell Publishing; Mazzarella, S.R. (ed.) (2007). *20 Questions About Youth & the Media.* New York: Peter Lang; Pecora, N., Murray, J.P. and Wartella, E.A. (eds) (2007). *Children and Television: Fifty Years of Research.* Mahwah, NJ: Lawrence Erlbaum.

56 Hall, S. (1991). Encoding/Decoding. In S. Hall, D. Hobson, A. Lowe, & P. Willis (eds), *Culture, Media, Language* (pp. 128–38). London: Routldge.

57 Butler, J. (1990). *Gender Trouble: Feminism and the Subversion of Identity*. London: Routledge.

2 Studying Producers of Quality Television Around the Globe

1 McCabe, J. & Akass, K. (eds) (2007). *Quality TV: Contemporary American Television and Beyond*. London: I.B. Tauris. For a recent discussion see Götz, M. (ed.) (2009). What is quality in children's television? *TelevIZIon, 22.*

2 Cardwell, S. (2007). Is quality television any good? Generic distinctions, evaluations and the troubling matter of critical judgment. In McCabe & Akass Ibid (pp. 19–34).

3 Mikos, L. (2009). Quality is a matter of perspective: Thoughts on how to define quality in children's television. *TelevIZIon, 22, 4–6.*

4 See also in Lemish, D. (2007). *Children and Television: A Global Perspective* (Chapter 6). Oxford: Blackwell.

5 Based on a description provided by Maya Götz (2007), Head of Prix Jeunesse, that appeared in A guide to international events in children's media. *Journal of Children and Media, 1*(1), 93–95. See also http://www.prixjeunesse.de/_neu/index.html. See also Commentaries on Prix Jeunesse 2008 by Kleeman and by Trujillo Caicedo, in *Journal of Children and Media, 3*(1), 101–7.

6 I have been an active member of the International Advisory Board since 2006.

7 Based on a description provided by Sachiko Kodaira (2007) senior researcher, NHK Broadcasting Culture Research Institute, that appeared in A guide to international events in children's media. *Journal of Children and Media, 1*(1), 96–97. See also http://www.nhk.or.jp/jp-prize/index_e.html

8 I was a member of the Youth Programming Jury at the 2006 event.

9 Based on http://www.bakaforum.net/

10 Based on a description provided by Firdoze Bulbia (2007), Chairperson of the Children and Broadcasting Foundation for Africa and Convener of the fifth World Summit on Media for Children, that appeared in A guide to international events in children's media. *Journal of Children and Media, 1*(1), 95–96. See also http://www.5wsmc.com/index.htm. See also commentaries on the fifth World Summit on Media and Children March 2007 by Prinsloo and by McMillin, *Journal of Children and Media, 1*(2), 192–98.

11 Quotations in the text follow very closely the spoken language of the interviewees, attempt to maintain the style and flavor of their speech, while correcting only for the most obvious grammatical mistakes in order to clarify the content.

12 However, due to the noisy recording circumstances in many instances, nine of the interviews were difficult to transcribe accurately. Efforts were made to reconstruct as much of the interview as possible.

13 For a discussion of theoretical concerns regarding interviews and related techniques see Lindlof, T.R. & Taylor, B.C. (2002). *Qualitative Communication Research Methods*. Thousand Oaks, CA: Sage Publications. More specifically, in regard to the influence of feminist thought on research methods, see Lemish, D. (2002). Gender at the forefront: Feminist perspectives on action theoretical approaches in communication research. *Communications: The European Journal of Communication Research, 27* (1), 63–78; Reinharz, S. (1992). *Feminist Methods in Social Research*. Oxford: Oxford University Press.

14 Milner IV, H.R. (2007). Race, culture, and researcher positionality: Working through dangers seen, unseen, and unforeseen. *Educational Researcher, 36*(7), 388–400.

15 For a discussion of relevant qualitative research procedures see, for example Glaser, B.G. & Strauss, A.L. (1967). *The Discovery of Grounded Theory: Strategies for Qualitative Research*. Chicago: Aldine; Lindlof, T.R. & Taylor, B.C. 2002.

Qualitative Communication Research Methods. Thousand Oaks, CA: Sage Publications.

16 Freire, P. (1970). *Pedagogy of the Oppressed.* NY: Continuum; Lemish, P. (1988). The praxis process for understanding-acting in relation to social problems. Haifa: Praxis Institute.

17 Spivak, G.C. (1988). Can the subaltern speak. In C. Nelson & L. Grossberg (eds), *Marxism and the Interpretation of Culture* (pp. 271–317). Chicago: University of Illinois Press.

3 What Does Gender Mean?

1 Valdivia, A.N. (1995). Feminist media studies in a global setting: Beyond binary contradictions and into multicultural spectrums. In A.N. Valdivia (ed.), *Feminism, Multiculturalism, and the Media: Global Diversities* (pp. 7–29). Thousand Oaks, CA: Sage Publications.

2 Appadurai, A. (1990). Disjuncture and difference in the global economy. *Theory, Culture and Society, 7,* 295–310.

3 For a discussion of this issue, see, for example, Barber, B.R. (1995). *Jihad vs. McWorld.* New York: Times Books; Featherstone, M. (ed.) (1990). Global culture: Nationalism, globalization and modernity. London: Sage; Feguson, M, (1992). The mythology about globalization. *Journal of European Communication, 7,* 69–93; Robertson, R. (1994). Globalization of glocalization? *Journal of International Communication, 1, 33–52;* Tomilsin, J. (1999). *Globalization and culture.* Cambridge, UK: Polity Press.

4 Sreberny-Mohammadi, A. (1991). The global and the local in international communications. In J. Curran and M. Gurevitch (eds), *Mass Media and Society* (pp. 118–38). London: Edward Arnold.

5 Ritzer, G. (1998). *Enchanting Disenchanted World: Revolutionizing the Means of Consumption.* London: Fine Forge Press.

6 The American twin actresses Mary-Kath and Ashley Olsen, who became famous as they grew up from infants to pre-schoolers in the situation comedy *Full House.*

7 Data presented by Mima Perisic, the United Nations Interagency Task Force on Adolescent Girls, UNICEF Headquarters, NY, March, 2009.

8 Brooks, D.E. & Hébert, L.P. (2006). Gender, race and media representation. In B.J. Dow & J.T. Wood (eds), *Handbook of Gender and Communication* (pp. 297–317). Thousand Oaks, CA: Sage.

9 Signorielli, N. & Morgan, M. (eds)(1990). *Cultivation Analysis: New Directions in Media Effects Research.* Newbury Park, CA: Sage.

10 Said, E. (1978). *Orientalism.* New York: Vintage Books.

11 Bloch, L.R. & Lemish, D. (2003). The Megaphone Effect: The international diffusion of cultural media via the USA. In P.J. Kalbfleisch (ed.), *Communication Yearbook 27.* Mahwah, NJ: Lawrence Erlbaum Associates, p. 159.

12 Ibid; see also Tobin J. (ed.)(2004). *Pikachu's Global Adventure: The Rise and Fall of Pokémon.* Durham: NC: Duke University Press.

13 See Lemish, D. (2007). *Children and Television: A Global Perspective,* Chapter 4. Oxford, UK: Blackwell.

14 See for example, the revolutionary writings of 1792 by Mary Wollstonecraft, entitled "A vindication of the rights of woman."

15 Data presented by Mima Perisic, the United Nations Interagency Task Force on Adolescent Girls, UNICEF Headquarters, NY, March, 2009.

16 The central figure of Alam Simsim, the Egyptian coproduction of *Sesame Street.*

17 Wolf, N. (1991). *The Beauty Myth: How Images of Beauty are Used Against Women.* William Morrow, New York.

18 See for example Frith, K., Shaw, P.M & Cheng, H. (2005). The construction of beauty: A cross-cultural analysis of women's magazine advertising. *Journal of Communication, 55*(1), 56–70; Kim, K.K., & Cha, H. (2008). Being a "good" woman in Korea: The construction of female beauty and success. In K Firth & K. Karan (eds), *Commercializing Women: Images of Asian Women in Advertising* (pp.33–54). Cresskill, NJ: Hampton Press.

19 American pop singer.

20 Hall, S. (1997). *Representation: cultural representations and signifying practices.* UK: Open University.

21 Nayak, A. & Kehily, M.J. (2007). *Gender, Youth and Culture: Young Masculinities and Femininities.* Hampshire, UK: Palgrave, p. 24.

22 Banks, T.L. (2000). Colorism: A darker shade of pale. *UCLA Law Review, 47*(6), 1705–46.

23 See for example, Celious, A. & Oyserman, D. (2001). Race from the inside: An emerging heterogeneous race model. *Journal of Social Issues, 57*(1), 149–65.

24 See discussion of McRobbie's contribution to this debate in Mazzarella, S.R. & Pecora, N. (2007). Revisiting girls' studies: Girls creating sites for connection and action. *Journal of Children and Media, 1*(2), 105–25; see also Nayak, A. & Kehily, M.J. (2007). *Gender, youth and Culture: Young Masculinities and Femininities.* Hampshire, UK: Palgrave, Chapter 4.

25 See for example Jordan, A.B. (2007). Heavy television viewing and childhood obesity. *Journal of Children and media, 1*(1), 45–54; Vanderwater, E.A. & Cummings, H.M. (2008). Media use and childhood obesity. In S.L. Calvert & B.J. Wilson (eds), *The Handbook of Children, Media, and Development* (pp. 355–80). Oxford, UK: Blackwell.

26 American actress.

27 An American actress and singer of Latina descent.

28 A mixed-race American R & B singer and actress.

29 Molina Guzmán, I. & Valdivia, A.N. (2004). Brain, brow or booty: Latina iconicity in U.S. popular culture. *Communication Review, 7*(2), 205–21.

30 Data presented by Mima Perisic, the United Nations Interagency Task Force on Adolescent Girls, UNICEF Headquarters, NY, March, 2009.

31 Information about Kami was gathered from several internal Sesame Workshop documents which were provided to me by one of the participants.

32 UNAIDS/WHO (2007). UNAIDS 2007 Report on the global AIDS epidemic, http://data.unaids.org/pub/EPISlides/2007/2007_epiupdate_en.pdf.

33 Raimodo, M. & Patton, C. (2002). Guest editors' introduction, Special issue: Women, HIV/AIDS, globalization, and media. *Feminist Media Studies, 2*(1), 5–18. Quotes from p. 5.

34 Ibid., p. 10.

35 Gill, R. (2007). *Gender and Media* (pp. 249–71). London: Polity Press; Lotz, A.D. (2001). Postfeminist television criticism: Rehabilitating critical terms and identifying postfeminist attributes, *Feminist Media Studies, 1*(1), 105–21.

36 Benyon, J. (2002). *Masculinities and Culture.* Buckingham and Philadelphia, PA: Open University Press; Jackson, P., Stevenson, N., & Brooks, K. (2001). *Making Sense of Men's Magazines.* Cambridge: Polity Press; Hanke, R. (1998). Theorizing masculinity with/in the media. *Communication Theory, 8*, 193–203.

37 Nayak, A. & Kehily, M.J. (2007). *Gender, Youth and Culture: Young Masculinities and Femininities.* Hampshire, UK: Palgrave, Chapter 3.

38 Callister, M.A., Robinson, T., & Clark, B.R. (2007). Media portrayals of the family in children's television programming during the 2005–6 season in the US. *Journal of Children and Media, 1*(2), 142–61.

39 Adam Sandler is an American comedian, best known for his roles in films such as *The Wedding Singer* (1998); *Punch-Drunk Love* (2002), *Spanglish* (2004), and *Reign Over Me* (2007). Will Ferrell is an American comedian, best known for his roles in films such as *A Night at the Roxbury* (1998), *Old School*, *Elf* (both 2003), *Anchorman* (2004), *Kicking & Screaming* (2005), *Talladega Nights*, *Stranger than Fiction* (both 2006), *Blades of Glory* (2007), *Semi-Pro*, *Step Brothers* (both 2008), and *Land of the Lost* (2009).

40 Sax, L. (2007). *Boys Adrift: The Five Factors Driving the Growing Epidemic of Unmotivated Boys and Underachieving Young Men*. New York, NY: Basic books.

41 Faludi, S. (1992). *Backlash: The Undeclared War Against Women*. London: Chatto & Windus; Whelehan, I. (2000). *Overloaded: Popular Culture and the Future of Feminism*. London: Women's Press.

42 See for example, Chodorow, N.J (1978). *The Reproduction of Mothering: Psychoanalysis and the Sociology of Gender*. Berkeley, CA: University of California Press.

43 Skeggs, B. (2001). The toilet paper: Femininity, class and mis-recognition. *Women's Studies International Forum, 24*(3/4), 297.

44 Bhabha, H. (1994). *The Location of Culture*. London: Routlegde; Gilroy, P. (1995). *Modernity and Double Consciousness*. Cambridge, MA: Harvard University Press; Kraidy, M.M. (2002). Hybridity in cultural globalization. *Communication Theory, 12*, 316–39.

4 The Big No-No

1 Semonche, J.E. (2007). *Censoring Sex: A Historical Journey Through American Media*. NY: Rowman & Littlefield.

2 For reviews of scholarly findings, see Brown, J. (ed.) (2008). *Managing the Media Monster: The Influence of Media (From Television to Text Messages) on Teen Sexual Behavior and Attitudes*. Washington, DC: National Campaign to Prevent Teen and Unplanned Pregnancy.

3 For a comprehensive overview of the issues, see Duggan, L. & Hunter, N.D. (1995). *Sex Wars: Sexual Dissent and Political Culture*. Routledge; Gunter, B. (2002) *Media Sex: What Are the Issues*. Mahwah, NJ: Lawrence Erlbaum; Lerum, K. & Dworkin, S.L. (2009). "Bad girls rule": An interdisciplinary feminist commentary on the report of The APA Task Force on the Sexualization of Girls. *Journal of Sex Research, 46*(4), 250–63.

4 Millwood Hargrave, A. & Livingstone, S. (2006). *Harm and Offence in Media Content: A Review of the Evidence*. Bristol: Intellect.

5 McNair, B. (2002). *Striptease Culture: Sex, Media and the Democratization of Desire*. London: Routledge.

6 Ibid.

7 Ragoné, H. (1997). Chasing the Blood Tie. In L. Lamphere, H. Ragoné, & P. Zavella (eds), *Situated Lives* (pp. 110–27). New York: Routledge.

8 The most prominent sources in this tradition are Dworkin, A. (1981). *Pornography: Men Possessing Women*. NY: Putnam; Dworkin, A. & MacKinnon, C.A. (1988). *Pornography and Civil Rights: A New Day for Women's Equality*. Published by Organizing Against Pornography; McKinnon, C.A. (1991). Pornography as defamation and discrimination. *Boston University Law Review, 71*, Rev. 793.

9 McNair, Ibid., p. ix.

10 See for example the discussion of Marcuse, among others, in Giddens, A. (1993). *The Transformation of Intimacy: Sexuality, Love and Eroticism in Modern Societies*. Cambridge: Polity press.

11 Foucault, M. (1976). *The History of Sexuality: Volume 1: The Will to Knowledge*. London: Penguin.

12 For critical discussions of sex education see Arthurs, J. & Zacharias, U. (2006). Sex education and the media: Introduction. *Feminist Media Studies, 6*(4), 539–41; Bragg, S. (2006). Young women, the media, and sex education. *Feminist Media Studies, 6*(4), 546–51; Irvine. J. M. (2002). *Talk About Sex: The Battles Over Sex Education in the United States.* Berkley: University of California; Nayak, A. & Kehily, M.J. (2008). *Gender, Youth and Culture: Young Masculinities and Femininities.* New York, NY: Palgrave Macmillan.

13 Sweeney, K. (2003). *Maiden USA: Girl Icons Come of Age.* New York: Peter Lang.

14 Buckingham, D. & Bragg, S. (2004). *Young People, Sex and the Media: The Facts of Life?* New York: NY: Palgrave Macmillan; Nayak & Kehily, Ibid.

15 Bragg (2006). Ibid.

16 Irvine, J.M. (ed.) (1994). *Sexual Cultures and the Construction of Adolescent Identities.* Philadelphia, Penn: Temple University Press; Shary, T. (2005). *Teen Movies: American Youth on Screen.* London and NY: Wallflower.

17 Jackson, S. (2006). "Street Girl": "New" sexual subjectivity in a NZ soap drama? *Feminist Media Studies, 6*(4), 469–86 (quote on page 474).

18 Kelly, D.M. (2006). Frame work: Helping youth counter their misrepresentations in media. *Canadian Journal of Education, 29*(1), 27–48.

19 Brown, J.D., Steele, J.R., & Walsh-Childers, K. (eds)(2002). *Sexual Teens, Sexual Media: Investigating Media's Influence on Adolescent Sexuality.* Mahwah, NJ: Lawrence Erlbaum; Greenberg, B.S., Brown, J.D., & Buerkel-Rothfuss, N.L. (eds) (1993). *Media, Sex and the Adolescent.* Cresskill, NJ: Hampton Press, Inc.; Gunter (2002) Ibid.

20 See for example, several chapters in D. Zillman, J. Braynt, J., & A.C. Huston (eds), *Media, Children and the Family: Social Scientific. Psychodynamic and Clinical Perspectives.* Hillsdale, NJ: Lawrence Erlbaum; and the integrative summary in Lemish, D. (2007). *Children and Television: A Global Perspective.* Oxford, UK: Blackwell.

21 Carleton, G. (2004). *Sexual Revolution in Bolshevik Russia.* Pittsburgh, PA: University of Pittsburgh Press.

22 See the elaborated discussions in Berenstein, F.L. (2007). *Dictatorship of Sex: Lifestyle Advice for the Soviet Masses.* Dekalb, IL: Northern Illinois University Pres; Kon, I.S. (1995). *The Sexual Revolution in Russia: From the Age of the Czars to Today.* New York: The Free Press; Kon, I.S. & Riordan, J. (eds) (1993) *Sex and Russian Society.* London: Pluto.

23 Giddens, Ibid.

24 Ilouz, E. (1997). *Consuming the Romantic Utopia: Love and the Cultural Contradictions of Capitalism.* Berkley: University of California Press.

25 Arthurs, J. (2004). *Television and Sexuality: Regulation and the Politics of Taste.* Maidenhead, UK: Open University Press.

26 Giddens (1993), Ibid., p. 38.

27 Gender dysphoria is a strong sense experienced by an individual that his/her assigned gender is not consistent with his/her sense of self. A recent estimate suggests that 1 out of 500 children exhibit significant gender variance/transgenderism; and one out of 2,000 adults have had gender-transformaing surgeries, according to Robinson Willimas, A. (2008). Transgender considerations: A clinical primer for the generalist working with trans and LGB patients. www.MyRightSelf.org. See also Newton, E. (1989). The mythic mannish lesbian: Radclyffe Hall and the new woman. In M.B. Duberman, M. Vicinius & G. Chauncey Jr. (eds), *Hidden from History: Reclaiming the Gay & Lesbian Past* (pp. 281–93). New York: New American Library Books.

28 Douglas, M. (1966). *Purity and Danger: An Analysis of Concepts of Pollution and Taboo.* New York: Praeger.

29 Irvine (1994). Ibid.

30 I have chosen to use the term homo/lesbian rather than gay, for two main reasons: first, this was the term mostly used by the interviewees, and second, and probably closely related to it, the fact that homosexuality was framed in sexual terms and not in cultural terms, as the term "gay" conceptually implies.

31 Rich, A. (1980). Compulsory heterosexuality and lesbian existence. *Journal of Women in Culture and Society, 5*(4), 631–60. For a discussion of heteronormativiy in children's films, see Martin, K.A. & Kazyak, E, (2009). Hetero-romantic love and heterosexiness in children's G-rated films. *Gender & Society, 23*(3), 315–36.

32 Sedgwick, E.K. (1993). *Tendencies.* Portland, OR: Book News.

33 See for example, Gross, L. (1998). Minorities, majorities and the media. In T. Liebes, J. Durran, & E. Katz (eds), *Media, Ritual and Identity* (pp. 87–102). London: Routldege; Gross, L. (2001). Out of the mainstream: Sexual minorities and the mass media. In M.G. Durham & D.M. Kellner (eds), *Media and Cultural Studies: Keyworks* (pp. 405–23). Oxford, UK: Blackwell; Kama, A. (2005). LGBT youth in Israel. In J.T. Sears (ed.), *Youth, Education and Sexualities: An International Encyclopedia* (pp. 453–57). Westport, CT: Greenwood; Kielwasser, A.P. & Wolf, M.A. (1992). Mainstream television, adolescent homosexuality and significant silence. *Critical Studies in Mass Communication, 9*, 350–73;

34 Arthurs (2004). Ibid.

35 Butler, J. (1990). *Gender Trouble: Feminism and the Subversion of Gender.* London: Routledge.

36 See for example, Kitzinger, J. (2004). *Framing Abuse: Media Influences and Public Understanding of Sexual Violence Against Children.* London: Pluto Press.

37 "Angro" is an urban term referring to the rebellion against the "Emo" (emotional) masculinity portrayed by men expressing their feelings, crying over an emotional TV scene, looking out of windows melancholically, etc. "Angro" expresses anger and rage and is typified by harsh language, a preference for hard-metal music, "talking dirty" and the like.

38 Shilling, C. (2003). *The Body and Social Theory (Second Edition).* Thousand Oaks, CA: Sage, pp. 48–51.

39 Arthurs (2004) Ibid.

40 See for example, Akass, K. & McCabe, J. (eds) (2004). *Reading* Sex and the City. London: I.B.Tauris; Arthurs, J. (2003). *Sex and the City* and consumer culture: re-mediating postmodernist drama. *Feminist Media Studies 3*(1), 83–98; Gill (2007), Ibid.; Hermes, J. (2006). *Ally McBeal, Sex and the City* and the tragic success of feminism. In J. Hollows & R. Moseley (eds), *Feminism in popular culture* (pp. 79–96). Oxford, UK: Berg; Moseley, R & Read, J. (2002). Having It *Ally*: Popular Television (Post)Feminism. *Feminist Media Studies 2*(2), 231–49.

41 McRobbie, A. (1996). More!: New sexualities in girls' and women's magazines. In J. Curran, D. Morley, & V. Walkkerdine, V. (eds), *Cultural Studies and Communications* (pp. 172–94). London: Arnold.

42 Stern, S. & Brown, J.D. (2008). From twin beds to sex at your fingertips: Teen sexuality in movies, music, television, and the Internet, 1950–2005. In P.E. Jamieson & D. Romer (eds), *The Changing Portrayal of Adolescents in the Media Since 1950* (pp. 313–43). New York: Oxford University Press.

43 Ibid., p. 335.

44 Bancroft, J. (ed.) (2003). *Sexual Development in Childhood.* Bloomington, Indiana: Indiana University press.

45 Pinheiro, P.S. (2006). *World report on violence against children.* New York: United Nations Publications.

46 Holland, P. (2008). The child in the picture. In K. Drotner & S. Livingstone (eds), *International Handbook of Children, Media and Culture* (pp.36–54). London: Sage; Jenks, C. (1996). *Childhood*. London: Routledge; Prout, A. (2008). Culture-nature and the construction of childhood. In K. Drotner & S. Livingstone (eds), *International Handbook of Children, Media and Culture* (pp. 21–35). London: Sage; Jenks, C. (1996). *Childhood*. London: Routledge.

47 Moran, J. (2001). Childhood sexuality and education: The case of Section 28. *Sexualities 4* (1), 73–89.

48 Mills, S. (2003). *Michel Foucault*. London: Routledge, p. 84.

49 McNair (2002). Ibid.

50 Henderson, L. (2001). Sexuality, feminism, Media Studies. *Feminist Media Studies*, 1(1), 17–24.

51 Arthurs (2004), Ibid.

52 Semoncher, J.E. (2007). Censoring sex: A historical journey through American media. Lanham, MD: Rowman & Littlefield; Smith, S. (2005). *Children, Cinema & Censorship: From Dracula to Dead End Kids*. New York: I.B. Tauris.

53 Gauntlett, D. (2008). *Media, Gender and Identity: An Introduction (2nd edition)*. London: Routledge; Giddens (1993). Ibid.

54 Giddens (1993). Ibid.; McNair (2002). Ibid.

55 Semonche (2007). Ibid., p. 47.

56 Durham, G.M. (2008). *The Lolita Effect: The Media Sexualization of Young Girls and What We Can Do About It*. Woodstock: The Overlook Press; Levine, D.E. & Kilbourne, J. (2008); *So Sexy So Soon: The New Sexualized Childhood and What Parents Can Do to Protect Their Kids*. NY: Ballantine Books; and the documentary film *Sexy inc. Our Children Under Influence*, a film by Sophie Bissonnette, a production of the National Film Board of Canada.

57 Stern & Brown (2008). Ibid., p. 337. See also suggestions for interventions in Brown (2008). Ibid.

58 McNair (2002). Ibid., p. 207.

59 Giddens (1993). Ibid., p. 181. For a much debated account about children's sexuality and the need for open discussion, see Levine, J. (2002). *Harmful to Minors: The Perils of Protecting Children from Sex*. Minneapolis, Minn: University of Minneapolis Press.

5 The Segregated Workplace and the Implied Audience

1 See for example: Byerly, C. M. & Ross, K. (2006). *Women and Media. A Critical Introduction*. Malden: Blackwell Publishing; Chambers, D., Steiner, L. & Fleming, C. (2004). *Women and Journalism*. London: Rutledge; Creedon, J. P. & Cramer J. (2006). *Women in Mass Communication. Third Edition*. Newbury Park: Sage; Gallagher M. (2008). At the Millennium: Shifting Patterns in Gender, Culture and Journalism. In R. Frohlich & S. A. Lafky (eds) *Women Journalists in the Western World. What Surveys Tell Us* (pp. 201–16). Cresskill, NJ: Hampton Press.

2 See the discussion of political economy in Meehan, E.R. & Riordan, E. (2002). *Sex & Money: Feminism and Political Economy in the Media*. Minneapolis, Minnesota: University of Minnesota Press.

3 As provided by the Geena Davis Institute on Gender and Media website, accessed February 2007 http://www.thegeenadavisinstitute.org.

4 Buckingham, D. (2008). Children and media: A cultural studies approach. In Drotner, K. & Livingstone, S. (eds), *The International Handbook of Children, Media and Culture* pp. 219–36. Los Angeles: Sage. Quotation on p. 222.

5 See for example: Byerly, C. M. & Ross, K. (2006). *Women and Media. A Critical Introduction*. Malden: Blackwell Publishing; Mills, K. (1997). What Difference Do

Women Journalists Make? In P. Norris (ed.), *Women, Media and Politics* (pp. 41–55). Oxford: Oxford University Press; Rhodes, J. (2001). Journalism in the New Millennium: What's a Feminist to Do, *Feminist Media Studies*, *1*(1), 49–53; Van Zoonen, (1998). One of the girls? The changing gender of journalism. In C. Carter, G. Branston, & A. Stuart (eds), *News, Gender and Power* (pp.33–46). New York: Routledge.

6   See for example, Buckingham, D., Davies, H., Jones, K., & Kelley, P. (1999). *Children's Television in Britain: History, Discourse and Policy.* London: British Film Institute Publishing.

7   Thanks to Damien Spry, Ph.D. student at the University of Sydney, Australia, for the historical analysis and arguments.

8   See note 5 above.

9   Livingstone, S. (1998). Audience research at the crossroads: The "implied audience" in media theory. *European Journal of Cultural Studies, 9,* 3–16.

10 See for example: Alexander, A. & Owers, J. (2007). The economics of children's television. In J.A. Bryant (ed.), *The Children's Television Community* (pp. 57–74). Mahwah, NJ: Lawrence Erlbaum; Banet-Weiser, S. (2004). Girls rule!: Gender, feminism, and Nickelodeon. *Critical Studies in Media Communication, 21*(2), 119–39; Seiter, E. & Mayer, V. (2004). Diversifying representation in children's TV: Nickelodeon's model. In H. Hendershot (ed.), *Nickelodeon Nation: The History, Politics, and Economics of America's Only TV Channel for Kids* (pp. 120–33). New York: New York University press.

11 Buckingham, D., Davies, H., Jones, K., & Kelley, P. (1999). *Children's Television in Britain: History, Discourse and Policy* (Chapter 5). London: British Film Institute Publishing.

12 Lemish, D., Liebes, T. & Seidmann, V. (2001). Gendered media meaning and use. In S. Livingstone & M. Bovill (eds), *Children and Their Changing Media Environment* (pp. 263–82). Hillsdale, NJ: Lawrence Erlbaum.

13 Meehan, E.R. & Riordan, E. (eds) (2002). *Sex & Money: Feminism and Political Economy in the Media.* Minneapolis, Minnesota: University of Minnesota Press.

14 Kapur, J. (2004). *Coining for capital: Movies, marketing, and the transformation of childhood.* New Brunswick, NJ: Rutgers University Press, p. 162.

15 Kapur (2004), Ibid.; Linn, S. (2004). *Consuming Kids: The Hostile Takeover of Childhood.* New York: The new Press; Seiter, E. (1995). *Sold Separately: Parents & Children in Consumer Culture.* New Brunswick, NJ: Rutgers University Press; Wasko, J. (2008). The commodification of youth culture. In K. Drotner & S. Livingstone (eds), *The International Handbook of Children, Media and Culture* (pp. 460–74). Los Angeles: Sage.

16 Steemers, J. (2009). The thin line between market and quality. *TelevIZIon, 2,* 53–56.

17 Cross, G. (1997). *Kids' Stuff: Toys and the Changing World of American Childhood.* Cambridge, Mass: Harvard University Press.

18 Francis, B. (2008). Toys, Gender and Learning. Unpublished report to the Froebel Educational Institute. Roehampton University, London: UK.

19 Retrieved on April 28, 2009 http://www.ipetitions.com/petition/Dora_Makeover/index.html

20 See for example: White, C.L. & Hall Preston, E. (2005). The spaces of children's programming. *Critical Studies in Media Communication, 22*(3), 239–55.

21 The N is a network for teens owned by Nickelodeon. Its name was changed to TeenNick in September 2009.

22 Barnes, B. (April 14, 2009). Disney expert uses science to draw boy viewers. *The New York Times.*

23 Giroux, H.A. (April 15, 2009). Disney, casino capitalism and the exploitation of young boys: Beyond the politics of innocence. *Truthout*. http://www.truthout.org/041509J

24 Maccoby, E.E. (1998). *The Two Sexes: Growing Up Apart – Coming Together*. Cambridge, MA: The Belknap Press of Harvard University Press.

25 Alluding John Gray's (1991) highly popular book: *Men are from Mars, Women are from Venus: A Practical Guide for Improving Communication and Getting What You Want in Your Relationships*. HarperCollins, New York.

26 For a discussion of these themes as they relate to humor about gender on the Internet, see Shifman, L. & Lemish, D. (forthcoming). "Mars and Venus" in virtual space: Post-feminist humor and the internet.

27 Lemish, D., Liebes, T. and Seidmann, V. (2001). Gendered media meaning and use. In S. Livingstone & M. Bovill (eds), *Children and their Changing Media Environment* (pp. 263–82). Hillsdale, NJ: Lawrence Erlbaum.

28 Livingstone, S. (April, 2009). Media policy from the perspective of the audience: Reflections on the implied audience of communications policy making. Paper presented at the *Connections: Media studies and the New Interdisciplinarity Conference*, University of Virginia, Charlottesville, VA, US.

29 Pecora, N.O. (1998). *The Business of Children's Entertainment*. NY: The Guilford Press.

30 Lemish, D. (2007). *Children and Television: A Global Perspective*. Oxford, UK: Blackwell, p. 4.

6 Gender Representations in Children's Television

1 Winter, R. & Neubauer, G. (2008). Cool heroes or funny freaks. *TelevIZIon, 21*, 30–35.

2 Beynon, J. (2002). *Masculinities and Culture*. Buckingham and Philadelphia, OA: Open University Press; Hanke, R. (1998). Theorizing masculinity with/in the media. *Communication Theory, 8*, 193–203.

3 Media Education Foundation (mef) (2002).*Tough Guise: Violence, Media and the Crisis in Masculinity with Jackson Katz* (DVD) www.mediaed.org.

4 Valdivia, A.N. (2005). Geographies of Latinidad: Developments of radical hybridity in the mainstream. In W. Critchlow, G. Dimitriadis, N. Dolby, & C. McCarthy (eds), *Race, Identity, and Representation* (pp. 307–17). New York: Routledge.

5 Valdivia, A.N. (2009). Living in a hybrid material world: Girls, ethnicity and doll products. *Girlhood Studies, 2*(1),73–93; Valdivia, A.N. (2008). Mixed race on Disney Channel: From *Johnnie Tsunami* through *Lizzie McGuire* and ending with the *Cheetah Girls*. In M. Beltrán & C. Fojas (eds), *Mixed Race Hollywood: Multi-raciality in Film and Media Culture* (pp. 269–89). New York: NYU Press.

6 A recent content analysis of children's television programs in seven countries found that the vast majority of family representations are from middle class or higher. See Lemish, D. (2009). "Without family": The portrayals of families in children's television around the world. Paper presented at the annual conference of the International Communication Association, Chicago, Il. (May)

7 Gardner, H. (2008). *Five Minds for the Future*. Boston, MA: Harvard Business Press.

8 Cowgill, L. J. (1999) *Secrets of screenplay structure: How to recognize and emulate the structural frameworks of great films*. NY: Watson-Guptill; Dancyger, K. & Rush, J. (2007). *Alternative screenwriting: Successfully breaking the rules*. Amsterdam: Focal Press/Elsevier.

9 Lemish, D. (1998b) Spice Girls' talk: A case study in the development of gendered identity. In S.A. Inness (ed.), *Millennium Girls: Today's Girls Around the World* (pp. 145–67). New York: Rowman and Littlefield.

10 Written by Maya Götz, head of the Prix Jeunusse and the International Central Institute for Youth and Educational Television (IZI), Germany.

11 Shifman, L.& Lemish, D., Ibid.

12 Maccoby, E.E. (1998). *The Two Sexes: Growing Up Apart – Coming Together*. Cambridge, MA: The Belknap Press of Harvard University Press.

13 Kapur, J. (2004). *Coining, for Capital: Movies, Marketing, and the Transformation of Childhood*. New Brunswick, NJ: Rutgers University press; Lemish, D. (2009). "Without family": The portrayals of families in children's television around the world. Paper presented at the annual conference of the International Communication Association, Chicago, Il. (May)

14 See for example, Hochschild, A. (2003). *The Commercialization of Intimate Life: Notes from Home and Work*. Berkeley: University of California Press.

15 Fisch, S. (2004). *Children's Learning from Educational Television: Sesame Street and Beyond*. Mahwah, NJ: Lawrence Erlbaum.

16 Kapur, Ibid.

17 Such as Martin Heidegger, Jean-Paul Sartre, Carl Rogers and Carl Jung.

18 For a theoretical discussion of the concept of authenticity, see Ferrara, A. (1998). *Reflective Authenticity: Rethinking the Project of Modernity*. London: Routledge; Taylor, C. (1992). *The Ethics of Authenticity*. Cambridge: Harvard University Press; Vannini, P. & Williams, J.P. (eds) (2009). *Authenticity in Culture, Self, and Society*. Farnham, England: Ashgate Publishing.

19 And thus rehearsing claims made by Gilmore, J. H. & Pine, B. J. (2007). *Authenticity: What Consumers Really Want*. Boston: Harvard Business School Press.

20 See for example Nicholas, B. (1991). *Representing Reality: Issues and Concepts in Documentary*. Bloomington: Indiana University Press.

21 GLAAD – Gay & Lesbian Alliance Against Defamation.

22 White, C.L. & Preston, E.H. (2005). The spaces of children's programming. *Critical Studies in Media Communication, 22*(3), 239–55.

23 Turow, J. (1997). *Breaking up America: Advertisers and the New Media World*. Chicago: University of Chicago Press, p. 4.

24 Tuan, Y. (1977). *Space and Place: The Perspective of Experience*. Minneapolis, MN: University of Minnesota Press.

25 McKee, N., Aghi, M., & Shahzadi, N. (2004). Cartoons and comic books for changing social norms: *Meena*, the South Asian girl. In A. Singhal, M.J. Cody, E.M. Rogers, & M. Sabido (eds), *Entertainment-Education and Social Change: History, Research, and Practice* (pp. 331–49). Mahwah, NJ: Lawrence Erlbaum.

26 In reference to genital mutilation, see for example, Atiya, N. (1982). *Khul-Khaal: Five Egyptian Women Tell Their Stories*. Syracuse, NY: Syracuse University Press; and the literary writings of Egyptian feminist novelist and activist Nawal El Saadawi who wrote in 1977 about her own and her mother's part in it, in *The Hidden Face of Eve: Women in the Arab World*. London: Zed Books (2009 edition).

27 See for example Roded, R. (2006). Women and the Qur'an. *Encyclopedia of the Qur'an 5* (pp. 523–41). Leiden/Boston: E.J. Brill; Schussler, F.E. (2001). *Wisdom Ways: Introducing Feminist Biblical Interpretation*. New-York: Orbis Books.

28 For a recent discussion of the crisis of voice and democratization of societies, see Couldry, N. (2008). Media and the problem of voice. In N. Carpentier & B. De Cleen (eds), *Participation and Media Production: Critical Reflections on Content Creation* (pp. 15–26). New Castle, UK: Cambridge Scholars Publishing.

29 Currie, D.H. (2008). Talking with girls: Methodological challenges and the need to sharpen our methods of inquiry. *Journal of Children and Media, 2*(1), 76–77.
30 See for example, Bosch, T.E. (2007). Children, culture and identity on South African community radio. *Journal of Children and Media,* 1(3), 277–88; Chalfen, R. (2008). To see what it's like to live like you: The popularity of making kids make pictures. Paper presented at Emergent Seeing and Knowing: Mapping Practices of Participatory Visual Methods seminar. Harvard University: Radcliff Institute for Advanced Study. Kearney, M.C. (2006). *Girls Make Media.* New York: Routldge; Thiel Stern, S. (2007). *Instant Identity: Adolescent Girls and the World of Instant Messaging.* New York: Peter Lang.
31 For an integrative summary, see Lemish, D. (2007). *Children and Television: A Global Perspective.* Oxford: Blackwell, chapter 6.

7 Beyond the Principles

1 Hamelink, C.J. (2008). Children's communication rights: Beyond intentions. In K. Drotner & S. Livingstone (eds), *The International Handbook of Children, Media and Culture* (pp. 508–19). Los Angeles: Sage.
2 Critcher, C. (2008). Making waves: Historical aspects of public debates about children and mass media. In K. Drotner & S. Livingstone (eds), *The International Handbook of Children, Media and Culture* (pp. 91–102). Los Angeles: Sage.
3 See for example Hornik, R. (1988). *Development Communication: Information, Agriculture & Nutrition in the Third World.* New York: Longman; McPhail, T.L. (ed.) (2009). *Development Communication: Reframing the Role of the Media.* West Sussex, UK: Wiley-Blackwell; Prasad, K. (2009). *Communication for Development: Reinventing Theory and Action.* New Delhi, India: B.R. World of Books; as well as The Communication Initiative Network: Where communication and media are central to social and economic development on-line http://www.comminit.com/en/; and The Media & Gender Monitor published on line by the World Association of Christian Communicators (WACC) http://www.whomakesthenews.org/research/media_gender_monitor/
4 See for example, Singhal, A. & Rogers, E.M. (1999). *Entertainment-Education: A Communication Strategy for Social Change.* Mahwah, NJ: Lawrence Erlabaum; Singhal, A., Cody, M., Rogers, E., & Sabido, M. (eds) (2004). *Entertainment-Education and Social Change: History, Research, and Practice.* Mahwah, NJ: Lawrence Erlbaum.
5 Nayak, A. & Kehily, M.J. (2007). *Gender, Youth and Culture: Young Masculinities and Femininities.* Hampshire, UK: Palgrave.
6 Garter, L.M., Dutta, M.J., & Cole, C.E. (eds) (2009). *Communicating for Social Impact: Engaging Communication Theory, Research, and Pedagogy.* Cresskill, NJ: Hampton press.
7 Ultrich, L. T. (2007). *Well-Behaved Women Seldom Make History.* NY: Vintage Books.
8 Delivered by Martin Luther King, Jr. on 28 August 1963, at the Lincoln Memorial, Washington D.C.
9 *Larry King Live,* CNN, November 16, 2008.
10 See his autobiographical book: Beatie, T. (2008). *Labor of Love: The Story of One Man's Extraordinary Pregnancy.* US: Memoris.

Bibliography

Akass, K. & McCabe, J. (eds) (2004). *Reading Sex and the City*. London: I.B.Tauris.

Alexander, A. & Owers, J. (2007). The economics of children's television. In J.A. Bryant (ed.), *The Children's Television Community* (pp. 57–74). Mahwah, NJ: Lawrence Erlbaum.

American Psychological Association (2007). APA Report on the sexualization of girls www.apa.org/pi/wpo/sexualization.html.

Appadurai, A. (1990). Disjuncture and difference in the global economy. *Theory, Culture and Society, 7*, 295–310.

Arthurs, J. (2003). Sex and the City and consumer culture: re-mediating post modernist drama. *Feminist Media Studies 3*(1), 83–98.

—— (2004). *Television and Sexuality: Regulation and the Politics of Taste*. Maidenhead, UK: Open University Press.

—— & Zacharias, U. (2006). Sex education and the media: Introduction. *Feminist Media Studies, 6*(4), 539–41.

Atiya, N. (1982). *Khul-Khaal: Five Egyptian Women Tell Their Stories*. Syracuse, NY: Syracuse University Press.

Bancroft, J. (ed.) (2003). *Sexual Development in Childhood*. Bloomington, Indiana: Indiana University press.

Banet-Weiser, S. (2004). Girls rule!: Gender, feminism and Nickelodeon. *Critical Studies in Media Communication, 21*(2), 119–39.

—— (2007). *Kids rule!: Nickelodeon and Consumer Citizenship*. Durham, NC: Duke University Press.

Banks, T.L. (2000). Colorism: A darker shade of pale. *UCLA Law Review, 47*(6), 1705–46.

Barber, B.R. (1995). *Jihad vs. McWorld*. New York: Times Books.

Barner, M.R. (1999). Sex-role stereotyping in FCC-mandated children's educational television. *Journal of Broadcasting & Electronic Media, 43*, 551–64.

Barnes, B. (April 14, 2009). Disney expert uses science to draw boy viewers. *The New York Times*.

Barthes, R. (1957). *Mythologies*. Paris: Seuil.

Beatie, T. (2008). *Labor of Love: The Story of One Man's Extraordinary Pregnancy*. US: Memoris.

Benyon, J. (2002). *Masculinities and Culture*. Buckingham and Philadelphia, PA: Open University Press.

Berenstein, F.L. (2007). *Dictatorship of Sex: Lifestyle Advice for the Soviet Masses.* Dekalb, IL: Northern Illinois University Press.

Bhabha, H. (1994). *The Location of Culture.* London: Routledge.

Bloch, L.R. & Lemish, D. (2003). The Megaphone Effect: The international diffusion of cultural media via the USA. In P.J. Kalbfleisch (ed.), *Communication Yearbook 27* (pp. 159–90). Mahwah, NJ: Lawrence Erlbaum Associates.

Bosch, T.E. (2007). Children, culture and identity on South African community radio. *Journal of Children and Media,* 1(3), 277–88.

Bragg, S. (2006). Young women, the media, and sex education. *Feminist Media Studies,* 6(4), 546–51.

Brooks, D.E., & Hébert, L.P. (2006). Gender, race and media representation. In B.J. Dow & J.T. Wood (eds), *Handbook of Gender and Communication* (pp. 297–317). Thousand Oaks, CA: Sage.

Brown, J. (ed.) (2008). *Managing the Media Monster: The Influence of Media (From Television to Text Messages) on Teen Sexual Behavior and Attitudes.* Washington, DC: National Campaign to Prevent Teen and Unplanned Pregnancy.

Brown, J.D., Steele, J.R., & Walsh-Childers, K. (eds) (2002). *Sexual Teens, Sexual Media: Investigating Media's Influence on Adolescent Sexuality.* Mahwah, NJ: Lawrence Erlbaum.

Brown, L.M., Lamb, S., & Tappen, M. (2009). *Packaging Boyhood: Saving Our Sons from Superheroes, Slackers, and Other Media Stereotypes.* New York: St. Martin's Press.

Browne, B.A. (1998). Gender stereotypes in advertising on children's television in the 1990s: A cross-national analysis. *Journal of Advertising, 27,* 83–96.

Buckingham, D. (2008). Children and media: A cultural studies approach. In K. Drotner & S. Livingstone (eds), *The International Handbook of Children, Media and Culture* (pp. 219–36). Los Angeles: Sage.

Buckingham, D., Davies, H., Jones, K., & Kelley, P. (1999). *Children's Television in Britain: History, Discourse and Policy* (chapter 5). London: British Film Institute Publishing.

Butler, J. (1990). *Gender Trouble: Feminism and the Subversion of Identity.* New York: Routledge.

Byerly, C.M. & Ross, K. (2006). *Women and Media. A Critical Introduction.* Malden: Blackwell Publishing.

Callister, M.A., Robinson, T., & Clark, B.R. (2007). Media portrayals of the family in children's television programming during the 2005–6 season in the US. *Journal of Children and Media,* 1(2), 142–61.

Cardwell, S. (2007). Is quality television any good? Generic distinctions, evaluations and the troubling matter of critical judgment. In J. McCabe & K. Akass (eds), *Quality TV: Contemporary American Television and Beyond* (pp. 19–34). London: I.B. Tauris.

Carleton, G. (2004). *Sexual revolution in Bolshevik Russia.* Pittsburgh, PA: University of Pittsburgh Press.

Celious, A. & Oyserman, D. (2001). Race from the inside: An emerging heterogeneous race model. *Journal of Social Issues,* 57(1), 149–65.

Chalfen, R. (2008). To see what it's like to live like you: The popularity of making kids make pictures. Paper presented at Emergent seeing and knowing: Mapping practices of participatory visual methods seminar. Harvard University: Radcliff Institute for Advanced Study.

Chambers, D., Steiner, L. & Fleming, C. (2004). *Women and Journalism*. London: Routledge.

Chodorow, N.J (1978). *The Reproduction of Mothering: Psychoanalysis and the Sociology of Gender*. Berkeley, CA: University of California Press.

Cirksena, K. & Cuklanz, L. (1992). Male is to female as _ is to _: A guided tour of five feminist frameworks for communication studies. In L.F. Rakow (ed.), *Women Making Meaning: New Feminist Directions in Communication* (pp. 18–44). New York: Routledge.

Clark, L. & Tiggemann, M. (2007). Sociocultural influences and body image in 9- to 12-year-old girls: the role of appearance schemas. *Journal of Clinical Child and Adolescent Psychology, 3*(1), 76–86.

Couldry, N. (2008). Media and the problem of voice. In N. Carpentier & B. De Cleen (eds), *Participation and Media Production: Critical Reflections on Content Creation* (pp. 15–26). New Castle, UK: Cambridge Scholars Publishing.

Cowgill, L.J. (1999) *Secrets of Screenplay Structure: How to Recognize and Emulate the Structural Frameworks of Great Films*. New York: Watson-Guptill.

Craig, S. (ed.). (1992). *Men, Masculinity, and the Media*. Newbury Park, CA: Sage;

Creedon, J. P. & Cramer, J. (2006). *Women in Mass Communication. Third Edition*. Newbury Park: Sage.

Critcher, C. (2008). Making waves: Historical aspects of public debates about children and mass media. In K. Drotner & S. Livingstone (eds), *The International Handbook of Children, Media and Culture* (pp. 91–102). Los Angeles: Sage.

Cross, G. (1997). *Kids' Stuff: Toys and the Changing World of American Childhood*. Cambridge, Mass: Harvard University Press.

Currie, D.H. (1997) Decoding femininity: Advertisements and their teenage readers. *Gender and Society, 11*(4), 453–57.

—— (2008). Talking with girls: Methodological challenges and the need to sharpen our methods of inquiry. *Journal of Children and Media, 2*(1), 76–77.

Dancyger, K. & Rush, J. (2007). *Alternative Screenwriting: Successfully Breaking the Rules*. Amsterdam: Focal Press/Elsevier.

de Beauvior, S. (1989[1949]). *The Second Sex*. New York: Vintage Books.

de Lauretis, T. (1987). *Technologies of Gender: Essays on Theory, Film, and Fiction* (pp. 1–30). Bloomington, Indiana: Indiana University Press.

Diaz-Wionczek, M., Lovelace, V., & Cortés, C.E. (2009). *Dora the Explorer:* Behind the scenes of a social phenomenon. *Journal of Children and Media, 3*(2), 204–9.

Douglas, M. (1966). *Purity and Danger: An Analysis of Concepts of Pollution and Taboo*. New York: Praeger.

Douglas, S. (1994) *Where the Girls Are: Growing Up Female with the Mass Media*. New York: Penguin Books.

Douglas, S.J. & Michaels, M.W. (2004). *The Mommy Myth: The Idealization of Motherhood and How it Has Undermined Women*. New York: Free Press.

Duggan, L. & Hunter, N.D. (1995). *Sex Wars: Sexual Dissent and Political Culture*. Routledge.

Durham, G. (2008). *The Lolita Effect: The Media Sexualization of Young Girls and What We Can Do About It*. Woodstock & New York: The Overlook Press.

Dworkin, A. & MacKinnon, C.A. (1988). *Pornography and Civil Rights: A New Day for Women's Equality*. Published by Organizing Against Pornography.

Dworkin, A. (1981). *Pornography: Men Possessing Women*. NY: Putnam.

Early, F.H. (2001). Staking her claim: *Buffy the Vampire* Slayer as transgressive woman warrior. *Journal of Popular Culture, 35*(3), 11–27.

El Saadawi, N. (1977[2009]) *The Hidden Face of Eve: Women in the Arab World.* London: Zed Books.

Herche, M. & Götz, M., (2008). The global girl's body. *TelevIZIon, 21*,18–19.

Faludi, S. (1992). *Backlash: The Undeclared War Against Women.* London: Chatto & Windus.

Featherstone, M. (ed.) (1990). *Global Culture: Nationalism, Globalization and Modernity.* London: Sage.

Feguson, M. (1992). The mythology about globalization. *Journal of European Communication, 7, 69–93.*

Ferrara, A. (1998). *Reflective Authenticity: Rethinking the Project of Modernity.* London: Routledge.

Fisch, S. (2004). *Children's Learning from Educational Television:* Sesame Street *and Beyond.* Mahwah, NJ: Lawrence Erlbaum.

Foucault, M. (1976). *The History of Sexuality: Volume 1: The Will to Knowledge.* London: Penguin.

Francis, B. (2008). *Toys, Gender and Learning.* Unpublished report to the Froebel Educational Institute. Roehampton University, London: UK.

Freire, P. (1970). *Pedagogy of the oppressed.* NY: Continuum.

Frith, K., Shaw, P.M. & Cheng, H. (2005). The construction of beauty: A cross-cultural analysis of women's magazine advertising. *Journal of Communication, 55*(1), 56–70.

Gallagher, M. (2008). At the Millennium: Shifting Patterns in Gender, Culture and Journalism. In R. Frohlich & S. A. Lafky (eds), *Women Journalists in the Western World. What Surveys Tell Us* (pp. 201–16). Cresskill, NJ: Hampton Press.

Ganguly, K. (1992). Accounting for others: Feminism and representation. In L.F. Rakow (ed.), *Women Making Meaning: New Feminist Directions in Communication* (pp. 60–79). New York: Routledge.

Gardner, H. (2008). *Five Minds for the Future.* Boston, MA: Harvard Business Press.

Garter, L.M., Dutta, M.J., & Cole, C.E. (eds) (2009). *Communicating for Social Impact: Engaging Communication Theory, Research, and Pedagogy.* Cresskill, NJ: Hampton Press.

Gauntlett, D. (2008). *Media, Gender and Identity: An Introduction (2nd edition).* London: Routledge.

Giddens, A. (1993). *The Transformation of Intimacy: Sexuality, Love and Eroticism in Modern Societies.* Cambridge: Polity Press.

Gill, R. (2007). *Gender and the Media.* London: Polity Press.

Gilmore, J.H. & Pine, B.J. (2007). *Authenticity: What Consumers Really Want.* Boston: Harvard Business School Press.

Gilroy, P. (1995). *Modernity and Double Consciousness.* Cambridge, MA: Harvard University Press.

Giroux, H.A. (April 15, 2009). Disney, casino capitalism and the exploitation of young boys: Beyond the politics of innocence. *Truthout.* http://www.truthout.org/041509J

Glaser, B.G. and Strauss, A.L. (1967). *The Discovery of Grounded Theory: Strategies for Qualitative Research.* Chicago: Aldine.

Götz, M. (ed.)(2009). What is quality in children's television? *TelevIZIon, 22.*

Götz, M., Lemish, D., Aidman, A., and Moon, H. (2005) *Media and the Make Believe Worlds of Children: When Harry Potter met Pokémon in Disneyland*. Mahwah, NJ: Lawrence Erlbaum.

——, Hofmann, O., Brosius, H.B., Carter, C., Chan, K., Donald, S.H., Fisherkeller, J., Frenette, M., Kolbjørnsen, T., Lemish, D., Lustyik, K., McMillin, D.C., Walma van der Molen, J.H., Pecora, N., Prinsloo, J., Pestaj, M., Ramos Rivero, P., Mereilles Reis, A.H., Sweys, F., Scherr, S., & Zhang, H. (2008). Gender in children's television worldwide. *TelevIZIon* 21, 4–10.

Gray, J. (1991). *Men are from Mars, Women are from Venus: A Practical Guide for Improving Communication and Getting What You Want in Your Relationships*. HarperCollins, New York.

Greenberg, B.S., Brown, J.D., & Buerkel-Rothfuss, N.L. (eds) (1993). *Media, Sex and the Adolescent*. Cresskill, NJ: Hampton Press, Inc.

Gross, L. (1998). Minorities, majorities and the media. In T. Liebes, J. Durran, & E. Katz, (eds), *Media, Ritual and Identity* (pp. 87–102). London: Routldege.

—— (2001). Out of the mainstream: Sexual minorities and the mass media. In M.G. Durham & D.M. Kellner (eds), *Media and Cultural Studies: Keyworks* (pp. 405–23). Oxford, UK: Blackwell.

Gunter, B. (2002) *Media Sex: What Are the Issues*. Mahwah, NJ: Lawrence Erlbaum.

Hains, R.C. (2007). "Pretty smart": Subversive intelligence in girl power cartoons. In S.A. Inness (ed.), *Geek Chic: Smart Women in Popular Culture* (pp. 65–84). New York: Palgrave Macmillan.

—— (2008). Power(Puff) feminism: The Powerpuff girls as a site of strength and collective action in the third wave. In M. Meyers (ed.), *Women in Popular Culture: Representation and Meaning* (pp. 211–35). Cresskill, NJ: Hampton Press.

Hall, S. (1991). Encoding/Decoding. In S. Hall, D. Hobson, A. Lowe & P. Willis, (eds), *Culture, Media, Language* (pp. 128–38). London: Routldge.

—— (1997). *Representation: Cultural Representations and Signifying Practices*. UK: Open University.

—— (2003). The spectacle of the other. In M. Wetherell, S. Taylor & S. Yates. (eds), *Discourse Theory and Practice: A Reader* (pp. 72–81). London: Sage.

Hamelink, C.J. (2008). Children's communication rights: Beyond intentions. In K. Drotner & S. Livingstone (eds), *The International Handbook of Children, Media and Culture* (pp.508–19). Los Angeles: Sage.

Hanke, R. (1998). Theorizing masculinity wit/in the media. *Communication Theory, 8*, 193–203.

Hargreaves, D.A. and Tiggemann, M. (2004). Idealized media images and adolescent body image: "Comparing" boys and girls. *Body Image, 1*(4), 351–61.

Harrison, K. and Cantor, J. (1997). The relationship between media consumption and eating disorders. *Journal of Communication, 47*(1), 40–67.

Harrison, K. (2000). NWL – The body electric: Thin-ideal media and eating disorders in adolescents. *Journal of Communication, 50*(3), 119–43.

—— (2003). Television viewers' ideal body proportions: The case of the curvaceously thin female. *Sex Roles, 48*(5), 255–64.

Hegde, R.S. (1998). A view from elsewhere: Locating difference and the politics of representation from a transnational feminist perspective. *Communication Theory, 8*(3), 271–97.

Henderson, L. (2001). Sexuality, feminism, Media Studies. *Feminist Media Studies, 1*(1), 17–24.

Hermes, J. (2006). *Ally McBeal, Sex and the City* and the tragic success of feminism. In J. Hollows & R. Moseley (eds), *Feminism in Popular Culture* (pp. 79–96). Oxford, UK: Berg.

Hochschild, A. (2003). *The Commercialization of Intimate Life: Notes from Home and Work*. Berkeley: University of California Press.

hooks, b. (2000). *Feminism is for Everybody: Passionate Politics*. UK: Pluto Press.

Holland, P. (2008). The child in the picture. In K. Drotner & S. Livingstone (eds), *International Handbook of Children, Media and Culture* (pp.36–54). London: Sage.

Hornik, R. (1988). *Development Communication: Information, Agriculture & Nutrition in the Third World*. New York: Longman.

Ilouz, E. (1997). *Consuming the Romantic Utopia: Love and the Cultural Contradictions of Capitalism*. Berkley: University of California Press.

Inness, S.A. (1999). *Tough Girls: Women Warriors and Wonder Women in Popular Culture*. Philadelphia: University of Pennsylvania Press.

Inness, S.A. (ed.) (2004). *Action Chicks: New Images of Tough Women in Popular Culture*. New York, NY: Palgrave Macmillan.

—— (2007). *Geek Chic: Smart Women in Popular Culture*. New York: Palgrave Macmillan.

Irvine, J.M. (ed.) (1994). *Sexual Cultures and the Construction of Adolescent Identities*. Philadelphia, Penn: Temple University Press.

—— (2002) *Talk About Sex: The Battles over Sex Education in the United States*. Berkley: University of California.

Jackson, P., Stevenson, N., & Brooks, K. (2001). *Making Sense of Men's Magazines*. Cambridge: Polity Press; Hanke, R. (1998). Theorizing masculinity with/in the media. *Communication Theory, 8*, 193–203.

Jackson, S. (2006). "Street Girl": "New" sexual subjectivity in a NZ soap drama? *Feminist Media Studies, 6*(4), 469–86.

Jenks, C. (1996). *Childhood*. London: Routledge.

Jordan, A.B. (2007). Heavy television viewing and childhood obesity. *Journal of Children and Media, 1*(1), 45–54.

Kama, A. (2005). LGBT youth in Israel. In J.T. Sears (ed.), *Youth, Education and Sexualities: An International Encyclopedia* (pp. 453–57). Westport, CT: Greenwood.

Kapur, J. (2004). *Coining for Capital: Movies, Marketing, and the Transformation of Childhood*. New Brunswick, NJ: Rutgers University Press.

Kearney, M.C. (2006). *Girls Make Media*. London: Routledge.

Kelly, D.M. (2006). Frame work: Helping youth counter their misrepresentations in media. *Canadian Journal of Education, 29*(1), 27–48.

Kielwasser, A.P. & Wolf, M.A. (1992). Mainstream television, adolescent homosexuality and significant silence. *Critical Studies in Mass Communication, 9*, 350–73.

Kim, K.K., & Cha, H. (2008). Being a "good" woman in Korea: The construction of female beauty and success. In K. Firth & K. Karan (eds), *Commercializing Women: Images of Asian Women in Advertising* (pp.33–54). Cresskill, NJ: Hampton Press.

Kitzinger, J. (2004). *Framing Abuse: Media Influences and Public Understanding of Sexual Violence Against Children*. London: Pluto Press.

Kon, I.S. & Riordan, J. (eds) (1993). *Sex and Russian society*. London: Pluto.

Kon, I.S. (1995). *The Sexual Revolution in Russia: From the Age of the Czars to Today*. New York: The Free Press.

Kraidy, M.M. (2002). Hybridity in cultural globalization. *Communication Theory, 12*, 316–39.

Lamb, S. & Brown, L.M. (2007). *Packaging Girlhood: Rescuing our Daughters' from Marketers' Schemes*. NY: Macmillan.

Lemish, D. (1998b) Spice Girls' talk: A case study in the development of gendered identity. In S.A. Inness (ed.), *Millennium Girls: Today's Girls Around the World* (pp. 145–67). New York: Rowman and Littlefield.

—— (2002). Gender at the forefront: Feminist perspectives on action theoretical approaches in communication research. *Communications: The European Journal of Communication Research, 27* (1), 63–67.

—— (2003). Spice World: Constructing femininity the popular way. *Popular Music and Society,* 26(1), 17–29.

—— (2007). *Children and Television: A global Perspective*. Oxford UK: Blackwell Publishing.

—— (2007). Gender roles in music. In J.J. Arnett (ed.), *Encyclopedia of Children, Adolescents, and the Media* (pp. 365–67). London: Sage.

—— (2008). Gender, representation in media. In W. Donsbach (ed.), *International Encyclopedia of Communication* (pp. 1945–51). Oxford: Blackwell Publishing.

—— (2009). "Without family": The portrayals of families in children's television around the world. Paper presented at the annual conference of the International Communication Association, Chicago, IL. (May)

Lemish, D., Liebes, T. & Seidmann, V. (2001). Gendered media meaning and use. In S. Livingstone & M. Bovill (eds), *Children and their Changing Media Environment* (pp. 263–82). Hillsdale, NJ: Lawrence Erlbaum.

Lemish, P. (1988). *The Praxis Process for Understanding – Acting in Relation to Social Problems*. Haifa: Praxis Institute.

Lerum, K. & Dworkin, S.L. (2009). "Bad girls rule": An interdisciplinary feminist commentary on the report of The APA Task Force on the Sexualization of Girls. *Journal of Sex Research, 46*(4), 250–63.

Levine, D.E. & Kilbourne, J. (2008); *So Sexy So Soon: The New Sexualized Childhood and What Parents Can Do to Protect Their Kids*. NY: Ballantine Books.

Levine, J. (2002). *Harmful to Minors: The Perils of Protecting Children from Sex*. Minneapolis, MN: University of Minnesota Press.

Lindlof, T.R. & Taylor, B.C. (2002). *Qualitative Communication Research Methods*. Thousand Oaks, CA: Sage Publications.

Linn, S. (2004). *Consuming Kids: The Hostile Takeover of Childhood*. New York: The New Press.

Livingstone, S. (1998). Audience research at the crossroads: The "implied audience" in media theory. *European Journal of Cultural Studies, 9,* 3–16.

—— (April, 2009). Media policy from the perspective of the audience: Reflections on the implied audience of communications policy making. Paper presented at the *Connections: Media Studies and the New Interdisciplinarity Conference*, University of Virginia, Charlottesville, VA, US.

London, R. (2007). Producing children's television. In J.A. Bryant (ed.), *The Children's Television Community* (pp. 77–93). Mahwah, NJ: Lawrence Erlbaum Associates.

Lotz, A.D. (2001). Postfeminist television criticism: Rehabilitating critical terms and identifying postfeminist attributes. *Feminist Media Studies, 1*(1), 105–21.

Maccoby, E.E. (1998). *The Two Sexes: Growing Up Apart – Coming Together*. Cambridge, MA: Harvard University Press.

Macdonald, M. (1995). *Representing Women: Myths of Femininity in Popular Media*. New York, NY: Arnold.

Martin, K.A. and Kazyak, E. (2009). Hetero-romantic love and heterosexiness in children's G-rated films. *Gender & Society, 23*(3), 315–36.

Mazzarella, S. (ed.) (2005). *Girls Wide Web: Girls, the Internet, and the Negotiation of Identity*. New York: Peter Lang.

Mazzarella, S. and Pecora, N. (eds) (1999). *Growing Up Girls: Popular Culture and Theconstruction of Identity*. New York: Peter Lang.

Mazzarella, S.R. & Pecora, N. (2007). Revisiting girls' studies: Girls creating sites for connection and action. *Journal of Children and Media, 1*(2), 105–25.

Mazzarella, S.R. (ed.) (2007). *Twenty Questions About Youth & the Media*. New York: Peter Lang.

McKee, N., Aghi, M., & Shahzadi, N. (2004). Cartoons and comic books for changing social norms: *Meena*, the South Asian girl. In A Singhal, M.J. Cody, E.M. Rogers & M. Sabido (eds), *Entertainment-Education and Social Change: History, Research, and Practice* (pp. 331–49). Mahwah, NJ: Lawrence Erlbaum.

McKinnon, C.A. (1991). Pornography as defamation and discrimination. *Boston University Law Review, 71*, Rev. 793.

McNair, B. (2002). *Striptease Culture: Sex, Media and the Democratization of Desire*. London: Routledge.

McPhail, T.L. (ed.)(2009). *Development Communication: Reframing the Role of the Media*. West Sussex, UK: Wiley-Blackwell.

McRobbie, A. (1996). More!: New sexualities in girls' and women's magazines. In J Curran, D. Morley, & V. Walkkerdine (eds), *Cultural Studies and Communications* (pp. 172–94). London: Arnold.

Media Education Foundation (me*f*) (2002). *Tough Guise: Violence, Media and the Crisis in Masculinity with Jackson Katz* (DVD) www.mediaed.org

Meehan, E.R. & Riordan, E. (2002). *Sex & Money: Feminism and Political Economy in the Media*. Minneapolis, Minnesota: University of Minnesota Press.

Meyers, M. (ed.) (1999). *Mediated Women: Representations in Popular Culture*. Cresskill, NJ: Hampton Press.

Mikos, L. (2009). Quality is a matter of perspective: Thoughts on how to define quality in children's television. *TelevIZIon, 22*, 4–6.

Mills, K. (1997). What Difference Do Women Journalists Make? In P. Norris (ed.), *Women, Media and Politics* (pp. 41–55). Oxford: Oxford University Press.

Mills, S. (2003). *Michel Foucault*. London: Routledge.

Millwood Hargrave, A. & Livingstone, S. (2006). *Harm and Offence in Media Content: A Review of the Evidence*. Bristol: Intellect.

Milner IV, H.R. (2007). Race, culture, and researcher positionality: Working through dangers seen, unseen, and unforeseen. *Educational Researcher, 36*(7), 388–400. Minneapolis, MN: University of Minneapolis Press.

Molina Guzmán, I. & Valdivia, A.N. (2004). Brain, brow or booty: Latina iconicity in U.S. popular culture. *Communication Review, 7*(2), 205–21.

Moseley, R. & Read, J. (2002). Having It *Ally*: Popular Television (Post)Feminism. *Feminist Media Studies, 2*(2), 231–49.

Nayak, A. & Kehily, M.J. (2008). *Gender, Youth and Culture: Young Masculinities and Femininities*. New York, NY: Palgrave Macmillan.

Newton, E. (1989). The mythic mannish lesbian: Radclyffe Hall and the new woman. In M.B. Duberman, M. Vicinius, & G. Chauncey (eds), *Hidden from History: Reclaiming the Gay & Lesbian Past* (pp. 281–93). New York: New American Library Books.

Nicholas, B. (1991). *Representing Reality: Issues and Concepts in Documentary*. Bloomington: Indiana University Press.

Owen, A. (1999). Vampires, postmodernity, and postfeminism: Buffy the Vampire Slayer. *Journal of Popular Film and Television, 27*(2), 24–31.

Pecora, N. (1998). *The Business of Children's Entertainment*. NY: The Guilford Press.

Pecora, N., Murray, J.P. and Wartella, E.A. (eds) (2007). *Children and Television: Fifty Years of Research*. Mahwah, NJ: Lawrence Erlbaum.

Pinheiro, P.S. (2006). *World Report on Violence Against Children*. New York: United Nations Publications.

Portman, T.A. & Herring, R. (2001). Debunking the Pocahontas paradox: The need for a humanistic perspective. *Journal of Humanistic Counseling, Education and Development, 40*(2), 185–200.

Prasad, K. (2009). *Communication for Development: Reinventing Theory and Action*. New Delhi, India: B.R. World of Books.

Prout, A. (2008). Culture-nature and the construction of childhood. In K. Drotner & S. Livingstone (eds), *International Handbook of Children, Media and Culture* (pp. 21–35). London: Sage.

Ragoné, H. (1997). Chasing the Blood Tie. In L. Lamphere, H. Ragoné, & P. Zavella (eds), *Situated Lives* (pp. 110–27). New York: Routledge.

Raimodo, M. & Patton, C. (2002). Guest editors' introduction, Special issue: Women, HIV/AIDS, globalization, and media. *Feminist Media Studies, 2*(1), 5–18.

Rakow, L. & Wackwitz, L.A. (2004). Representation in feminist communication theory. In L. Rakow & L.A. Wackwitz (eds), *Feminist Communication Theory: Selections in Context* (pp. 171–86). Thousand Oaks, CA: Sage Publications.

Reinharz, S. (1992). *Feminist Methods in Social Research*. Oxford: Oxford University Press.

Rhodes, J. (2001). Journalism in the new millennium: What's a feminist to do? *Feminist Media Studies, 1*(1), 49–53.

Rich, A. (1980). Compulsory heterosexuality and lesbian existence. *Journal of Women in Culture and Society, 5*(4), 631–60.

Ritzer, G. (1998). *Enchanting Disenchanted World: Revolutionizing the Means of Consumption*. London: Fine Forge Press.

Robertson, R. (1994). Globalization of glocalization? *Journal of International Communication, 1*, 33–52.

Robinson Willimas, A. (2008). Transgender considerations: A clinical primer for the generalist working with trans and LGB patients. www.MyRightSelf.org.

Roded, R. (2006). Women and the Qur'an. *Encyclopedia of the Qur'an 5* (pp. 523–41). Leiden/Boston: E.J. Brill.

Ross, S. (2004). "Tough enough": Female friendship and heroism in *Xena* and *Buffy*. In S.A. Inness, (ed.), *Action Chicks: New Images of Tough Women in Popular Culture* (pp. 237–55). New York, NY: Palgrave Macmillan.

Russo, A. (1992). Pornography's active subordination of women: Radical feminists re-claim speech rights. In L.F. Rakow (ed.), *Women Making Meaning: New Feminist Directions in Communication* (pp. 144–66). New York: Routledge.

Said, E. (1978). *Orientalism*. London: Routledge & Kegan Paul.

Sax, L. (2007). *Boys Adrift: The Five Factors Driving the Growing Epidemic of umotivated Boys and Underachieving Young Men.* New York, NY: Basic Books.

Schussler, F.E. (2001). *Wisdom Ways: Introducing Feminist Biblical Interpretation.* New-York: Orbis Books.

Sedgwick E.K. (1990). *Epistemology of the Closet.* Berkeley: University of California Press.

—— (1993). *Tendencies.* Portland, OR: Book News.

Seiter, E. & Mayer, V. (2004). Diversifying representation in children's TV: Nickelodeon's model. In H. Hendershot (ed.), *Nickelodeon Nation: The History, Politics, and Economics of America's only TV Channel for Kids* (pp. 120–33). New York: New York University Press.

Seiter, E. (1995). *Sold Separately: Parents & Children in Consumer Culture.* New Brunswick, NJ: Rutgers University Press.

Semonche, J.E. (2007). *Censoring Sex: A Historical Journey through American Media.* NY: Rowman & Littlefield.

Shary, T. (2005). *Teen Movies: American Youth on Screen.* London and NY: Wallflower.

Shifman, L. & Lemish, D. (forthcoming). "Mars and Venus" in virtual space: Postfeminist humor and the Internet.

Shilling, C. (2003). *The Body and Social Theory (second edition)* (pp. 48–51). Thousand Oaks, CA: Sage.

Signorielli, N. (1989). Television and conceptions about sex roles: Maintaining conventionality and the status quo. *Sex Roles, 21,* 341–60.

—— and Morgan, M. (eds) (1990). *Cultivation Analysis: New Directions in Media Effects Research.* Newbury Park, CA: Sage.

Singhal, A. & Rogers, E.M. (1999). *Entertainment-Education: A Communication Strategy for Social Change.* Mahwah, NJ: Lawrence Erlbaum.

Singhal, A., Cody, M., Rogers, E., & Sabido, M. (eds) (2004). *Entertainment-Education and Social Change: History, Research, and Practice.* Maywah, NJ: Lawrence Earlbum.

Skeggs, B. (2001). The toilet paper: Femininity, class and mis-recognition. *Women's Studies International Forum, 24*(3/4), 297.

Smith, S. (2005). *Children, Cinema & Censorship: From Dracula to Dead End Kids.* New York: I.B. Tauris.

Smith, S.L. & Cook, C.A. (2008). Children and gender in film and television. Presented at the conference of the Geena Davis Institute on Gender in Media. Los Angles, CA.

—— & Moyer-Gusé, E. (2005). Voluptouous vixens and macho males: A look at the portrayal of gender and sexuality in video games. In T. Reichert & J. Lambiase (eds), *Sex in Consumer Culture: The Erotic Content of Media and Marketing* (pp. 51–65). NY: Routledge.

Spivak, G.C. (1988). Can the subaltern speak. In C. Nelson & L. Grossberg (eds), *Marxism and the Interpretation of Culture* (pp. 271–317). Chicago: University of Illinois Press.

Sreberny-Mohammadi, A. (1991). The global and the local in international communications. In J. Curran and M. Gurevitch (eds), *Mass Media and Society* (pp. 118–38). London: Edward Arnold.

Steemers, J. (2009). The thin line between market and quality. *TelevIZIon, 2,* 53–56.

Stern, S. & Brown, J.D. (2008). From twin beds to sex at your fingertips: Teen sexuality in movies, music, television, and the Internet, 1950–2005. In P.E. Jamieson &

D. Romer (eds), *The Changing Portrayal of Adolescents in the Media Since 1950* (pp. 313–43). New York: Oxford University Press.

Stipp, H. (2007). The role of academic advisors in creating children's television programs: The NBC experience. In J.A. Bryant (ed.), *The Children's Television Community* (pp.111–28). Mahwah, NJ: Lawrence Erlbaum Associates.

Sweeney, K. (2003). *Maiden USA: Girl Icons Come of Age*. New York: Peter Lang.

Taylor, C. (1992). *The Ethics of Authenticity*. Cambridge: Harvard University Press.

Thiel Stern, S. (2007). *Instant Identity: Adolescent Girls and the World of Instant Messaging*. New York: Peter Lang.

Thomson, T.L. & Zerbinos, E. (1995). Gender roles in animated cartoons: Has the picture changed in 20 years? *Sex Roles, 32*, 651–73.

Tobin, J. (2004). *Pikachu's Global Adventure: The Rise and Fall of Pokémon*. Durham: NC: Duke University Press.

Tomilsin, J. (1999). *Globalization and Culture*. Cambridge, UK: Polity Press.

Tuan, Y. (1977). *Space and Place: The Perspective of Experience*. Minneapolis, MN: University of Minnesota Press.

Turow, J. (1997). *Breaking up America: Advertisers and the New Media World*. Chicago: University of Chicago Press.

Ultrich, L.T. (2007). *Well-Behaved Women Seldom Make History*. NY: Vintage Books.

UNAIDS/WHO (2007). UNAIDS 2007 Report on the global AIDS epidemic, http://data.unaids.org/pub/EPISlides/2007/2007_epiupdate_en.pdf

Urla, J. & Swedlund, A.C. (1995). The anthropometry of Barbie: Unsettling ideals of the feminine body in popular culture. In L. Schiebinger (ed.), *Feminism and the Body* (pp. 397–428). Oxford, UK: Oxford University Press.

Valdivia, A.N. (1995). Feminist media studies in a global setting: Beyond binary contradictions and into multicultural spectrums. In A.N. Valdivia (ed.), *Feminism, Multiculturalism, and the Media: Global Diversities* (pp. 7–29). Thousand Oaks, CA: Sage Publications.

Valdivia, A. (1999). A guided tour through one adolescent girl's culture. In S.R. Mazzarella & N.O. Pecora (eds), *Growing Up Girls: Popular Culture and the Construction of Identity* (pp. 159–71). New York: Peter Lang.

Valdivia, A.N. (ed.) (1995). *Feminism, Multiculturalism, and the Media: Global Diversities*. Thousand Oaks, CA: Sage Publications.

—— (2005). Geographies of Latinidad: Developments of radical hybridity in the mainstream. In W. Critchlow, G. Dimitriadis, N. Dolby, & C. McCarthy (eds), *Race, Identity, and Representation* (pp. 307–17). New York: Routledge.

—— (2008). Mixed race on Disney Channel: From *Johnnie Tsunami* Through *Lizzie McGuire* and Ending With the *Cheetah Girls*. In M. Beltrán & C. Fojas (eds), *Mixed Race Hollywood: Multiraciality in Film and Media Culture* (pp. 269–89). New York: NYU Press.

—— (2009). Living in a hybrid material world: Girls, ethnicity and doll products. *Girlhood Studies, 2*(1), 73–79.

Van Zoonen, (1998). One of the girls? The changing gender of journalism. In C. Carter, G. Branston, & A. Stuart (eds), *News, Gender and Power* (pp.33–46). New York: Routledge.

Vanderwater, E.A. & Cummings, H.M. (2008). Media use and childhood obesity. In S.L. Calvert & B.J. Wilson (eds), *The Handbook of Children, Media, and Development* (pp. 355–80). Oxford, UK: Blackwell.

Vannini, P. & Williams, J.P. (eds) (2009). *Authenticity in Culture, Self, and Society*. Farnham, England: Ashgate Publishing.

Wasko, J. (2008). The commodification of youth culture. In K. Drotner & S. Livingstone (eds), *The International Handbook of Children, Media and Culture* (pp. 460–74). Los Angeles: Sage.

Whelehan, I. (2000). *Overloaded: Popular Culture and the Future of Feminism*. London: Women's Press.

White, C.L. & Preston, E.H. (2005). The spaces of children's programming. *Critical Studies in Media Communication, 22*(3), 239–55.

Winter, R. & Neubauer, G. (2008). Cool heroes or funny freaks. *TelevIZIon, 21*, 30–35.

Wittig, M. (1992). One is not born a woman. In *The Straight Mind and Other Essays* (pp. 9–20). Boston: Beacon Press.

Wolf, N. (1991). *The Beauty Myth: How Images of Beauty are Used Against Women*. New York: Doubleday.

Zillman, D., Braynt, J., & Huston, A.C. (eds) (1994), *Media, Children and the Family: Social Scientific. Psychodynamic and Clinical Perspectives*. Hillsdale, NJ: Lawrence Erlbaum.

Index